HALLOWEEN PROPMAKER'S HANDBOOK

To my parents
who first taught me the joys of Halloween

To Marilyn
who convinced me I really could write a book

And most of all
to my wife, Judy
for putting up with skeletons in the closets,
corpses in the bed,
Frankenstein's monster in the kitchen,
piles of bones in the basement
and other assorted eccentricities

HALLOWEEN PROPMAKER'S HANDBOOK

KEN PITEK

McFarland & Company, Inc., Publishers
Jefferson, North Carolina, and London

Library of Congress Cataloguing-in-Publication Data

Pitek, Ken, 1955–
Halloween propmaker's handbook / Ken Pitek.
p. cm.
Includes index.

ISBN-13: 978-0-7864-2463-4
ISBN-10: 0-7864-2463-X (softcover : 50# alkaline paper) ∞

1. Halloween. 2. Halloween decorations. 3. Haunted houses.
I. Title.
GT4965.P58 2006 394.2646—dc22 2006015608

British Library cataloguing data are available

Manufactured in the United States of America

McFarland & Company, Inc., Publishers
Box 611, Jefferson, North Carolina 28640
www.mcfarlandpub.com

TABLE OF CONTENTS

I. TECHNIQUES

II. PROJECTS

III. REFERENCES

PREFACE: WELCOME TO MY CRYPT

Welcome to my crypt! Here you will find the stuff of which nightmares are made. Here I will guide you through all the steps needed to create many of your own frightening Halloween props as well as how to take some store-bought props and turn them from just a little scary to totally frightening. But be warned these are not your cutesy little Halloween arts and crafts items. These are meant to be scary and even gruesome. If this is not for you, please go no further!

If you are still with me, let me tell you a little about what you will find in this book. The prop ideas I will present should be well within the capabilities of most people. The props will, for the most part, require a very little in the way of tools and use common, everyday, readily available items. Where you will need items that can be a little harder to come by, say a life-size anatomically correct skeleton (plastic of course), I will tell you where you can find those items at reasonable prices.

I have tried, where possible, to use common household items which will probably be familiar to you. Where I do get into things like lights and motors, I will have you use either safe battery power or UL approved pre-wired motors and lights. I have endeavored to keep the tools needed to simple hand tools (pliers, knife, hammer, paintbrush, screwdriver, drill and bits). If you have power tools, and are competent in their use, they most certainly may be used to speed things along, but for the most part they will not be required.

The time needed to complete a project will range from just a few minutes to several days. You will often find it necessary to start a project and let paint or some other material dry. I will try to warn you when this time may be excessive so you may plan accordingly.

At the beginning of each project, you will find a list of tools and materials needed, as well as some items which may be substituted. I will often mention brand names in my instructions; this is not meant to be a plug for any particular brand. I mention brand names only for those people who just have to know exactly what I used. I will often give you general guidelines and leave you to use your imagination to create truly one-of-a-kind props.

Each project will be laid out in step-by-step detail with many pictures to help you understand the instructions. At the end, I will always show you a picture of one of my finished projects so that you may see how much better yours turned out.

I will also give you a number of tips and show you some techniques so that you can design your own original props. This to me is the most fun, because when people ask, "Where did you get that great prop?" you can say, "I made it myself."

How to Use This Handbook

Before we get started building our props, let me give you a quick overview on how to use this book. You will notice the book is laid out in several sections. First comes the techniques section, where I will discuss basic techniques you can use to design and build your own props. After that, you will find the projects section, where I will guide you step by step through a number of projects. Lastly, you will find a reference section where I will give you helpful information such as where to find materials and what types of materials can be used.

Before we go any further, let me address the issue of safety. First, the only guarantee I can give you, with regard to the safety of the procedures detailed here, is that I performed them and lived to tell about it. You must know yourself, and your abilities, and decide whether you can safely complete the project.

Once you have decided to take on the project, you should stop and think about just what precautions you will take. I can give you a few general guidelines to help you along; however, ultimately it is you who must decide how to proceed safely. A few general safety rules are:

- Always wear safety glasses or goggles. No matter what you are doing, protect your eyes.
- When working with liquids, sprays or powders, wear goggles.
- When working with chemicals, wear protective gloves. This includes paints, stains, latex, etc.
- When using chemicals, work out of doors or use plenty of ventilation.
- When using sprays, wear a respirator or mask.
- Always read and follow all manufacturers directions and cautions.

These are meant to be only a basic set of rules. You must, of course, think for yourself about how to keep a project safe.

Once you have decided what safety precautions must be taken, you will need to assemble the tools and materials you will need. It is always a good idea to make sure you have everything you will need for the project before you start. Next, you will need to decide where you will work on your project. Make sure you have adequate room and that there are no hazards in the way. If you are working with chemicals, paints, etc., make sure you have sufficient ventilation and proper eye protection.

Once you have everything you will need for your prop and a place to work, read through all the directions and make sure you understand them. Only then should you begin. Now you can simply follow along with the step-by-step directions.

PART I
TECHNIQUES

SCAREOLOGY 101

Welcome to Scareology 101! You might ask, "What is Scareology?" Scareology is my term for the study of how to scare and in particular how to scare people with your Halloween display. This section will be a brief introduction into the subject of what makes an effective Halloween haunt.

First, we need to look at what fear is and what causes it. Then you must decide just how much fear you wish to generate. What we call fear is really the mind's way of reacting to a perception of possible danger. When confronted by a situation perceived as potentially dangerous, people's pulse rates increase, they breathe a little faster and their hearts begin to race. All this is to prepare the body for what may come. It is called a flight-or-fight reflex. Everybody is afraid of something; some people are afraid of the dark, others of spiders, while still others are afraid of fluffy little bunnies. Whatever someone is afraid of, there is a way to take advantage of it to give them a good scare.

Actually, you really do not want people to be truly in fear of your display. If they were, they would never approach it, thus depriving you of the joy of watching their reactions. What you really want is for them to be apprehensive, with all their senses heightened. The more alert they are, the more they will notice all the hard work you went through. Someone who is apprehensive will still approach your display but will be much easier to startle. And that is really what you want to do. It should be your objective to catch your victims off guard. The surprise of something totally unexpected happening is what will make people scream and jump back. That is how you will know you have had a successful scare.

So how do you place someone in an apprehensive state? Whether you are operating a professional haunt or simply haunting your yard for Halloween, it really starts before a person reaches your display. I have found that eerie music or sound effect recordings are very effective anytime, day or night, while lighting effects are highly effective only at night or in a darkened environment.

There are a large number of Halloween sound effects tapes and CDs available at most any store that has a Halloween section. I have found most of these to be quite effective at setting the mood. With the volume turned up a bit, they can be heard before most of your display can be seen (be sure not to turn the volume up too much or you won't be able to hear the screams of your victims). The most effective way to utilize these recordings is with a player with remote speakers which may be placed away from the actual player. When I set up my haunt, I place the player in the house so that I may easily change recordings, adjust the volume, etc. (This also allows you to completely stop the sound

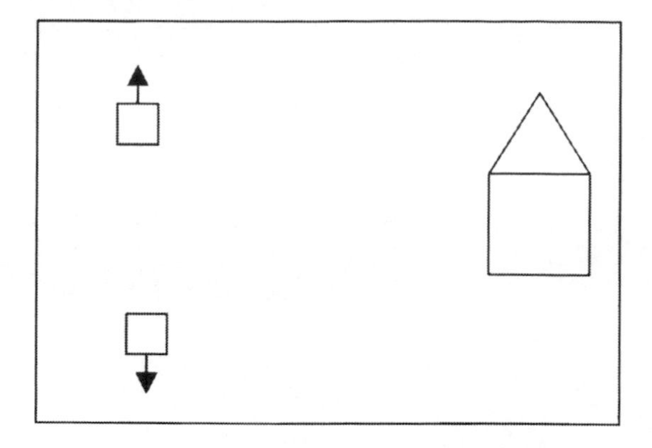

Speakers for background music and sound effects should be placed to the outside of your haunt area, facing away, so as not to interfere with any audio scares you may be using.

Every year the author transforms his kitchen into a mad scientist laboratory.

effects if they are too intense for some of your youngest visitors.) I then place the speakers at the corners of my property facing away from my other props (just make sure any wires are placed where no one will trip over them). This allows people to hear the effects long before reaching my haunt and yet leaves the sound level close in so that it does not drown out any sound effects used with individual props.

With the proper sound effects playing, I have found many younger children actually have to be coaxed up to the house by their parents (I often wonder if these children ever forgive their parents for this). It is of course best if the speakers are well hidden; it adds to the mystery if no one can tell where the sound is coming from. Often, with a little planning, you can really take advantage of your sound effects. Say your display includes a group of ghosts, and the left channel of your recording contains numerous ghostly moans. By placing your left speaker in with the ghosts, it will seem as if the ghosts are the ones moaning. It is the attention to little details like this which truly adds impact to your haunt.

You may wish to add a second player close to the house with sounds like screams, rattling chains (said to be one of the most unsettling of sounds), scratching and general mayhem. Done properly, it can appear as if the sounds are coming from within the house. Here the volume need not be very loud; after all, if the sounds are coming from inside, they should be rather muted. This also allows you to hear people's comments and does not drown out the sounds of other props along the approach.

Lighting effects can also often be seen from a distance, but only at night. While this is a limitation of sorts, daylight itself is a limitation. Night is truly the best time for haunting; just ask any ghost.

When lighting your haunt, you want to keep several things in mind. If you do not have enough light for people to see adequately, it can be dangerous. If the light level is not enough that you can easily find your way around your own haunt, how can you expect a stranger to be able to? Yet, too much light will not allow you to capitalize on the fear of the dark that everyone possesses to one degree or another. There are several options here. You can use black lights which still allow enough visible light for people to find their way around (see section on working with black light). You can use spotlights to light individual props, reflecting enough light to make your haunt navigable. You can use colored lights to give everything a very different appearance. Or, you can use any combination of the above.

It is often advisable to have some form of bright light at the very front of your display. This will attract attention from a distance and if properly focused will not overly light the rest of the area. This can be a spotlighted prop, a flashing strobe light, strobe lights sequenced to flash in response to recorded thunder, or whatever your imagination can dream up. Remember that you want to start giving your victims an uneasy feeling as soon as possible — the sooner the better.

A skeleton lying on the ground is much harder to spot from a distance than, say, one hanging in a cage.

In keeping with the idea of developing apprehension while people are still approaching your haunt, you may wish to consider placing some of your largest props at the entrance or where they may easily be seen from a distance. After all, the larger the prop the greater the distance it can be seen from. Of course, how you position these props can make a real difference. Take for instance a skeleton; if you lay it down on the ground, it will not be visible very far off. Take the same skeleton and put it in a chair or stand it up, and it will be seen from a much greater distance. You will also want to take into consideration from what angles people may approach. You do not want trees, parked cars, etc., to block their view.

Once your victims finally reach your entrance, you will want to guide them along a path of your choice rather than one of their choosing. For years, I was frustrated by trick-or-treaters taking a shortcut across my front lawn, when many of my best effects depended on their approaching down the driveway. Then I came up with the idea of using a section of cemetery fence to cut them off. After this, they had no choice but to go along the path I wanted them to.

If you have the room and the time to set it up, it can be interesting to lead

Once the author installed the fence shown, victims were forced to approach down the driveway rather than cutting across the lawn.

your guests down a winding and confusing path. This will help to add to their sense of uneasiness; after all, people do not like to be confused. While your victims try to find their way along your twisting and turning path, it is a prime time for someone or something to leap out at them. They will be concentrating on how to get to their destination and less likely to be watching out for your little surprises.

Many of your scares will probably depend on people blocking light to a photo sensor, stepping on a pressure mat or being in the right spot for something to drop on their heads, or for an actor to jump out at them. To do this they must be carefully guided, without knowing they are being set up. Besides the obvious ways such as using fences or walls, victims can be led by their own curiosity. If you give them something to look at they will follow what they believe is a path of their choice from prop to prop. If you give them something especially good to look at, they should pause right where you want them to, and then you can pounce. One of my favorite and most successful scares is also one of the easiest. I call it the spider drop, and as the name implies it involves a dropping spider (I will detail this effect in the projects section of this book). Basically, the way I work it is to set the victim up by providing a convenient spot for them to look through a window into Frankenstein's lab. While they stand there admiring my work on the lab, a giant spider lands directly on their heads.

Just what kinds of props are the most effective? It has been my experience that most every time I use a store-bought prop someone, if not several someones, comments, "I have one of those" or "I know someone who has one of those." Needless to say, that means they are less than impressed with mine. For this reason, I believe it is best to use props of your own making or an unusual adaptation of a commercial prop. Of course, one exception to this would be some of the high-end props meant for commercial haunted houses. These tend to be rare enough that most people have not seen them. They also tend to be priced outside of most people's budgets. In short you want everything about your haunt to be as unique as possible.

Props can be divided into two categories: stationary and moving. The moving category can be further divided into continuous motion and intermittent motion. In addition, the intermittent category can be divided into timed, triggered and controlled. We will discuss each category briefly and the advantages and drawbacks of each.

A stationary prop is one that just sits there. It has no moving parts, though it may have parts that can be adjusted or posed. The advantages of a stationary prop are that they tend to be less expensive and more durable. Since a stationary prop has no motors or gears to wear out, they tend to be maintenance free. You will not need to run a power cord for them or change batteries. An example of a stationary prop would be a skeleton or skull.

While stationary props may be easy to use and durable, they do have the drawback of not being an effective scare. It is rather difficult to startle a victim with something that just sits there. They are best suited to setting the mood and building apprehension. Use your stationary props to lead visitors and misdirect their attention. If you give them a trail of props, most people will follow it just like you want them to. While someone is looking to the left to see your corpse, an actor or concealed moving prop can jump out at them from the right.

There are times when you can use a stationary prop for a good scare. If the prop can be hidden in such a way that the victim turns a blind corner and sees a large prop blocking the way, you can often get a very nice reaction. In a totally dark environment, you can suddenly illuminate a prop with a spotlight and perhaps add a sound effect at the same time. Both these techniques require a lot of planning and very careful placement. It may take you some time to get things right, but when you do you will be well rewarded.

Not surprisingly a moving prop is anything which moves (an actor can be considered a moving prop; we will discuss the use of actors later). Advantages of moving props include the fact that they tend to draw more attention, can be more lifelike, may do unexpected things, and give an overall feel of realism. Disadvantages include the fact that they usually require a power source, are prone to breakage or wearing out, and some may be able to injure people if improperly used.

The human eye has a real tendency to pick out objects that are moving over those which do not. This probably goes back to basic survival instincts; food and predators move, rocks do not. This means that if your props move they will more likely be noticed. When you see something move, you have more of a tendency to think of it as being alive. A stationary monster can appear to be no more dangerous than the tree next to it. However, a moving monster is more likely to appear as if it is about to chase you down and eat your heart. If you can use at least a few moving props, you can add a certain amount of excitement and realism to your haunt which will be well worth the time and expense.

When placing any moving prop there are several things to keep in mind. First and foremost is safety. Power cords or pneumatic lines must be kept out of the way, and props must not move in such a way as to pose a hazard to anyone. When setting out your props do not forget you will be dealing with people of all sizes, shapes and ages. A prop which zooms by just over your head may nearly decapitate a person who is 6'4". Likewise, a small child may grab at things an adult would never touch. Always, with any of your props, try to anticipate what people may do, remembering that even intelligent people can do some very dumb things. You also need consider how you will run power or pneumatic lines out to props, which require them; a little planning here goes a long way. If you intend to use an item outside, make sure it is appropriate for the weather it may encounter. Also, consider any line you run to power it; just because your prop is designed to withstand rain does not mean the extension cord is. It is wise to never use electrical devises outside when rain, heavy dew or even very high humidity is anticipated.

Let us consider the different types of moving props. The first we will look at are the continuous motion moving props. As the name implies these are props which move continuously, repeating the same motion over and over again. In some cases this repeated motion can mimic what you would expect in real life, say in the case of a flying bat that circles repeatedly. In other cases, the repeated motion does not look very lifelike at all — for instance, a monster whose head moves back and forth as if it is planning to cross a street it never crosses. While a continuous motion prop can add some realism, you should carefully consider just how cost effective it is before putting down your hard-earned money.

An intermittent moving prop is one which performs a specific action, stops and then repeats the action, either after waiting a prescribed period of time, or in response to some outside influence. This type of prop can be far more effective than a continuous motion prop in that the action is more sudden and realistic. After all, living things tend to perform an action and stop rather than repeating it over and over again. This works best when the prop performs its action just as the victim approaches.

Let us consider the ways in which an intermittent moving prop is made to move. The first option is to use a simple timer which is set to turn the prop on for so many seconds, turn it off, and wait so many seconds before turning it back on. This action tends to be a little more effective than continuous motion; however, much of the effect depends on where in the cycle the victim first sees the prop. The best effect would be for the prop to be first seen while stationary, then begin to move just as the victim is right next to it. The approaching victim will think he is walking up to a stationary prop; when it suddenly moves he can receive quite a startle. If the victim first sees the prop moving from a distance, he will be prepared for it to move when he gets close and thereby, be less surprised. The problem with a timed prop is that it is next to impossible to time it so that all of your victims arrive just as the prop begins to move. In fact, if you get any at all it is probably just luck.

A step up from the timed props are the triggered ones. These props are triggered by the victim in one way or another and are probably the second most effective form of moving props. They will usually allow you to determine almost exactly where your victim will be when the prop is triggered. One small problem is that the triggers have no way of knowing what direction your victim is facing when they reach the trigger point. If your scare depends on a victim facing a specific direction, you will need to plan carefully to lead them into your trap. This probably will not be a large problem with most props, as most people are startled whenever something begins moving suddenly, whether it is in front of them, behind them or off to the side.

Another problem can be that it usually is not to difficult to figure out what the trigger is and people (especially children) will tend to stay in one spot, setting off the effect again and again and again. This would not be a problem if they were the only ones in your haunt. The problem is that if you build a truly well-planned and well-executed haunt, you will have a steady stream of visitors, and if one person keeps triggering a prop, others will not see it in the way you intended. Remember, it is often very important to trigger a prop when the victim is close. The closer one is to a perceived threat, the greater the fear induced. You can overcome this drawback by using controlled props, which we will discuss a little later.

Now let us look at the different ways in which props may be triggered. One of the oldest and best ways is with a pressure mat. You have probably seen these in the form of the screaming doormats, the little mat you put by your door and when someone steps on it, it plays back a recorded scream. That is exactly what a pressure mat is — a mat which acts as a switch that closes with the weight of someone stepping on it. These mats can run in price from under $10.00 for the inexpensive home models to over $100.00 for high-quality professional mats.

The advantages of pressure mats include that they can be placed anywhere in relation to your prop. Many are weather resistant, which means they can be used indoors or out. They will work in bright light or dark, or even in constantly changing light. They require relatively little planning in placement. In addition, with a little know-how, you can adapt them to trigger several props simultaneously.

The drawbacks are that you must be very careful to make sure they are placed so that no one will trip over them. Remember, people will be distracted by your props and not paying full attention to where they are walking. You also need to make sure that the mat is placed where it will be stepped on directly; if the intended victim steps over or around the mat, the effect will not be triggered. You must also take care that the mat is concealed or blends in. If the mat is visible before it triggers your effect, people will figure something is coming and not be as startled.

There are also a large number of props which are triggered optically. These rely on the victim blocking or reducing light to a sensor. One advantage of this type of system is that it is pretty much impossible for the victim to detect the trigger. There is nothing that can be tripped over and no wires which need to be run for the triggering device.

The optically triggered props have some severe limitations however. For one, they need light to work, meaning they are next to worthless in the dark. Also, if used out of doors in daylight they can be temperamental as to the position of the sun, and at times can be set off by as little as a falling leaf passing close to the sensor. Also, do not forget that if you plan to use a strobe light, it will tend to constantly trigger an optically triggered prop. This type of trigger tends to work best indoors where you can control both the light and the direction of approach of the victim.

For most purposes, the controlled props will give you the best results. These props are, just as the name implies, those which are controlled by a person. The major advantage of a controlled prop is that it is can be set off at the exact perfect moment for any given circumstance. That is to say, you or someone you have trained will make the decision as to when the effect goes off, rather than it being triggered by the first person to enter the area. This allows you to wait until a group assembles at the prop, as well as offering you the opportunity to catch people on the way in or on the way out (if the haunt is set up so that victims must leave the way they entered). Another advantage is that it keeps people from repeatedly setting off an effect, something young children are especially fond of. After all, if one person is continually setting off the effect as a new batch of victims approaches, it will deprive the new arrivals of seeing the effect the way you intended. Also, controlling how often a prop is triggered can save a lot of wear and tear on it.

By now you have probably figured out the major drawback of a controlled prop, and that is that someone has to trigger it at just the right moment. This, of course, means you need a person in a position to do so. The trigger person will need an unobstructed view of the approach to the prop as well as access to the switching device.

Probably the most common device for setting off a triggered prop is with a hardwired switch, a switch that is either mounted on the prop or connected by a cable to the prop. If the switch is mounted on the device, this can be a drawback if the triggering person is visible and looks out of place. Of course at times it is easy to make the operator appear as if he belongs. Take for example an electric chair. If you dress the operator as an executioner he will blend right in and can even add to the effect. Other times, it is best to try to hide the operator, or use a remote switch wired to the device. If you choose this option remember first and foremost to be careful how you run the cable. Safety first. Make sure that the cable is not only out of the way of where you want your victims to go, but also of where they may go if they get scared or lost. It is usually best to run any cables, wires, air lines, etc., where there is a physical barrier to keep people away from them. A secondary consideration is to choose a spot where the operator can see but not be seen.

Another option for triggering a prop is a wireless remote. By now, it should not surprise you to know that you have several options. Some of the oldest remote control devices use sound waves to connect the controller to the device. These are usually less than ideal in that it is not unusual for a device to be triggered by a stray sound from a source other than the controller. This is for the most part old technology and you should not run into it very often.

Another option more common these days is a wireless infrared remote. These devices use light in the infrared spectrum (invisible to the human eye) to carry the control signal. These devices can still be set off by random stray signals but it is extremely uncommon. Drawbacks include the fact that these devices are pretty much line of sight. That is to say that you need to be able to see the receiver on the device from where the remote is. If any object blocks the path (this includes one of your victims, who may not be where you planned for him to be) the device will not be reliably triggered. You can also have a problem in bright light. If a bright light is shining on the receiver, it may block the signal from the remote. So again positioning is important and if the prop is used out of doors you must remember to take into account the changing position of the sun. If you use an infrared remote, remember to test it first not only for range but also for any lighting conditions you may possibly encounter.

Another option for a remote trigger is an RF (radio frequency) controller. These controllers use a radio frequency signal to connect the controller to the device. This type of device is often your best choice in that it often has the best range, is less susceptible to having its signal blocked by intervening objects and will work in any lighting conditions. As with any remote switching system, the operator must still have a clear view to know when to trigger the device and, unless somehow blended into the scene, should as much as possible be hidden from view.

One of the biggest drawbacks to using controlled props is that it is often difficult for one person to control more than one prop. Even if you can manage to get all the controls in one spot, it is difficult to keep track of several groups of people in different locations and trigger each effect at the perfect moment. This means that you will often need one person for each effect. Another consideration is that the person triggering the effect can get bored and fail to trigger the device. All this must be taken into account and planned for.

Let us now discuss one of the most versatile types of props: the actor. By actor, I do not mean a member of the Screen Actors Guild making union scale. Rather, I am referring to anyone who may run around your haunt yelling, "Boo!" rattling chains, triggering props, etc. So how should you use your actors? As we have already discussed, actors may be used to trigger props at the ideal moment. However, they can do much more.

My favorite way to use an actor is to make people think the actor is a stationary prop, until it is too late. I can best explain this by telling the story of my friend Gary. One Halloween he set a lawn chair out in his front yard, took some straw and tucked it in the cuffs of his pants and shirt, with just enough sticking out to make it look as if he were a dummy, stuffed with straw. He then put on a hockey mask, grabbed his chainsaw and sat very still in the chair. When children approached, he would wait until they came over and started poking at the apparent stuffed dummy. At this point, he would jump up, growl and start the chain saw (of course the chain had been removed). The effect was enough that kids would drop their candy and run off. In fact, there was one youngster who has not been seen since! The key, of course, is to lure the victim into a false sense of security and when he is relaxed and distracted, it is the perfect time to pounce!

Of course, actors do not need to be limited to jumping out and startling people. There are myriad ways in which they can be used. Actors can be used to set the mood simply by walking around in costumes or makeup. There is nothing like a zombie or two roaming around a graveyard scene to give it that apprehensive feel. While they are roaming around, apparently aimlessly, your actors can also be used to lead your victims in the direction you want them to go, as well as providing security for your props.

You may find it a good technique to have your actor hide in the shadows behind a prop. Then, while your victims are focusing on the prop, it will be easy for your actor to sneak up behind them. Another good trick is to have your actor illuminated by a strobe light. The resulting stop-motion effect can be very unsettling.

Another, less immediate, function of actors is to report back to you on just how well your haunt is working. At the end of the day, they can tell you what scares seem to work and which are a little lame. They can also advise you on traffic control through the haunt and what bottlenecks need to be addressed.

One final warning about the use of actors: we talked before about the flight-or-fight reflex; it is inevitable that eventually you will run into someone who wants to fight when frightened. It is not uncommon at all for patrons of a haunt to take a swing at an actor. The best advice I can give to prevent this is to keep out of reach of a victim. When jumping out, advance to just out of arms reach and then withdraw. Once a victim is startled, there really is no point to chasing them (if you scared them properly, they probably will not stop running for some time anyway). Stay out of reach and stay safe.

Once you finally have your haunt set up just the way you think you want it, it is important to walk your haunt. Approach from all the angles your victims may approach from. Look to see what props are properly positioned and which do not give the effect you are after. Test all your triggers, and make sure the lighting is what you expected. Position your actors and then have them perform for you as you walk through your haunt.

Once you have personally walked the haunt, have others do it. Try to get people of all ages and heights to go through as you follow them and observe their reactions. You may find that some of your effects are too intense for youngsters, or that an exceptionally tall or short person has difficulty seeing one or more effect. You may even want to try to find a person in a wheelchair to make sure he can safely navigate your haunt and still trigger all the effects.

A few final thoughts. It is not necessary to scare everyone in a group. If you do a good job on just one of them, he can jump enough to scare the entire group. A sudden motion is usually more effective then a slow, constant motion. Give your victims something to distract them and then pounce. Try to make effective use of shadows and dark spots. And most importantly, please: No cute pumpkins or smiling ghosts!

WORKING WITH BLACK LIGHT

Just what is black light? Black light is a term used to describe light in the UV (ultraviolet) spectrum. By definition, this light cannot be seen by the human eye; however, it does cause certain substances to "glow" when they are exposed to it. And therein lies its usefulness in the art of Scareology. Most black lights available today do give off a certain amount of light that is not in the UV spectrum. Most of this light is violet, to which the eye is only moderately sensitive, which means

Black light can be used to make many ordinary items seem to glow in the dark.

that people in a room lit only by black light can see well enough to get around and yet still have the feeling of being in the dark. When you add to this strategically placed items which stand out by glowing, you can place people in a state of uneasiness, making them ready for a good scare.

There are two basic types of black lights available today: incandescent and fluorescent. The incandescent type uses a hot wire filament to produce light, which is then passed through a filter coating to remove most of the visible light and allow only the UV light to pass. The fluorescent type uses a gas-filled tube to produce the light and then passes it through the filter coating. The incandescent variety is convenient to use in that it has a screw base to fit conventional lamp or ceiling fixtures. It does, however, have several drawbacks. For one, they get very hot and must be kept a good distance from any flammable or heat-sensitive substance. They also produce far less UV light and much more visible light than the fluorescent type. The fluorescent variety generally gives the best effect and quality fixtures are available at reasonable prices (yes, you can use a black light tube in any fluorescent fixture, providing the wattage rating and length are the same). When you add to this the fact that they never get too hot to touch, they really should be your first choice.

So just how do you go about using black light in your haunt? Don't worry, I'm not about to give you a bunch of complicated formulas. Instead I will just give you a few general guidelines to get you started and the rest will be up to your imagination. First, you must keep in mind that the glow effect caused by black light is most visible in a dark room lit only by black light or out of doors, after dark, with minimal other artificial lighting. If you do decide to use your

***Left:* An incandescent black light does little but give off a pretty purple light. *Below:* A fluorescent black light should be your first choice.**

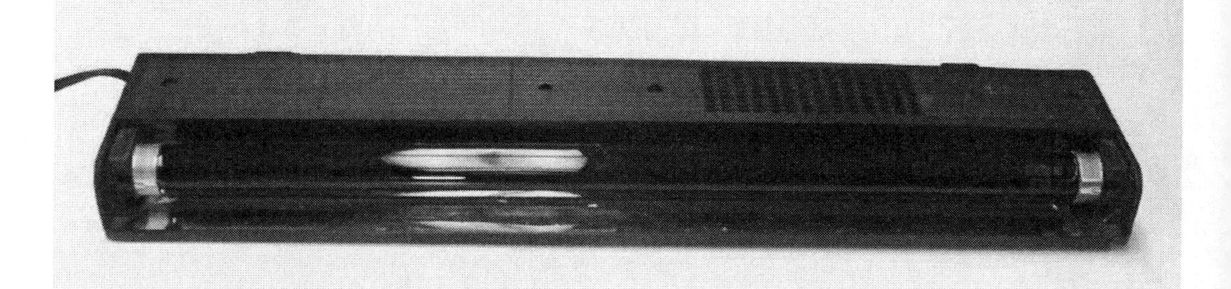

black lights out of doors, remember to keep your fixtures protected from any moisture. Rain or even a moderate dew can not only ruin your fixture, but also can be very dangerous.

Your fixtures should be located so that the light hits the object to be illuminated from the front rather than the rear. This will generally give you the most effect for any given amount of light. Also keep in mind that the closer the light to the object the brighter the glow. You should try to place your lights where no one will come between the light and the prop, thus blocking the light and causing the prop to stop glowing. It is often good to place your light at ceiling level if possible; this will give you good coverage and minimal interference from people and items in the room. Your prop will stand out better if placed in front of a dark background (a flat black is usually best) rather than a light one.

When placing your fixtures, you must keep in mind how you will run power to them and place them where they will not be a hazard. You do not want your lights placed where someone may trip over them or where a small child may decide to grab at them. In addition, most black light fixtures have an exposed bulb, made of glass, which can cause injury if broken. Remember, it is better to forgo an effect than risk having someone injured.

One more thing to keep in mind is that many everyday items appear different under black light. A white shirt for instance will seem to light up (I will explain why later) and many dental caps will appear to be a pink color. Upon entering a room lit by black light, it is natural for people to notice this and discuss it amongst themselves. If they do this, they will often miss seeing the props you spent so much time on. Therefore, if time, space and budget allow, it is best to first lead your victims into a room with nothing in it, just black lights everywhere. If you keep them there for a little while, they will spend the time talking about how different everything looks and when you lead them on to the next room with your props, they will be ready to pay attention.

So now that you know how to position your lights, just what are you going to point them at? That's a good question. Most people limit themselves to commercial glow-in-the-dark products. While these do indeed glow very well under black light, your choice is limited and the products tend to be somewhat boring and lacking in detail. You can often, with a little know-how and some imagination, come up with your own ideas which not only look better but also are far less expensive. Remember that a prop has its greatest effect the first time someone sees it. If you use a store-bought prop it is unique to you and about a million other people. If you build your own it is one of a kind. So what do you do when you find the perfect prop but it does not come in glow-in-the-dark? Well, do you remember earlier in this article I told you I would tell you why white shirts seem to glow in black light? The reason is that almost all laundry detergents contain whiteners which leave a residue on the shirts. Fortunately for us these whiteners also glow nicely under black light. So if you want your prop to glow, just paint it with liquid laundry detergent. I have found that if you use one that says it does not contain dyes it works a little better (the dyes seem to absorb some of the glow). To see just how well this does work, look at the picture at the beginning of this section, which was taken under black light. On the far right you will see a glow in the dark Petite Pete skeleton and just to the left of it you will see one painted in liquid Tide Free (I mention brand names only for those who wish to know exactly what I used; most any liquid detergent should work). Now look closely at the left side of the picture. Just behind the green bottle you can just make out a regular white skeleton. So you can see that not only does this work, but the skeleton, painted with detergent, glows with a very realistic white color. If you use this technique keep in mind that the detergent coat can easily wash or rub off, and after handling you could wind up with it on your hands, so be careful, especially around your eyes. To prevent or at least reduce this rubbing off you can coat your treated prop with several light coats of spray varnish or lacquer. Make sure to use very light coats to begin with to avoid washing off the detergent.

Another item many people use is glow-in-the-dark paints. These usually work very well under black light, but unfortunately they tend to be rather expensive. I have found that most any paint which claims to be fluorescent or neon will glow nicely under black light. I have been able to buy 16-ounce bottles of fluorescent paints at a local craft store for $3.99, a lot less than the glow-in-the-dark stuff. This paint can be seen applied to the exterior of two of the bottles in the first picture (one is made with stacked rings, just to the right of the largest bottle, and the other is at the lower right). Besides using it to paint on the outside of bottles, you can use your paint to make secret messages appear in a room that goes from white light to black light. To do this you will need two bottles of paint of the same color, one fluorescent and the other regular. Start by painting your background with the regular paint. You will want to keep this paint uneven with brush strokes (it will help the second layer to blend in). After the first layer dries the next step is to write your message in the fluorescent paint. Here again, use uneven coverage to help your message blend in with the background. To use this effect start with the regular lights on in the room, then switch them off at the same time you turn on the black light. Your message will seem to suddenly appear. There are other effects you can do with this paint I will tell you about later. For those who must know, the paint I used was Clean Colors by Rich Art (again, almost any paint that claims to be fluorescent should work). Another advantage of this paint is that it is water-soluble and non-toxic. Water-soluble, of course, means easy cleanup and non-toxic means it will be a little safer.

By now you have probably spent a lot of time looking at the first picture, and I bet you are wondering just how I got all those bottles to glow so nicely.

Left: **Can you read this sign under ordinary light?** ***Right:*** **How about now under black light?**

The first step is to find some really neat-looking bottles. You can always use old empty perfume bottles, or just shop around; many stores have a great variety of odd-shaped decorator bottles. But how do you get them to glow? It is a very difficult and time-consuming process. Take, for instance, the bottle at the lower left (as well as several of the other bottles pictured). To make this one glow involved the following steps. First was a trip to the local grocery store, where I purchased a bottle of tonic water (on sale for $0.79 for two liters). Then I had to bring it home, open it and pour it into my bottle. It turns out that tonic water glows a very nice whitish-blue color when exposed to black light. There are a few things you should keep in mind when working with tonic water. First is a very important safety consideration: tonic water is carbonated and can build up considerable pressure under the proper conditions. Therefore, you always want to use it in an open container or leave the bottle open for a few days before sealing it to let the carbonation escape (a little occasional shaking will help speed this up). Second is to make certain that you buy tonic water; seltzer water will not work. Third, you may be thinking that you can make glowing colored bottles using tonic water with food coloring. Wrong! Using food coloring to change the glow color of tonic water gives a very unsatisfactory effect. I will spare you all the technical details, but suffice to say the food coloring absorbs the glow. The same is true for using tonic water in a colored bottle. The only color you will have any luck with is a blue bottle (the closer it matches the color of the tonic glow the better the results).

So what do you do if you want colored bottles? How do you make them glow? These are a little more difficult than the tonic bottles. You will remember I told you I would tell you about some other effects using fluorescent paints. Well, they will look very nice when poured into a bottle of your choice. In fact, if you have chosen a water-based paint (as I suggest you do) you can mix it with water

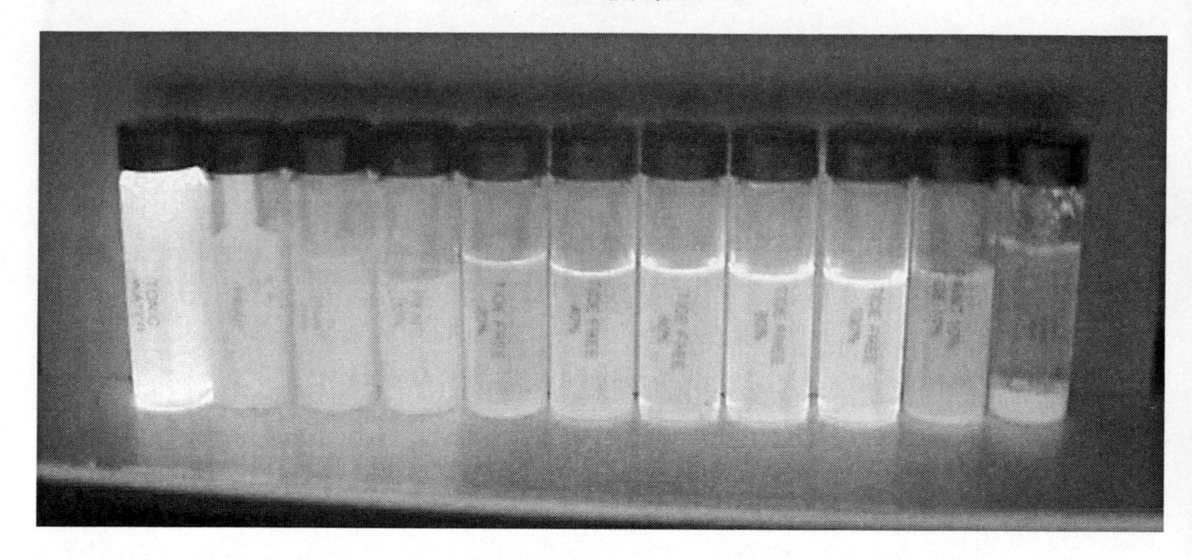

Pictured above are some samples of materials that "glow" under black light. Left to right are: tonic water, 100 percent paint, 10 percent paint, 30 percent paint, 20 percent liquid laundry detergent, 40 percent liquid laundry detergent, 50 percent liquid laundry detergent, 60 percent liquid laundry detergent, 100 percent liquid laundry detergent, 10 percent paint in 10 percent liquid laundry detergent, and 10 percent paint in tonic water.

and save some money. I have found that if you use as little as 10 percent paint (by volume) and 90 percent water, the glow is very nearly as bright as with pure paint. You should remember that the glow color of the paint is not always exactly the same as the color in room light. You should always check your colors under black light to be certain the color you will get is what you want. If you are planning to use a colored bottle, try matching the glow color to the color of the bottle; this should give you a fairly good glow.

I bet you were starting to think, "Wow! If all these things glow so well I will just mix them all together and have a super glow." Sorry, but it just does not work. As you can see from the picture above, they just will not mix (trust me, I have tried). There is one effect you can do by mixing paint and tonic water. If you fill your container part way with tonic water and then slowly squeeze in some paint, you can achieve a layered effect. This can be seen again in the first picture — the bottle second from right near the glowing skeletons. When first poured in the paint tends to float on the top. After some time it will settle to the bottom, maintaining some of the layered look (the bottle pictured had been sitting for over two weeks). Try to pour your bottle where you plan to use it as any agitation will break up the layered effect and just give you a powdery look at the bottom.

Now let us take our tonic water trick one step further and use it to improve on a store-bought prop. I am sure that if you are a true hauntaholic you have seen the numerous "thing in a bottle" props. These are usually some form of an alien, eyeballs, body parts or whatever, which come in a jar to which you add water to make them look like lab specimens. Most people who try to get creative with these items usually just add some food coloring to the water. This can definitely add to the prop, but if you are planning to use your prop in a black light environment, you can go one step further. Simply fill your bottle with some tonic water (after you have let it go flat). As can be seen in the pictures below this does give rather an impressive effect. Again, for those who just have to know, the critter I used is called "Evil New Born" and it came from The Anatomical Chart Company in Skokie, Illinois.

Another variation of the tonic water trick is glowing gelatin. This is a fun material that can be molded just as you would mold a gelatin dessert, only it survives a warm room much better, and of course your finished product will glow nicely under black light. To make this secret formula, you need only tonic water, unflavored gelatin and access to a kitchen. Simply prepare the gelatin according to the package directions except instead of tap water use tonic water. I like to use a little less liquid than the package calls for (about 25 percent less); it makes for a more durable finished product. You can add a little food coloring to change the color of the finished product, but it does seem to cut down on the glow substantially.

Left: **Evil New Born bottle prop shown under normal room light.** ***Right:*** **Evil New Born bottle prop, jar filled with tonic water, under black light.**

The items mentioned above are good if you need only a relatively small amount, but what do you do if you need a lot of glowing water, say for barrels of toxic waste? There is a handy solution, although you may have to look around a little to find it. Some boating and diving shops sell a product called Sea Dye. Sea Dye is a fluorescent dye meant to be tossed into the water to mark the location of a boat or diver in distress. It is an extremely concentrated dye that will color a large area of water a bright fluorescent yellow-green. A single package of Sea Dye should be enough to turn more than one-thousand gallons of water black light reactive.

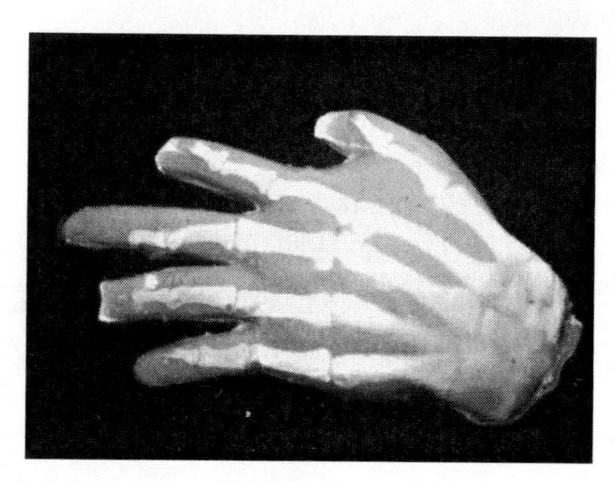

Tonic water gelatin used to make an X-ray hand.

Sea Dye is extremely simple to use; just open the outer protective package and remove the dye pack from within. Then just cut a small slit in the inner bag and remove as much dye as you need. Start with a very small amount as the dye is extremely concentrated.

There are numerous other everyday items which also work well for black light effects. For instance, mashed potato flakes seem to look quite nice

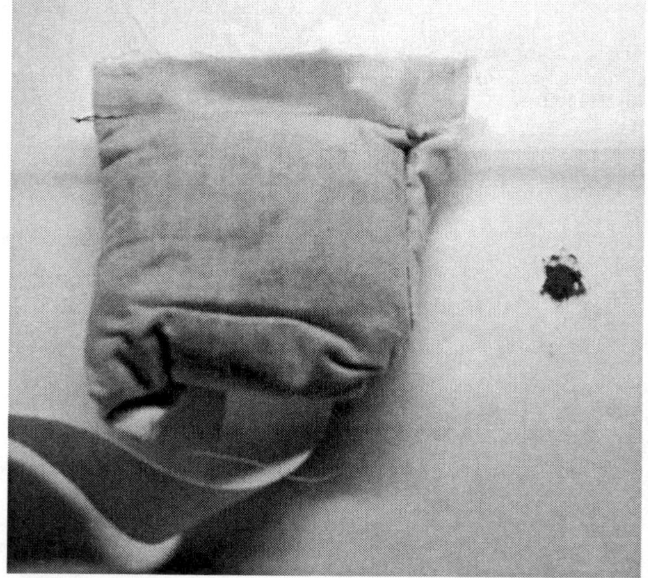

Left: **Sea Dye can be used to turn large quantities of water black light reactive.** ***Right:*** **The inside of a Sea Dye marker, showing the amount of dye removed and used to color two gallons of water.**

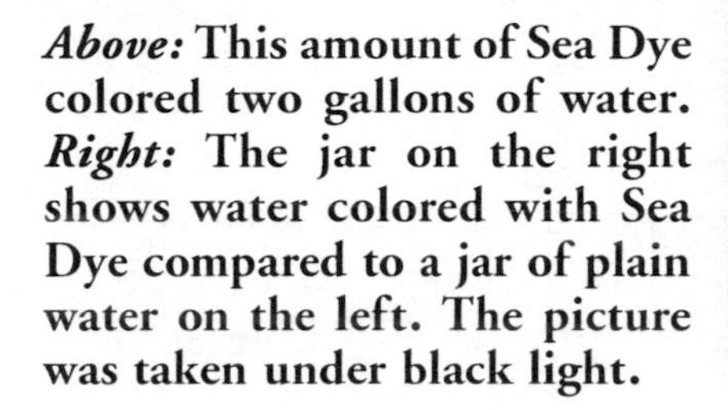

Above: **This amount of Sea Dye colored two gallons of water.** ***Right:*** **The jar on the right shows water colored with Sea Dye compared to a jar of plain water on the left. The picture was taken under black light.**

under black light (I use Hungry Jack brand). I have also found modeling clay and cordage that work nicely. I have included a list of some of my favorites in the back of this book; most can be found at your local grocery or hardware store. The list is by no means inclusive and I am sure you will be able to find many others on your own. My suggestion to you is to try everything you can get your hands on under your black light (especially if it claims to be fluorescent or neon) and see if it glows. Experiment, be bold, use your imagination, and try to come up with an idea no one has thought of before. Then you can have a truly original, one-of-a-kind prop.

One final warning: while most black lights sold for home use are safe, there are some commercial ones which can be dangerous. These use what is called shortwave UV, as opposed to the longwave UV, most commonly found. These are often used for scientific and medical use, and are not meant to be used where there will be any degree of human exposure. Be sure to check the warnings on any lights you may buy. It is also a good idea to limit your black light exposure (and that of others) to reasonable doses. Even so-called safe UV lights can be unhealthy if one is exposed to them for many hours a day over a period of many days.

SKULL PAINTING 101

Let us move on to the subject of basic skull painting. With an inexpensive plastic skull and some spray paint, you can make some great-looking props, like the ones pictured above, and in many more styles and colors. While some of these skulls may look like they are difficult and time consuming, they are really quick and easy to make. The only part that takes any real time is waiting for the paint to dry.

First let's get the safety issues out of the way. Always work outside, or with plenty of ventilation; paint fumes and mist simply are not good for you. It is also a good idea to wear a respirator and safety glasses. Of course, you will want to make sure you always aim the paint spray away from yourself. Read and follow the manufacturer's directions on any and all of the products you use. It is also a very good idea to wear old clothes (they inevitably will end up with paint on them) and even rubber gloves.

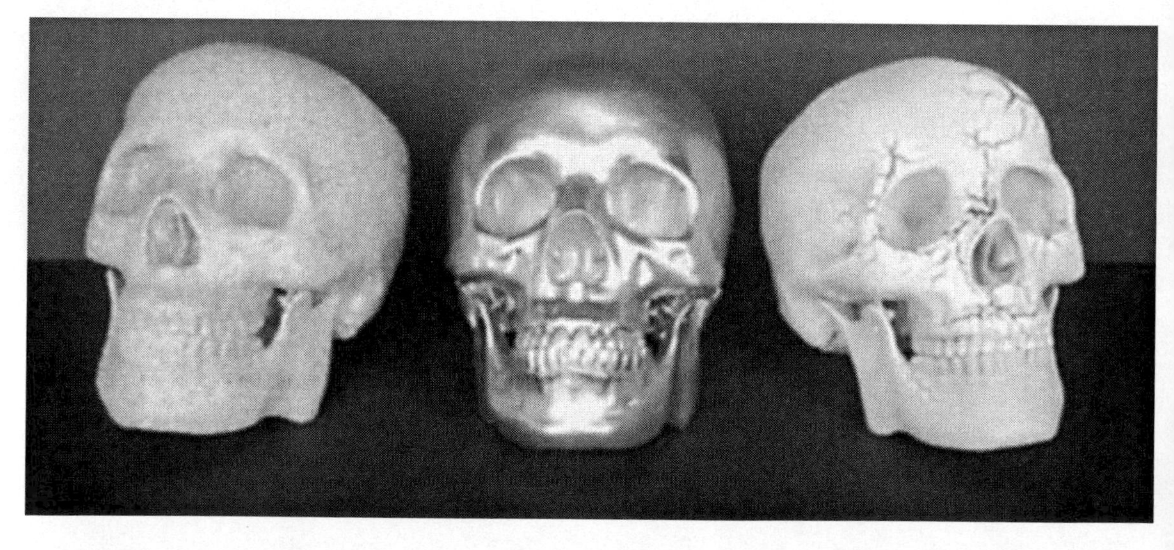

A little bit of spray paint can make an ordinary skull into an extraordinary prop.

The first thing you will need for skull painting is, of course, a skull. You should look for one that has a semi-rough bone-like finish, as some of the cheaper glossy plastic ones will not hold paint well, and you will end up with an uneven finish or a skull that peels and chips easily. I also prefer a skull without the calvarium cut, that is to say one on which the top of the skull is not removable. All the skulls I used for the props shown in this section are the 2-piece skulls from the Anatomical Chart Company.

After you have selected a skull to paint, the next thing you must select is your paint. The type and color of paint you select will depend on just what you want your finished prop to look like. There are, by far, too many paints out there for me to give you all the possibilities. Instead, I will do as I usually do and give you a few examples of what has worked for me and leave the rest up to your imagination.

By virtue of its shape, a skull can be rather difficult to paint. With a little planning, though, it can be made very simple. I always start painting my skull from the bottom up. Trying to paint the bottom of a skull can be a challenge, as if you try to stand it on its top it tends to roll around. This little problem is very easy to solve; all you need is a cardboard box and a knife. Simply take a box large enough and sturdy enough to hold your skull and cut an oblong hole in it, about 4" × 5". Then take your skull and place it upside down in the hole.

You will want to place your skull with the face angled slightly upwards;

***Left:* Cut a hole in a cardboard box about 4" × 5". *Right:* Place your skull in the hole and it will hold your skull securely.**

this will make it a little easier to get inside the eye sockets and nose area. If you are painting outside, face the skull so that the wind is blowing toward the face; this will help the paint get into the deep facial areas. Once your skull is positioned, take a moment to look it over and plan your painting strategy. It my sound a little strange to think you need a plan to paint such a seemingly simple object; however, skulls can be tricky. For instance, it can be a real trick to get paint all the way into the eye sockets and nose without it running. Another problem area is under the cheekbones.

So how do you get into some of the tough spots? Start by remembering to use many light coats. Do not layer the paint on so thickly that it runs. It may sound a little strange at first, but many parts you may think of as being the top should be painted when the skull is upside-down. Take, for instance, the top of the eye sockets and nose; you will have the best luck painting these when the skull is upside-down. Do not forget that as the paint moves forward out of the can it is also being pulled down by gravity. It is this slight falling motion which will help it to fill in the top of the eye sockets when they are upside-down. You will also want to hold the can at a slight angle to aim the spray toward the surface you wish to coat. Of course, you will do most of your painting on the bottom of the eye socket, etc., when the skull is right side up. Remember, you can always add another coat of paint, but a run can be much harder to get rid of. (If you do get a run, let the paint dry completely and then sand it smooth with fine sandpaper and recoat.) A good way to avoid runs is to keep the paint spray moving and come back to the same area several times to achieve a uniform coverage. Make sure to let the bottom of the skull dry completely before turning it over to paint the top.

Now that we have quickly covered the basics of painting techniques, let's see how to achieve specific effects.

THE GOLDEN SKULL

While it may look impressive, the golden skull is as easy as it gets when it comes to skull painting. The only trick here is to pick the right paint. For this skull just pick the proper paint and apply as directed above. The paint I used was Rust-Oleum Specialty Metallic Gold. The

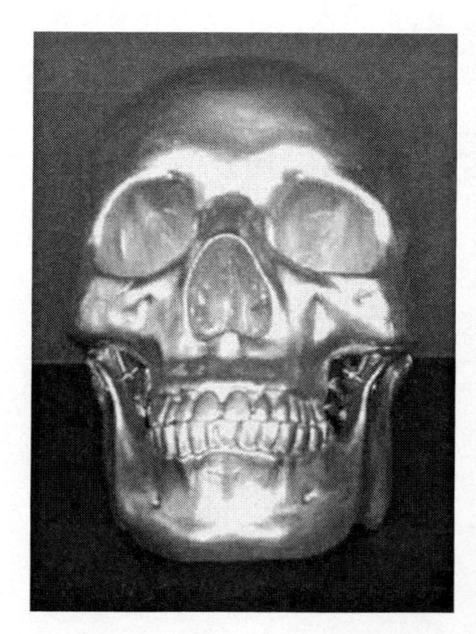

While it may look impressive, the golden skull is as easy as it gets!

company also makes silver, but I was disappointed in the results; it lacked the bright metal glow of the gold. Be sure to use several coats as it will give you a much better look than only one or two. I am sure there are many other gold metallic paints that will work well; I mention the brand only for those who want to know exactly what I used.

THE STONE SKULL

The stone skull is a little more difficult than your typical painted skull but I love the polished granite look you can get and it is still well within the ability of most anyone. For this skull, I used American Accents Stone Creations by Rust-Oleum. This paint and others like it are available at most craft and hardware stores. The product is designed to give a stone finish to almost any surface and comes in a wide range of colors. You apply it according to the directions on the can; the problem comes with the fact that you are trying to paint an object with many different angles and curves. This causes the finish to have a tendency to slide off your skull rather than sticking. The best advice I can give here is to never hold the can too close to your work and apply the paint in several layers, allowing the product to dry in-between coats. At first, I had a real tendency to get a base layer down and then moved the can closer to fill in the bare spots. This only resulted in blowing off the finish I had just applied. The key here is patience; apply, let dry and reapply until you are happy with the finished product.

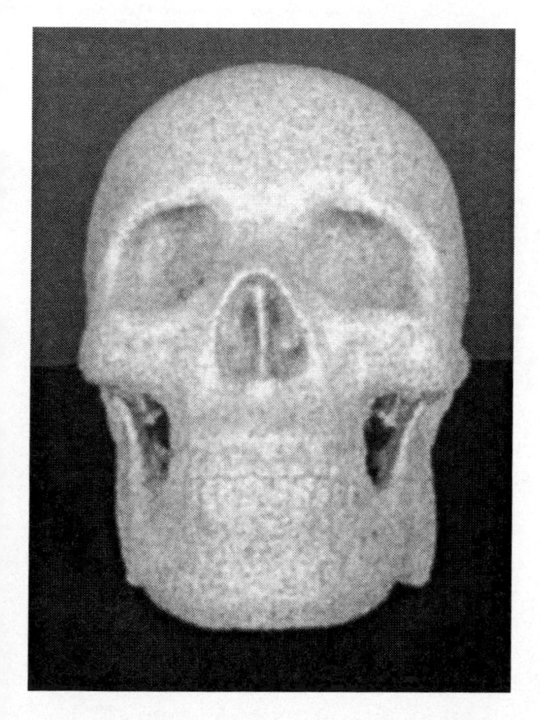

While it is still easy to do, the stone skull will require some patience to master.

Another little trick I learned is to prime the skull with a spray-on texture paint; the rougher surface helps considerably in keeping the stone finish from blowing right off the skull. Again the product I used was made by Rust-Oleum and is called Rust-Oleum Textured. When you are finished and have let your stone paint dry (two or three days at least) finish it off with several layers of clear coat. I recommend you use the clear coat the manufacturer makes specifically for this product. If you choose another brand, make sure you read the label on the stone finish can; some clear coats will cause your skull to turn a dingy yellow color.

THE CRACKLE SKULL

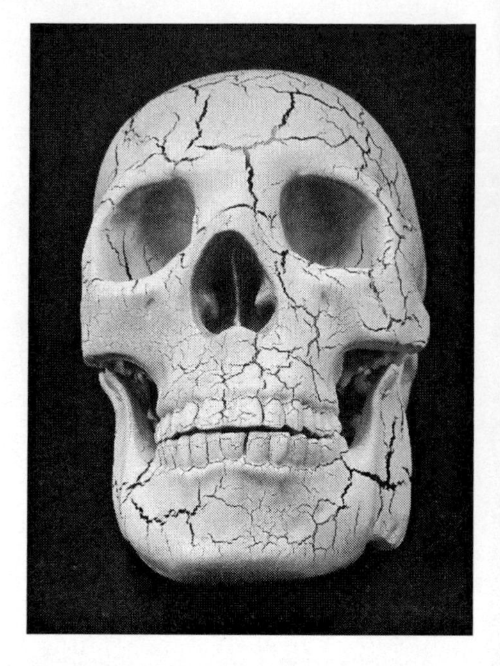

The crackle skull will take by far the most practice to get right, but it is worth it.

The crackle skull can take some practice to get right, but when you do you will have a very impressive one-of-a-kind prop. To make this skull I used a two-part paint kit, again by Rust-Oleum, called Crackle Creations. The application is simple enough; the practice comes in getting just the look you want. Follow the package directions when applying the base coat. I have found I need to vary in applying the crackle coat. For this, I like to use one rather heavy coat, almost to the point of running the paint. This will give the very large cracks as seen between the eyes and below the nose. The smaller cracks, as on the front of the jaw, were made by applying the top coat and then coming back a few seconds later and applying another light coat.

Remember also to paint the base coat on the entire skull first. Then when applying the top coat do only the parts of the bottom which cannot be reached with the skull right side up and avoid overspray. Then turn the skull over to do the top. Remember to plan your painting strategy and plan to have your best effect on the parts of the skull which will be seen.

LIMITLESS POSSIBILITIES

There are two other finishes I would like to mention briefly. Both are simple spray-on finishes which take only a few minutes but give great results. The first is Rust-Oleum Hammered; this paint will give your skull the look of hammered metal. The other is Rust-Oleum Chalkboard Paint; this paint gives your skull the look and feel of an old blackboard. The finished skull can be used as a chalkboard that you can write on in chalk and then erase. If you do use your skull to write on remember to read the can for the correct type of chalk to use as some chalks will scratch the surface.

I would hope that by now your imagination is running wild with ideas. I would expect you are thinking, "If skulls look this good with just a little paint, what about an entire skeleton?" If you are, you have the right idea. Full skeletons look great in any of these finishes, and I am sure there are many more that would look as good or better. I will leave it up to you, the reader, to experiment and find all the options.

I hope you find these few suggestions helpful and a good way to get you started on making some very unique props. Just look around at your local stores for new and unique finishes. Try them on skulls, skeletons or whatever and you may well come up with a one-of-a-kind prop that you will use to frighten the little children in your neighborhood for years to come.

PUT A LIGHT IN IT

People who know me will tell you I will put a light in just about anything. I often find it an easy and effective way to make a dull, lifeless prop come to life with new excitement; the best part is that it is usually very easy and very inexpensive. Take, for instance, a simple translucent skull. Ordinarily it just sits there, but add a simple light and it really shines. (For detailed instructions on lighting a transparent skull see section "Skull Light Skull Bright.")

In this section I will give you a few ideas as to where you can find inexpensive lights and give you some basic tips on how to wire them. Once you have mastered these basics, you can start using them to create ways to modify and build your own props.

Let us start by talking about where you can find a variety of inexpensive lights. One of the easiest ways is to use lights that you can buy pre-wired and ready to use. These can be the simple bulb-on-a-cord type used for the lighted skull or any of hundreds of other small lights you may find at any of a number of locations. These are about as easy to use as you can find. All you need to do is find a way to hold the bulb where you want it and then plug it in. Of course, you must

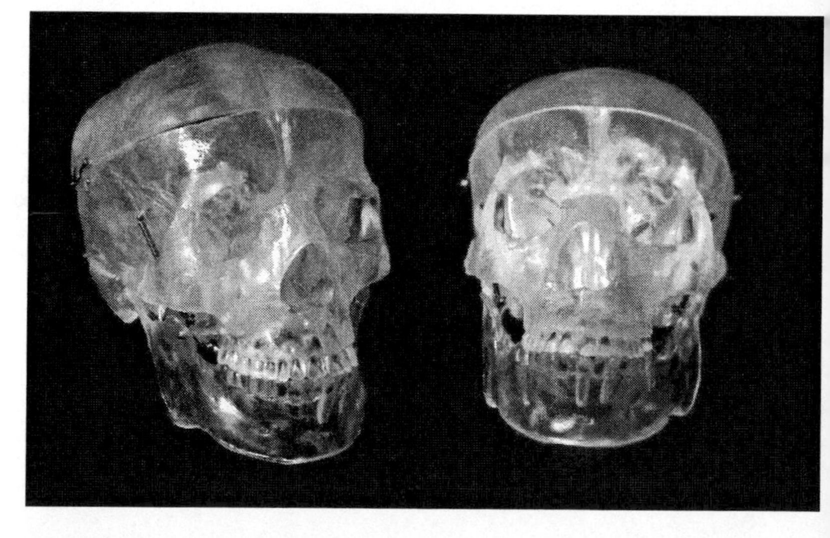

Simply adding a light to a prop can really make it stand out.

take into account the amount of heat your light will give off. As a general rule the brighter the light, the more heat it gives off. You must make sure to have enough space around your light and enough airflow to keep things from overheating. I also recommend you look for UL-approved products. Just keep your eyes open anytime you are out shopping and you will be surprised what you can find.

Another option is to find or buy loose bulbs or LEDs (light emitting diodes) and wire them in yourself. With what I show you later in this section, you should easily be able to do this. The only problem with buying all your components separately is the cost. By the time you buy a bulb, base, wire, etc., you will have spent a lot more money than you need to.

I prefer to buy strings of holiday lights and take them apart for what I need. This will give you everything you need with the exception of a battery pack and maybe some additional wire. In fact, in some cases you can even get a battery pack with your lights. Buying this way gets you a much better price and can even save you some work. I have seen miniature light sets for as low as $1.99 for one hundred bulbs, and the replacement bulbs for $0.99 for five.

Let me start with the basics of electricity and wiring. I apologize to any readers who may have a strong background in electronics. What I present here is for people with very little or no knowledge of electronics, and it is without a doubt oversimplified and in lay terms. If I use the term battery to refer to what is actually an electrochemical cell or use some other technically inaccurate term, please forgive me. I do it only to make the information easier to understand for the beginner. In fact, if you are versed in electronics you may skip reading this section. Flip through and look at the pictures for ideas instead.

Let us start by talking about the different components we will use to make our lights work. The first we will discuss is the light source itself. For the projects you will do, you will most likely use either an incandescent bulb or an LED.

An incandescent bulb is what we normally just call a light bulb. These come in a variety of sizes, shapes, colors, voltages and wattage ratings.

The wattage rating tells us how much electricity the bulb will use. On larger bulbs, such as the ones you would use in a lamp in your home, the wattage rating is printed right on the bulb. For smaller bulbs you will have to rely on the package to tell you the wattage. For most of the projects we will discuss here, wattage will not be much of an issue.

The next important feature we will look at is the base. The base is the part of the bulb that connects to the socket which holds the bulb and provides a connection to the electrical wires.

Bulb bases come in a variety of styles; the most familiar is the screw base on next page. This is not the only type of base you will find. The bayonet base is also very common on smaller bulbs.

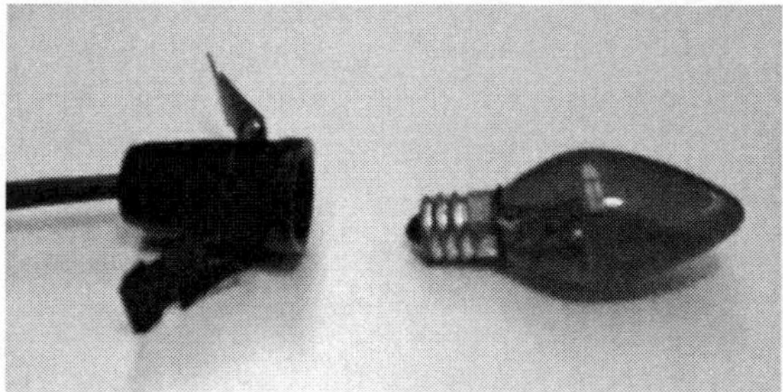

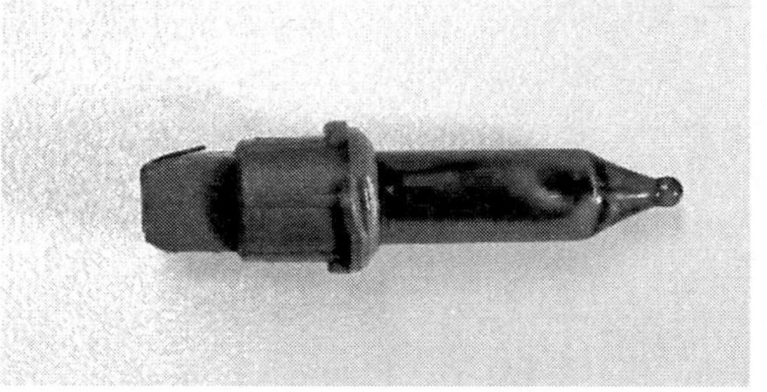

Left: **Incandescent bulbs come in a wide variety of sizes, shapes and colors.** ***Right, top:*** **A screw base bulb simply screws into a base.** ***Right, bottom:*** **A bayonet base bulb simply pushes into a base.**

There are other styles of bases as well, but you will find these to be the most common. Most bases also come in a variety of sizes as well. The problem of matching the type and size of the base of your bulb with the socket is eliminated if you buy them as a set. Again, my favorite way to do this is to buy a string of lights and remove the parts I want.

Many bulbs, especially those for holiday lights, also come in a wide variety of colors, giving you a lot of options when it comes to prop design. I myself, however, still believe you cannot beat red eyes for Halloween.

The final thing we will look at in our discussion of bulbs is the voltage rating. This number tells you the number of volts of electricity it will take to make your bulb light properly without burning out quickly. Voltage can be either AC (a wall outlet) or DC (a battery). AC voltage (actually AC current if you want to be correct) is a voltage which changes not only the number of volts but also the polarity (positive or negative). DC voltage remains the same and keeps the same polarity. This really means very little to us except that some AC devices will not work with DC, and some DC devices will not work with AC. In the case of bulbs, however, most will work equally well with AC or DC and for our purposes you can use an equal voltage of either.

The other type of light you may often wish to use is the LED or light emitting diode. These are semiconductor devices that allow electricity to flow in only one direction and emit light when electricity flows through them. This may

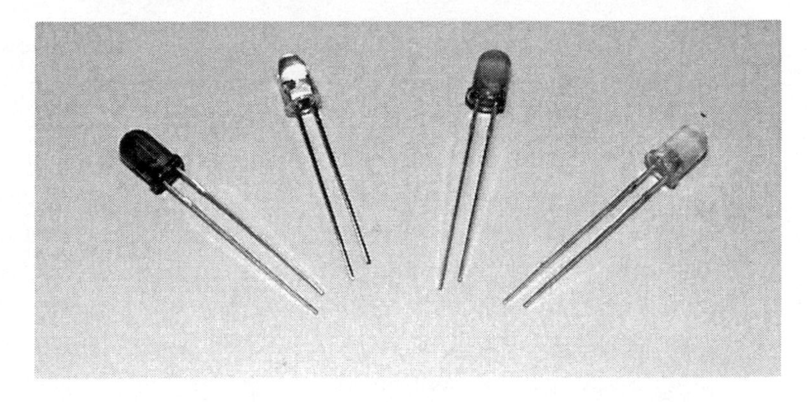

While there are fewer colors, sizes and shapes to choose from, LEDs are a great choice where low power consumption is important.

sound complicated, and the inner workings of an LED actually are somewhat complicated; however, LEDs are extremely easy for us to use.

The only real differences in using an LED as opposed to a bulb are that the LED will light only with the plus and minus sides properly hooked up, and LEDs come in fewer colors and sizes. A big plus for LEDs is that for a given amount of light, they use far less electricity and generate much less heat than an incandescent bulb. While new LEDs are getting bigger and brighter, they are still suitable only for effects such as glowing eyes or other effects which do not demand a large amount of light. If you need a very bright light, or need to light a large area, you will most likely want to use a large bulb which plugs into an AC wall outlet. If you need a not-too-bright light that will last a very long time on a battery, an LED is just what you need.

Another advantage of LEDs is that they have a much longer life than bulbs, making them a great choice for building into a prop where they would be difficult or impossible to change. This, and the fact that they can light for a very long time when run off a small battery, makes them a very useful item to have in your prop-building parts kit.

The next component I would like to talk about briefly is wire. There really is not a whole lot you need to know about wire. It comes in a variety of thicknesses, called the gauge. The somewhat confusing thing about wire gauge is the higher the gauge number the thinner the wire (most people would expect the opposite). For most props powered by only a couple of small batteries, a wire gauge of between 26 and 22 should be about right. You can never use too thick of a wire, but you must take care not to use too thin of a wire. If your wire is too thin for the load you put on it, it may overheat, creating a fire hazard. A properly sized wire should never feel warm while carrying its load.

The next thing you need to know about wire is that it comes either solid or stranded. Solid wire is just as the name implies — a solid piece of copper covered with an insulator. Stranded wire has a number of very thin wires covered in insulation.

Stranded wire is generally more flexible and can better withstand repeated bending back and forth than solid wire, while solid wire will better retain any bend you put in it. For most of the applications we will discuss, you may use either solid or stranded wire. For most of the props I build, I use solid wire because it's a little easier to strip off the insulation to connect the wire.

So far, we have a bulb or LED that will use electricity to make light, and wire to move the electricity to the bulb. Where will that electricity come from? You have two basic choices: household AC current (electricity from the outlet in your home) or DC current from batteries. The only use of AC current we will talk about here is the use of pre-wired UL-listed lights, which you buy ready to plug in and use. We will not discuss altering or rewiring these lights, as the voltage from an AC wall outlet can be dangerous. Our discussion of using AC will cover nothing more dangerous than plugging a cord into the wall, just as you would a lamp or toaster. Of course, just as with a lamp or toaster, it is your responsibility to insure the device is not placed in such a way that the heat from it could cause a fire. So we have two basic rules for the use of AC: use only unaltered UL-listed lights and make sure you place them where the heat will not be a problem. We can add a third common-sense rule: electricity and water do not mix, so do not use an AC light anywhere near water!

Most batteries, on the other hand, do not produce enough electricity to be very dangerous. Very large batteries such as car batteries can be an exception. Here we will talk only about using smaller batteries, such as you might use in a flashlight. Batteries come in different sizes and produce different numbers of volts. For the projects discussed in this section, we will talk about batteries in the following sizes and voltages. The first are the batteries which produce 1.5

Left: **Wire comes as either solid or stranded.** ***Right:*** **One and a half volt batteries come in a variety of sizes.**

volts; these come in sizes of AAA, AA, C, and D as well as other less common sizes.

All these batteries produce the same number of volts and an AAA battery can be used to power the same devices as a D battery. The difference is in how long they can do it. The much smaller AAA battery will produce the 1.5 volts of electricity for far less time than a D battery. Smaller batteries are good when they must be hidden in a small space; larger batteries are better when you need to run a device for a longer time.

The other common battery voltage is nine volts; these are commonly called nine-volt batteries or transistor radio batteries. These are best when a device requires a higher voltage or you need to run a number of lower voltage devices in series (more about series circuits later).

Several batteries can be combined to give more volts or a longer life depending upon how they are wired together (more about how to do this later).

It is normally easiest to connect your batteries to your wire using a battery holder. This is a device that has metal contacts inside to connect to the battery or batteries, and wires coming out of it to connect to your project. These not only make battery hook-up easier, but also make it easier to change batteries when they run out of electricity.

Batteries have two contacts, usually one on each end. The exception is a nine-volt battery, which has both contacts on the same end. These contacts are where you tap into the battery to use the electricity they store. The contacts are called the plus (+) and minus (-) terminals. In order for the electricity to flow, it needs a path from the minus terminal to the plus terminal.

So, for our projects, we will need to connect our battery (usually in a battery holder) to a piece of wire, run the wire to our bulb or LED, then run another

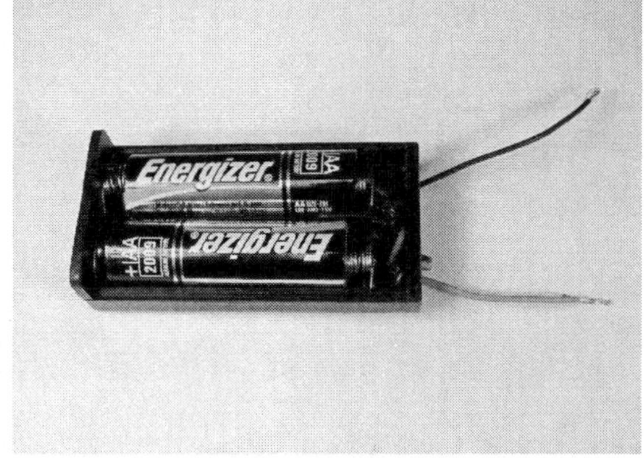

Left: **A nine volt battery.** ***Right:*** **A battery holder makes it easier to connect and change batteries.**

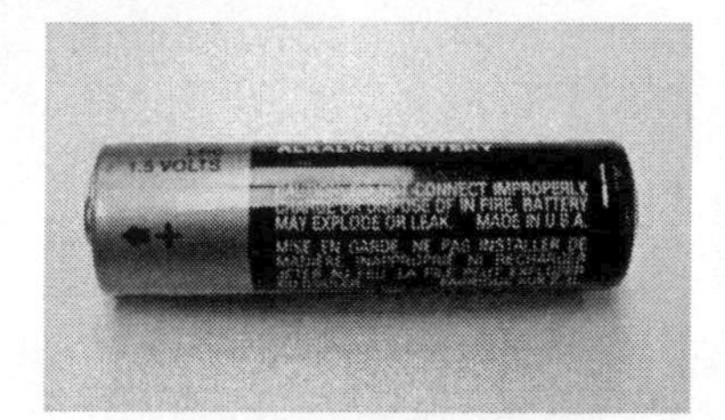

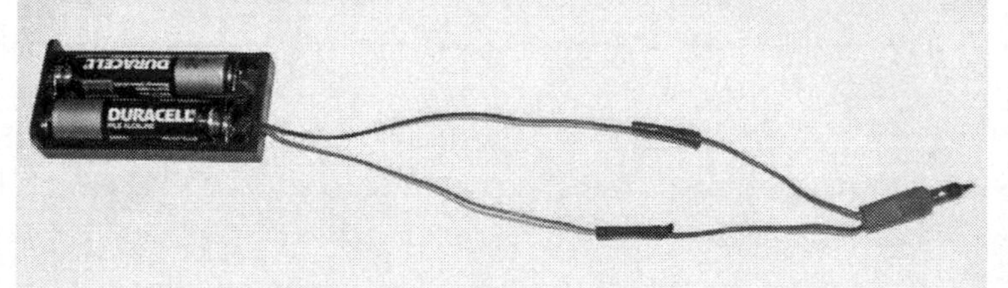

Left: **A battery has two terminals, called the positive and the negative terminals.** ***Right:*** **A battery for a power source, wire to run the power through, a bulb, and wire for a return path to the battery make a completed circuit.**

wire from the bulb back to the battery. While this is as simple as it sounds, if we have more than one battery or light, we need to connect them so that each light gets the voltage it needs to work correctly.

To show you how to correctly connect your components under different circumstances, I will be using what are called schematic diagrams. These are simply drawings where standard symbols are used to represent components, and lines are used to show the wires that connect them. For the schematic diagrams here, we will use the following standard symbols to indicate the following components.

For a battery see below and for a bulb or LED see below.

In order to make the math as easy as possible, we will always make our circuits using all batteries of the same voltage and all lights of the same voltage. Now that you are familiar with the symbols we will use and the limitations of the combinations we will talk about, we will discuss the two basic types of circuits, series and parallel. A series circuit is one in which the electricity flows from the source and all of the electricity must pass through each device to get back to the source.

In the series circuit shown on next page, electricity starts at the negative terminal of the battery. It then flows through a wire to the first light (L1 or lamp one), then through the light into another piece of wire. Next, it flows through a

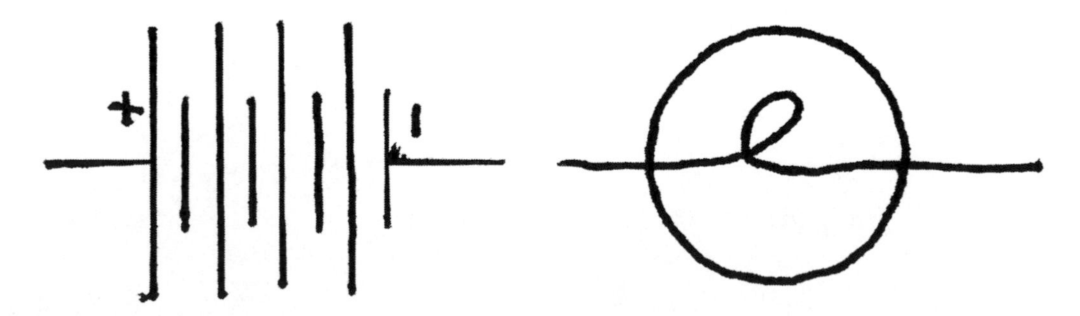

Left: **The schematic symbol for a battery.** ***Right:*** **The schematic symbol for a lamp.**

wire to the second light (L2). Then through the light, back into another wire and back to the positive terminal of the battery. Electricity can flow because it has an uninterrupted path from the negative terminal of the battery back to the positive terminal of the battery. If you have a break in any of the wires or a bulb burns out, the whole circuit goes down. Pictured below is how this series circuit would look if you built it.

The other basic type of circuit is a parallel circuit. A parallel circuit is one in which electricity leaves the negative terminal of the battery and flows through two or more paths back to the positive terminal.

In the parallel circuit pictured above, electricity flows from the negative terminal of the battery into a wire. The difference here is that this wire then connects directly to one side each of two different lights (L1 and L2). After passing through the two lights the electricity then goes into another wire and back to the positive terminal of the battery. If one of the lights burns out, the other will remain lit because the electricity still has an uninterrupted path from the negative terminal of the battery back to the positive terminal. This is what this parallel circuit looks like built.

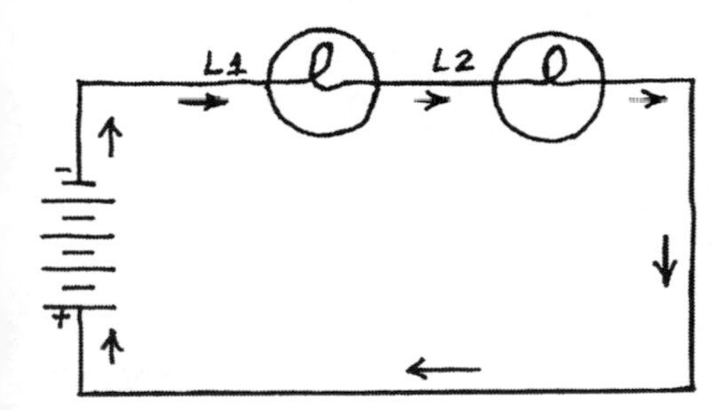

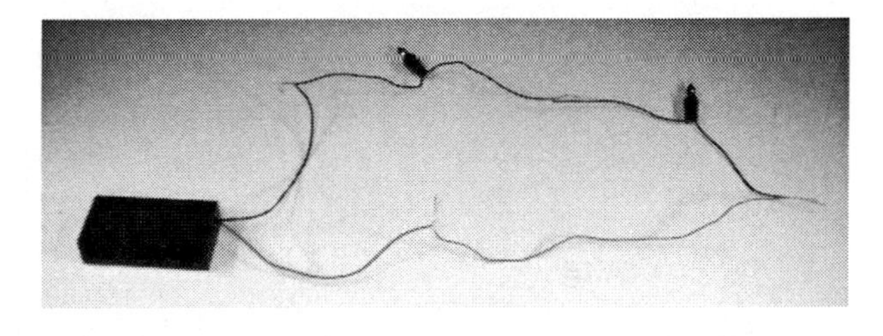

Left: **A schematic drawing for a completed series circuit.** ***Right:*** **A completed series circuit.**

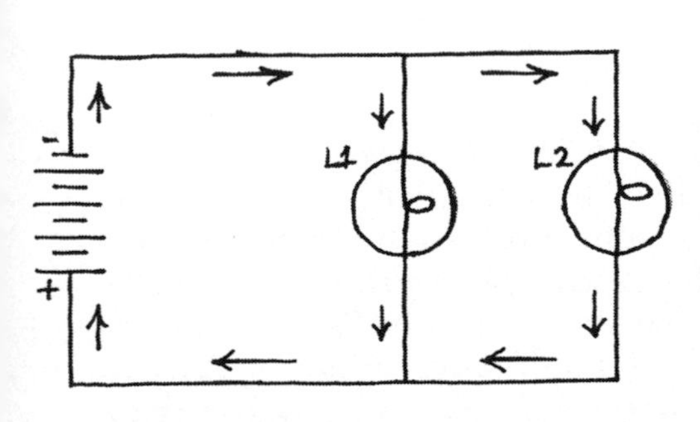

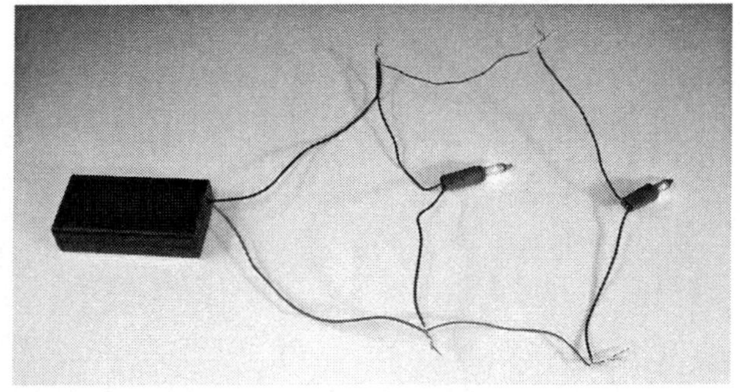

Left: **A schematic drawing for a completed parallel circuit.** ***Right:*** **A completed parallel circuit.**

Below, the same circuit is built a little differently. It is still a parallel circuit, because the electricity can pass through either of the two lights to get back to the battery. Remember, if all of the electricity must pass through each light, it is a series circuit. If the electricity can take more than one path, it is a parallel circuit.

It is possible to combine the two circuit types into what is called a series parallel circuit, but we will not discuss that type of circuit here. A simple series or parallel circuit will work for our needs. It is also important to know that lights are not the only things which can be combined in series or parallel. Batteries may also be combined in either way, and as with lights the results are different with different wiring.

When two batteries of equal voltage are wired together in parallel, the voltage supplied to the wires is the same as the voltage of either battery. That is to say, if you have two or more 1.5-volt batteries wired in parallel, the total voltage will be 1.5 volts.

The advantage of adding batteries in parallel is that each battery has to supply only a part of the electricity used. This means that your two batteries will last twice as long as one when used to light the same light or lights. In theory, you can add as many batteries as you like in parallel to make your lights last as long as you need.

By contrast, if you take the same two 1.5-volt batteries and wire them in series, the result is quite different. When wired in series, the voltages of the two

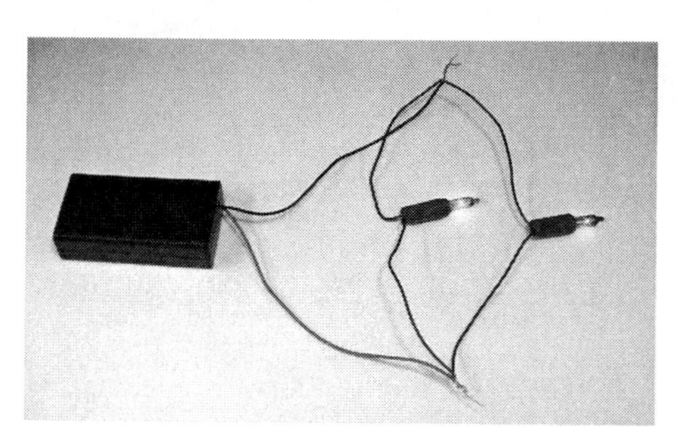

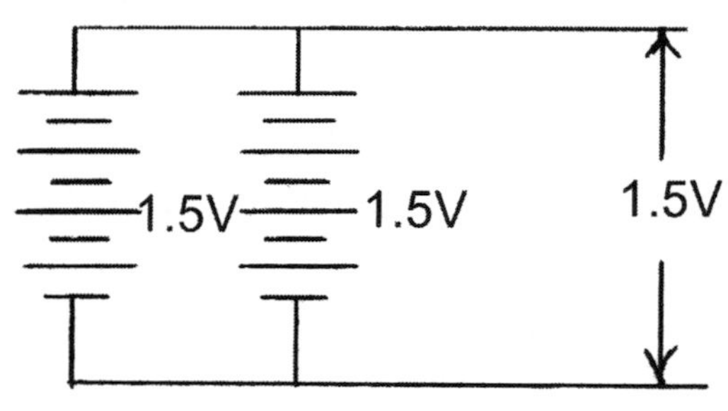

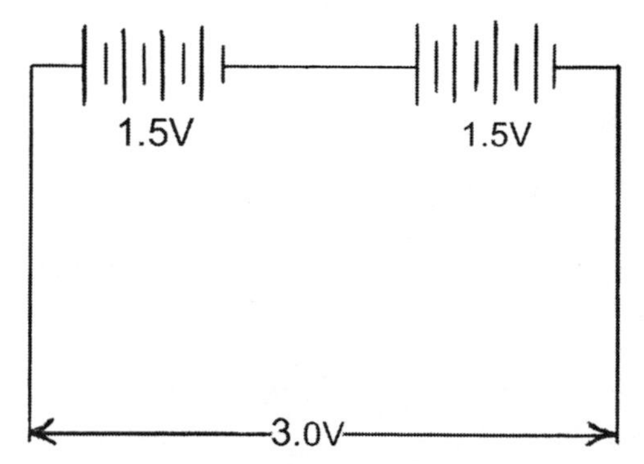

Top, left: **Another way of building a parallel circuit.** ***Above:*** **A schematic drawing for two batteries wired in parallel, showing how two one-and-a-half-volt batteries wired in Parallel supply one and a half volts of power.** ***Left:*** **A schematic drawing for two batteries wired in series, showing how two one-and-a-half-volt batteries wired in series supply three volts of power.**

batteries add. So now you will have 1.5 volts from the first battery and 1.5 volts from the second battery which adds up to 3 volts.

In theory, you could keep adding more batteries to reach any voltage you might want. In practice, adding too many batteries can be dangerous as the inside of a battery can handle only so much voltage. Try to limit your 1.5-volt batteries to no more than six in a series.

We have seen how the total voltage of combined batteries can vary depending upon how they are wired, but what about the bulbs? No matter where it is placed in any kind of circuit, a light will still need the same number of volts to light properly. The catch is that depending upon the type of circuit, a different number of volts will be available to each light when using the same voltage from the battery or batteries.

Matching the voltage of the battery to the voltage of lights is easiest in a parallel circuit. In a parallel circuit, the same voltage is applied to all the lights, so that the voltage of the battery simply needs to equal the voltage rating of the lights. If you have six three-volt lights wired in parallel, you would need a three-volt battery to power them. In fact, no matter how many three-volt lights you have in parallel (one or one hundred), you still need a three-volt battery to make them work.

Again, in the case of a series circuit, it gets a little trickier. In a series circuit, the voltage of the battery (batteries) should equal the total of the voltage ratings of the lights in the circuit. That is to say, if you have two lights in your circuit rated at 1.5 volts each, you will need a three-volt source (two 1.5-volt batteries in series). If you have three 1.5-volt lights, you will need 4.5 volts of batteries. For two three-volt lights, you need six volts of batteries.

Now that we have discussed the theory of how our components will be wired together, let us look at how we will make the actual connections. Soldering is more or less the standard way to make an electrical connection, but for our

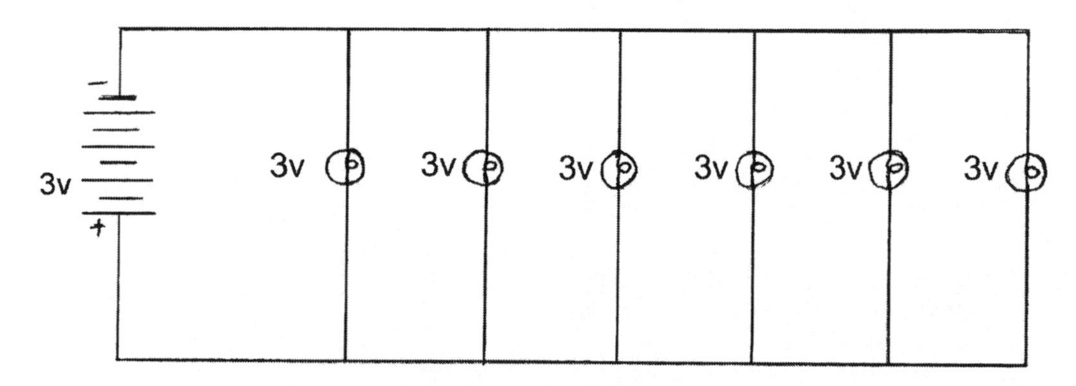

A schematic drawing for six lamps wired in parallel, showing how six three-volt lamps wired in parallel require three volts of power.

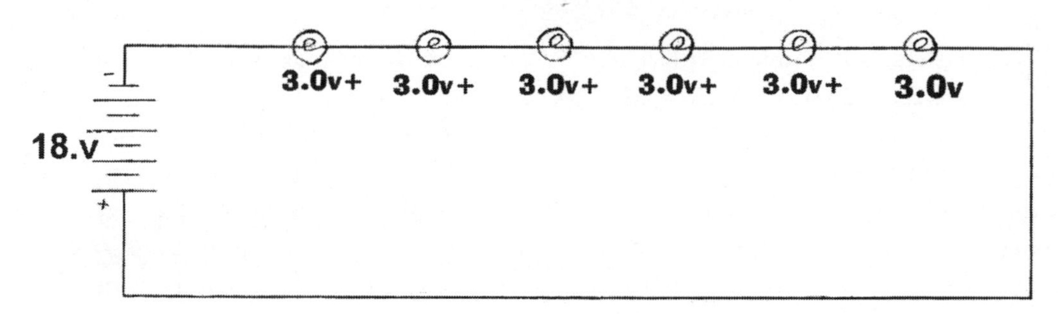

A schematic drawing for six lamps wired in series, showing how six three-volt lamps wired in series require eighteen volts of power.

props we can use an easier and quicker way. We can just strip some of the insulation off of the ends of the wires, twist the bare copper ends together and then tape over any exposed copper with electrical tape.

For those of you who have never worked with wiring, this is not at all difficult. One of the best tools for stripping insulation off of wire is a pair of wire cutters, but you can use long-nose pliers or a variety of other tools. The idea is to lightly cut or crush the insulation at the point you want to remove it, and then just pull off a short section of the insulation. With wire cutters, you must take care to cut only through the insulation and not the wire, by using only a light pressure.

It sometimes helps to lightly twist the wire cutters or pliers around the wire. While still exerting a light squeezing pressure on the tool, pull toward the cut end of the wire. Always pull the tool away from you, never toward you. If the tool slips, you do not want it to hit you in the face or elsewhere. The exact amount of insulation you strip off does not matter; around .75" should work just fine.

One of the best tools for stripping insulation off of wire is a pair of wire cutters.

Once you have stripped off insulation from both wires you wish to connect, simply twist the bare copper sections together.

Once you have your wires twisted together, you must cover the bare copper with electrical tape (available at any hardware store). Start by cutting a piece of tape about one inch long. Take the tape and wrap the very end of it once around the bare copper and a portion of the insulation.

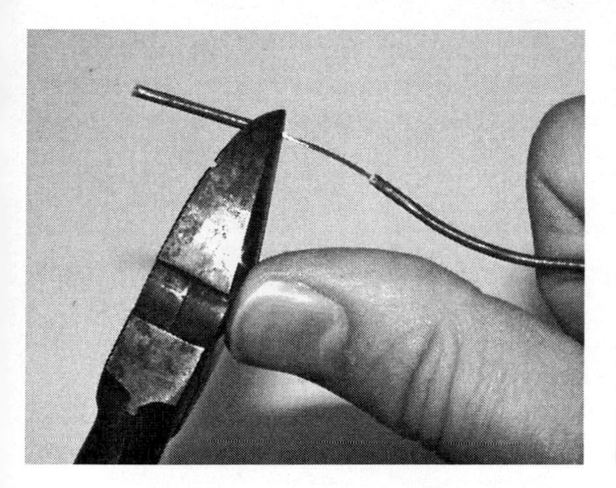

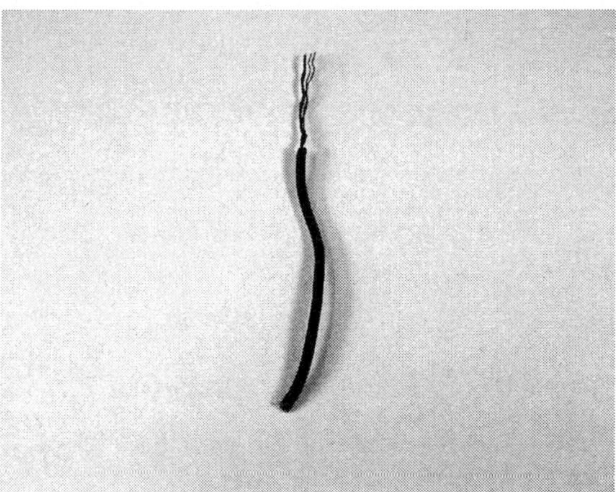

***Left:* Pull off the wire's insulation to expose the conductors within. *Right:* Wire with a section of the insulation removed to show the copper conductors.**

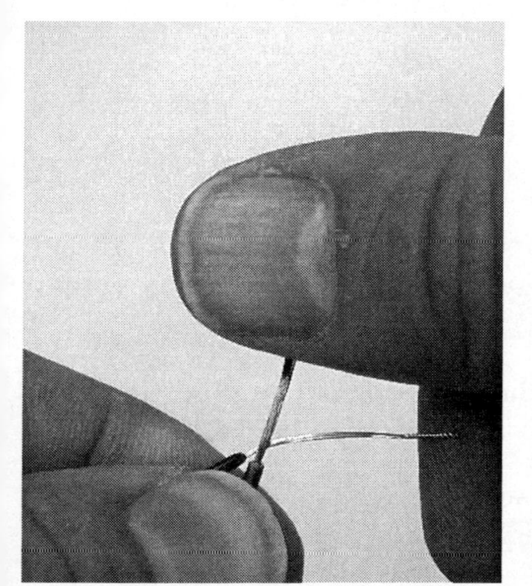

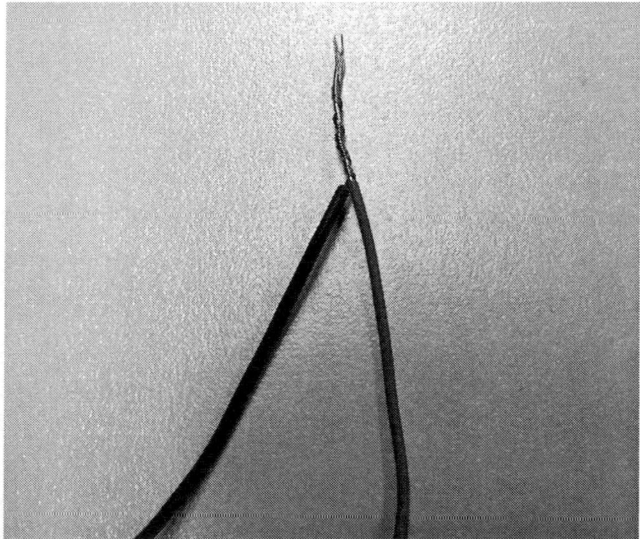

***Left:* To connect two wires, simply twist the stripped conductors together. *Right:* Two conductors twisted together to form a connection.**

Bend the copper and tape back against the insulation of one of the wires and continue to tape. Pull the tape taut, and be certain that all exposed copper is covered. Any exposed copper could touch other exposed copper, and could cause your lights not to work or present a fire risk.

So far you know about the different types of circuits and how to make wire connections, but what about the kind of lights you can use? As I have stated before, one of my favorite sources of lights is to take apart strings of holiday lights and use the components in my props. The easiest to use are the miniature lights often called Italian lights.

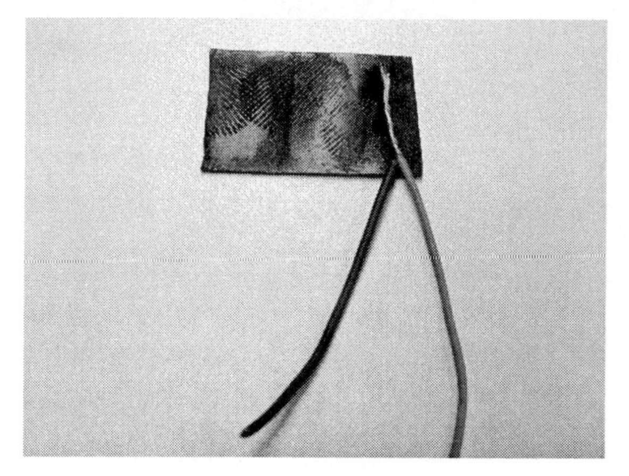

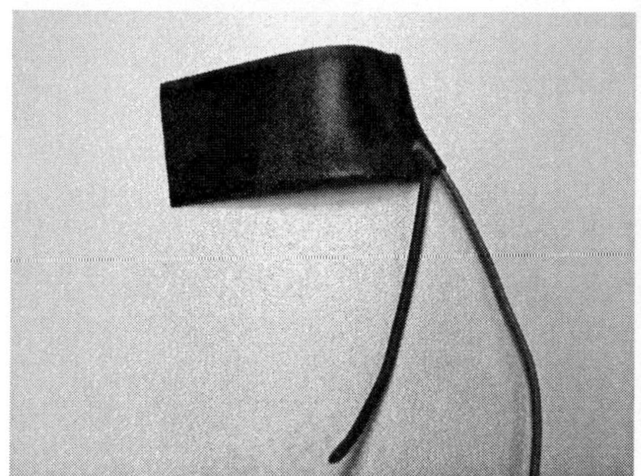

Left: **Lay the bare copper portion of your wire on the electrical tape.** ***Right:*** **Fold the electrical tape over the bare copper.**

Left: **Bend the copper and tape back against the insulation of one of the wires, and continue to tape.** ***Right:*** **When done your splice should look like this.**

These little lights are great for eyes and all sorts of other props. They come in a larger variety of sizes, colors and shapes every year, and seem to get less expensive every year. It used to be about the only time you could find these lights was around Christmastime. Now, however, it seems they have different color sets for every holiday. And after every holiday it seems you can pick up the leftovers at a bargain price.

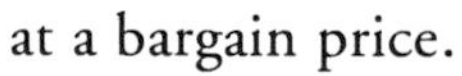

Say you find a set of 100 lights that you think would make great eyes. The problem is you do not want to make a hundred-eyed

Light sets sold for a variety of holidays are a great source of lights to add to props.

Christmas lights come in literally dozens of different sizes, shapes and colors, allowing for hundreds of Halloween uses.

monster, just a two-eyed one! It couldn't be easier to harvest two of the bulbs and bases for your prop and convert them to battery power. The first thing you need to do is to determine the voltage of the bulbs in your string. Often this is as easy as looking at the tag that is often located on the light string near the plug. This will often tell you what voltage replacement bulb to use; this of course is the voltage you will want to deliver to your bulbs from a battery pack.

If you cannot find a replacement lamp voltage on the tag, all is not lost; just check the following table and it will give you the most likely voltages for your bulbs. You will just need to count the number of bulbs on your string and determine the number of circuits. Counting the bulbs is as easy as 1,2,3. Determining the number of circuits is almost as easy. First, plug your set into an outlet and all the bulbs should light. Now, remove the bulb closest to the plug. All or some of the bulbs should go out. If all of the bulbs went out, you have just one circuit. If all of the lights did not go out, go to the first lit bulb closest to the plug and remove it. If the remainder of the bulbs go out, you have two circuits. If some of the bulbs remain lit, again remove the first lit bulb nearest the plug. Continue this process until all the bulbs are unlit. The number of circuits is the number of bulbs you had to remove to get all the bulbs to go out. Once you have the number of bulbs and the number of circuits, just look at the table below for the most likely voltage for your bulbs. These numbers are for light sets designed for use in the U.S.A. and other countries using 120-volt outlets.

Now that you know what the voltage of your bulbs is, you can begin to remove them from the string. **Make sure your light set is unplugged!** You may have several wires running from the plug, but you will usually have only two going into the base which holds the bulb. It is these two wires going into the base that you want to cut. If you want to get the maximum number of usable bases, you will want to cut these two wires halfway between the bulb you are removing and the next bulb. If you do not care if you need to throw some of the bases out, cut the wires next to the

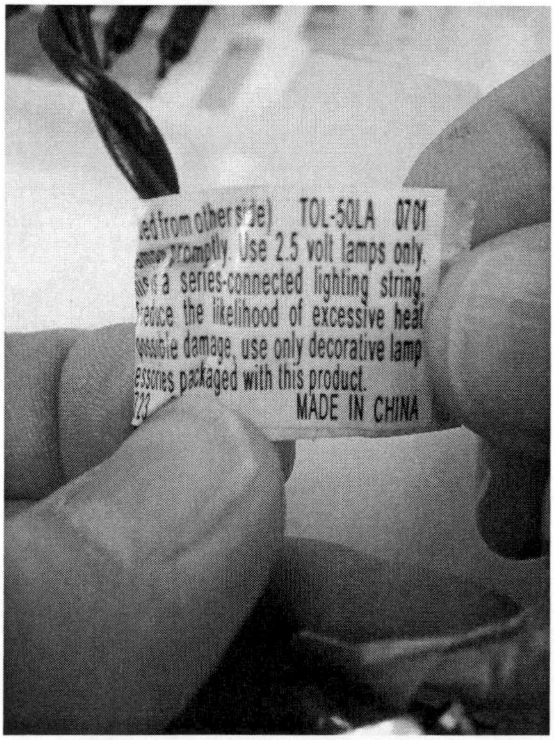

# OF BULBS	# OF CIRCUITS	MOST LIKELY VOLTAGES
10-12	1	12
15	1	8
20-25	1	6
35	1	3.5
35	2	8
40	1	2.5 OR 3.5
50	1	2.5
50	3	8
100	5	6
100	4	6
100	2	2.5
105	3	3.5
150	3	2.5
200	4	2.5

Left: **A tag on most light sets will tell you the correct voltage for the bulbs.** ***Right:*** **The above table will help you determine the voltage of bulbs from light sets when you cannot find the voltage on a tag.**

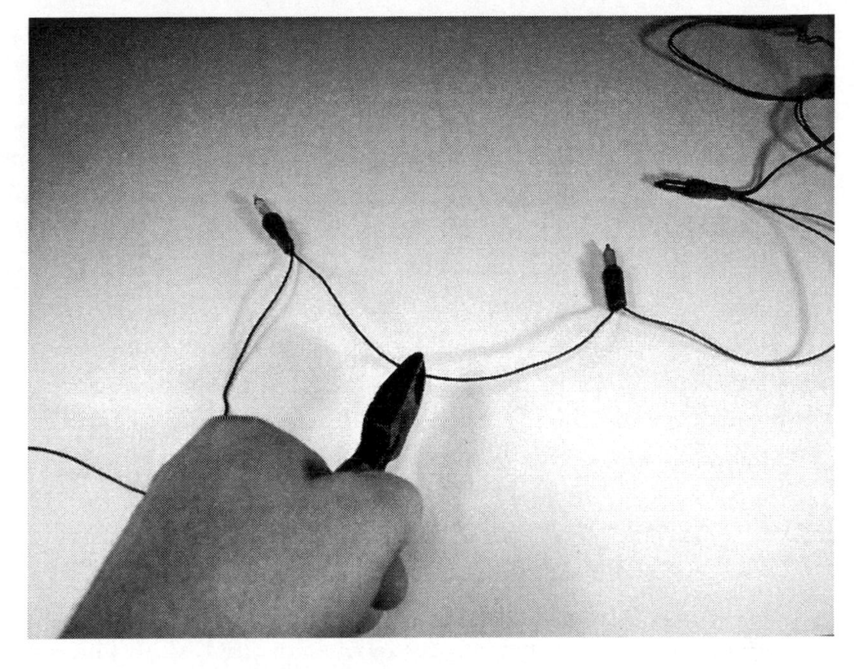

Cutting the bulbs out of a light set will allow you to use them individually for your projects.

base of the next bulb in either direction. This will give you longer leads on the sockets (more wire to work with).

Continue cutting out bulbs and bases until you have as many as you need, or just go ahead and cut them all out for future use. You now have a supply of very inexpensive lights ready to be hooked up to battery packs and put into your props. But wait a minute. What if your bulb is a 2.5-volt bulb? How can you power it with a 1.5-volt battery or two 1.5-volt batteries wired in series for a total of three volts? Actually, you could use either. Light bulbs are really rather tolerant of voltage variations. A bulb designed to work at 2.5 volts will light at 1.5 volts but rather dimly. It will also light at three volts though it may not last as long as at the designed 2.5 volts. Just try to come as close as you can to the designed voltage and you should have satisfactory results. As long as you are keeping the total voltage of all the batteries in your circuit under, say, 20 volts, the worst that can happen is that if your voltage is too low your bulb will not light. If you use too high of a voltage, your bulb may burn extremely brightly for about a second and then burn out. In very rare cases, if your applied voltage is greatly higher than the designed voltage, a bulb may pop, sending small pieces of glass flying. Of course, you will be wearing your safety glasses just in case.

When wiring in your lights, remember what we said earlier about how lights work differently when wired in series and parallel. If you have two or more 2.5-volt bulbs in parallel, you will want to use a voltage of around 2.5 volts. Since we cannot do that with 1.5-volt batteries, we come as close as we can by wiring two 1.5-volt batteries in series for a total of three volts.

If you take the same two 2.5-volt bulbs and wire them in series, you will need a total of five volts from your batteries. Again, there is no combination of

1.5-volt batteries that comes to five volts, so we take three 1.5-volt batteries wired in series for a total of 4.5 volts. If you want the bulbs extra bright, you could use four 1.5-volt batteries for a total of six volts. The bulbs should tolerate this higher voltage well; just remember the bulb life will be dramatically shorter. Sometimes, it is worth the shorter bulb life for the brighter light. After all, bulbs are cheap and easy to change unless they are buried deep within a prop.

When wiring in a bulb, it does not matter which wire goes to the plus and which goes to the minus side of the battery. If you are using LEDs, however, it does make a difference. An LED will light only when you have the correct polarity. That is to say, just like a battery, an LED has a plus and a minus side. These leads from the LED must be wired plus from the LED to the plus from the battery, and minus from the LED to the minus of the battery. I will tell you how to tell which is which on an LED a little later.

In the past few years, a new type of holiday light string has appeared on the market. These use LEDs instead of light bulbs, and are a great way to get cheap LEDs when compared to buying them at your local electronics store. Again, it is a great way to get inexpensive bases with the LEDs. The only problem with taking the LEDs from these sets is that often the leads are not marked to tell you which lead is plus and which is minus. This is an easy problem to solve. Just take one lead from the LED and connect it to the plus and the other to the minus side of your battery. If it lights, you have the polarity correct. If the LED does not light, take the lead you had on the plus and move it to the minus and move the one from the minus to the plus and your LED should now light. Once your LED lights, you can now mark your leads to indicate which must be connected to the plus and which to the minus of your battery.

If you cannot find an LED light set, you can still buy them from an electronics supply store like Radio Shack. On these LEDs, the minus side is either the shorter lead coming from the LED or the lead closest to the flat side of the LED.

If you buy your LEDs at an electronics supply store, they should be able to tell you the operating voltage at the time you buy them. If you remove them from a string of LED lights, it will be more difficult. LED light sets usually do not give a replacement voltage, as LEDs last so long no replacement is needed. Many LED sets also use a transformer to change the voltage from the wall outlet and do not show the secondary voltage on the transformer. So how do you determine the correct voltage for an LED harvested from a light set? If you are knowledgeable in electronics, you can measure the voltage drop across an LED while it is still in the set using a volt-ohmmeter. A less technical way is to observe how bright the LED is when lit in the set, and then adjust the voltage to get the same brightness when it is removed. An even easier way is to just use three volts; it seems to work well on most LEDs.

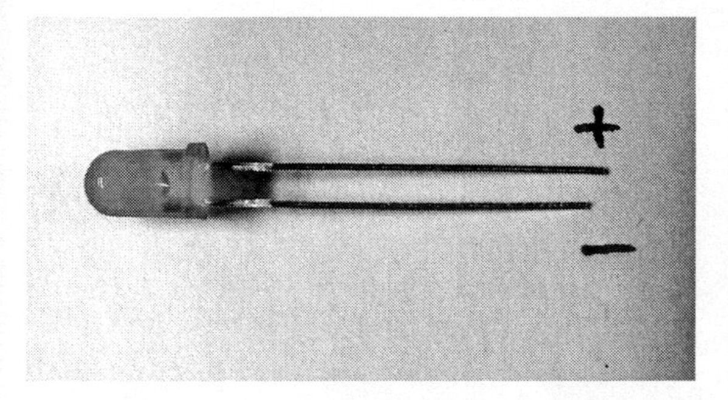

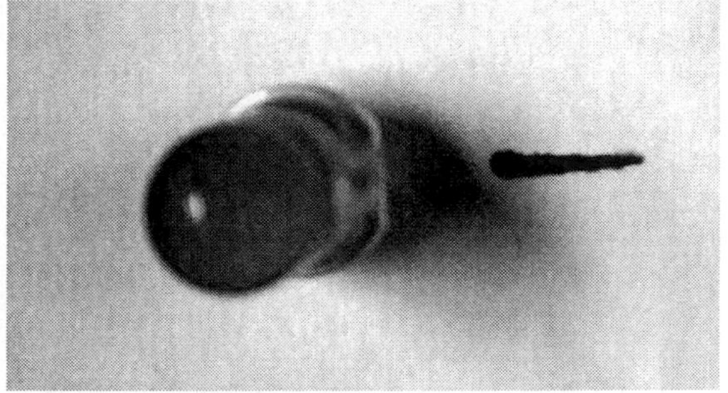

Left: **The short lead on an LED is the minus side.** ***Right:*** **Some LEDs have their minus lead closest to the flat side of the LED.**

If you removed your LED from a light set and have it in a holder with wires already attached, you are ready to begin wiring your circuit the same as with a bulb. If you bought a loose LED, you need to connect wire to the leads coming out of the LED. You can solder wire to these leads but must take care not to damage the LED by overheating it. Another way is to wrap wire around the lead. This is easy if you have a wire wrap tool; just use the right gauge wire for your tool and wrap away.

If you are like most people and do not know what a wire wrap tool is, let alone own one, you can still wrap your connection. Start by stripping off about 1.5 inches of insulation from one end of your wire. Place the stripped wire next to one of the leads of the LED so that the end of the insulation just touches the lead.

Holding the LED and insulated section of the wire firmly, take a pair of long-nose pliers and carefully wrap the wire around the lead. You will want to use solid wire for this because stranded just will not hold.

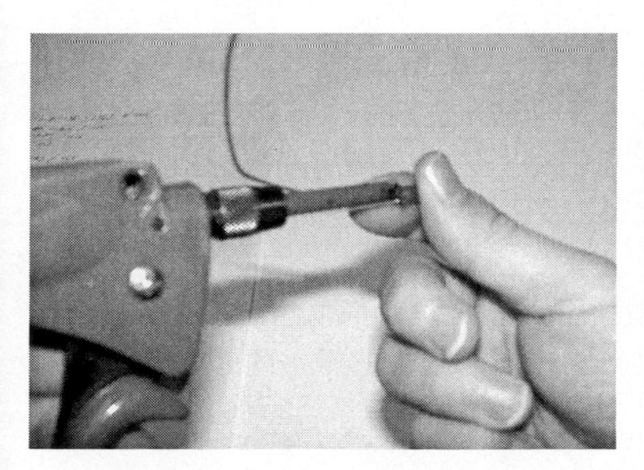

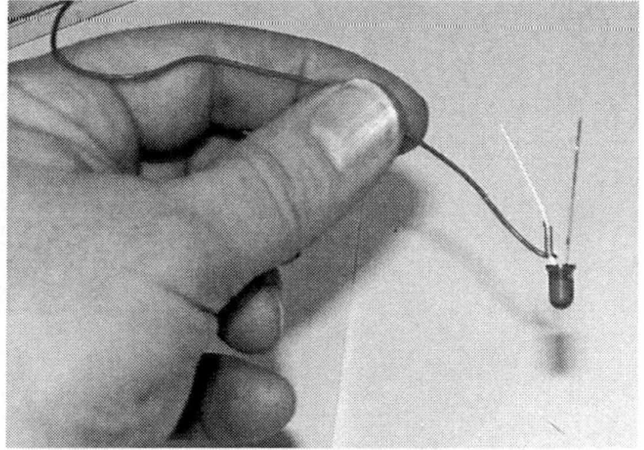

Left: **If you have a wire wrap tool it is easy to wrap wire around the leads of your LEDs.** ***Right:*** **Using a wire wrap tool gives you a neat finished wrap when wrapping the leads of LEDs.**

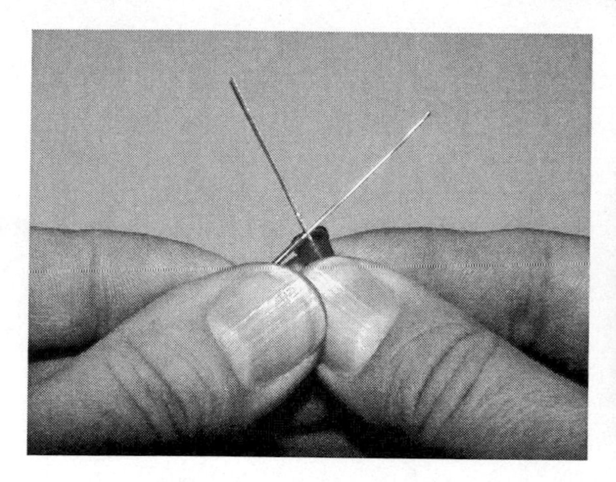

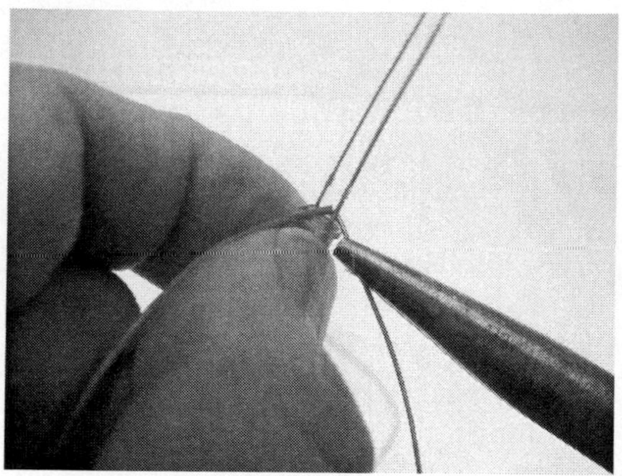

***Left:* Place the stripped wire next to one of the leads of the LED so that the end of the insulation just touches the lead. *Right:* Holding the LED and insulated section of the wire firmly, take a pair of long nose pliers and carefully wrap the wire around the lead. You will want to use solid wire for this; stranded just will not hold.**

Make sure you pull the wire tightly against the lead to make good contact. Once you have the first loop around the lead, use your pliers to push the wire around the lead. To do this, place one side of the pliers against the loop and the other against the unwrapped wire. Now, squeeze on the handles of the pliers to force the wire against the lead. You will have to work in very small sections and it will take a long time to get all the way around the lead. Just keep working your way slowly around the lead until all of the stripped section of the wire is used. If you like, you can add a small drop of solder to hold the wrap in place (if you get a nice tight wrap this is not needed).

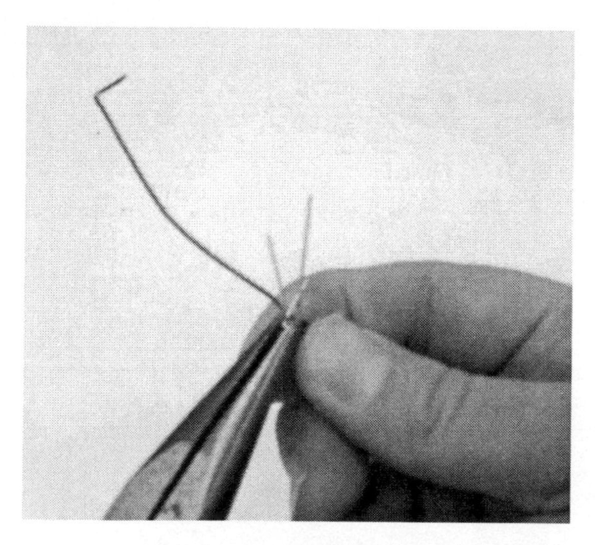

Continue wrapping the lead of your LED until you have several wraps.

Once you have completed your first lead, take another piece of wire and wrap it to the other lead the same way.

Now that your wires are connected, you must insulate the bare copper from touching anything else. Start by trimming off any excess lead.

It is very difficult to wrap in-between the leads with electrical tape, though it can be done. Another option is to use liquid electrical tape. This is paint-on tape, but it can be hard to find. I myself like to use the coffee

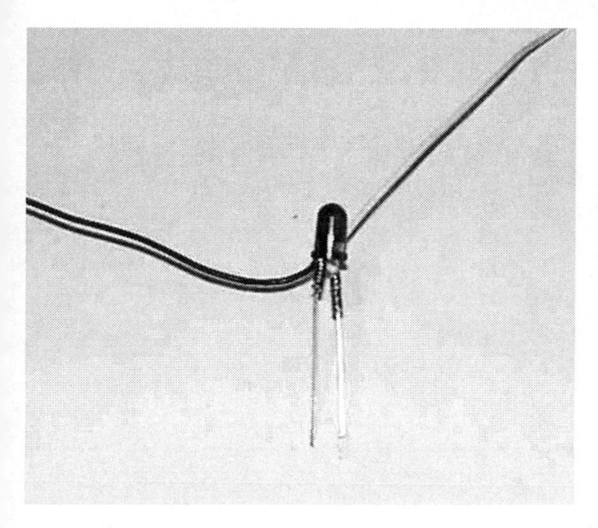

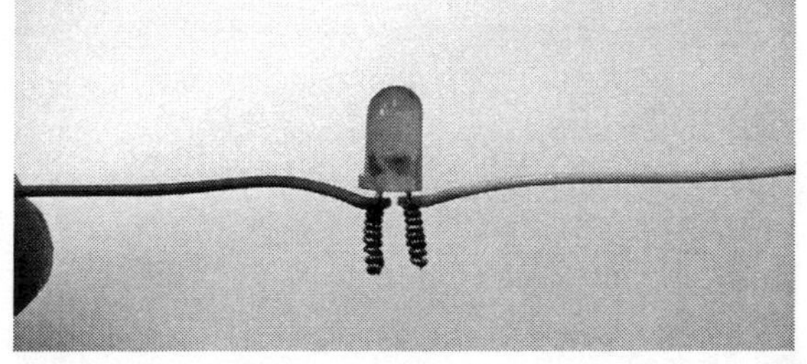

Left: **Hand wrapping an LED may not give you as neat of a finished product, but it can hold just as well.** ***Above:*** **When done wrapping, use wire cutters to trim off any excess from your leads.**

stirrer method. Take a one-holed coffee stirrer and cut off a piece a little longer than your trimmed lead.

Take the wire and fold it back against the lead, then slide the cut section of coffee stirrer over the free end of the wire. Slide the stirrer down the wire and cover the wire wrapped lead.

Repeat the process for the other lead, and your connections are insulated.

If you are unaccustomed to working with electricity, all this may seem a little overwhelming. But it is not as hard as it may sound. If you want to keep it real easy, just use two 1.5-volt batteries in a battery pack and then wire two lights in parallel like in the picture on the next page. This should work well for most any small bulb or LED.

Now that you know more than you ever wanted to know about how to wire lights, how can you use them in a prop? I guess my all-time favorite way is to put

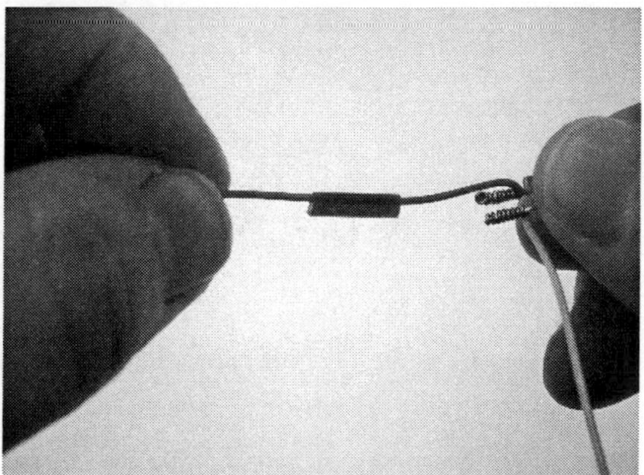

Left: **Using scissors, cut two small lengths of coffee stirrer to insulate your leads.** ***Right:*** **Slide your cut piece of coffee stirrer over the free end of one wire.**

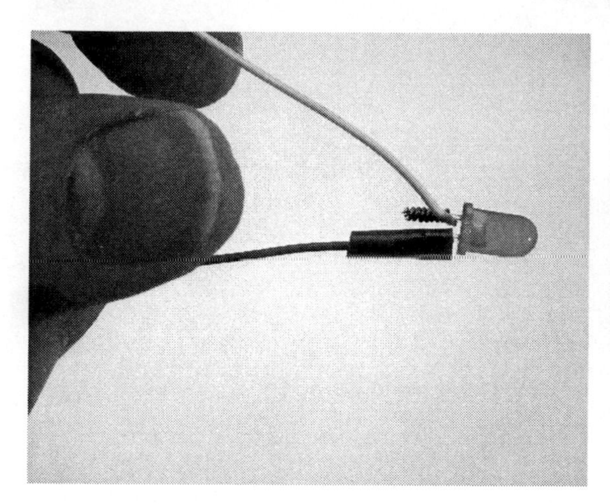

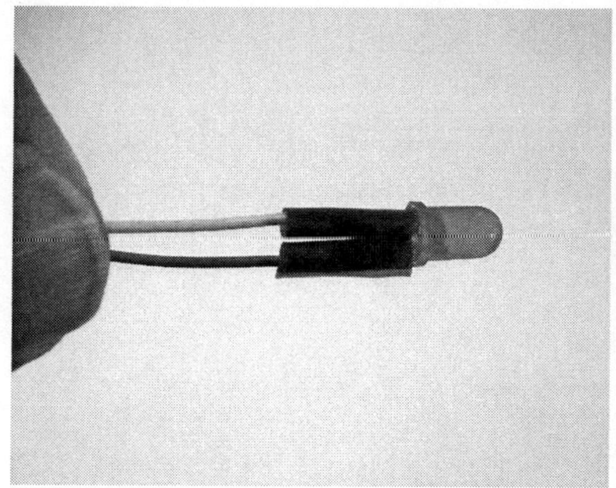

***Left:* Slide the cut piece of coffee stirrer over one of the wrapped leads on your LED. *Right:* Use the second piece of coffee stirrer to cover the other lead.**

lighted eyes in a skull. The eyes I like best are the Demon Eyes that I show you how to make in the section of this book by the same name. Demon Eyes are not the only lights you can use. You can also use the bulbs you harvest from holiday lights for eyes. On the next page are a few pictures of eyes I have put into skulls using holiday lights. The insert in the lower right corner of each picture shows a close-up of the type of bulb I used for the eyes in that skull.

Just how do you get the eyes and wire into the skulls? Easy! For skulls with a cut calvarium (removable skull top), start by removing the top of the skull.

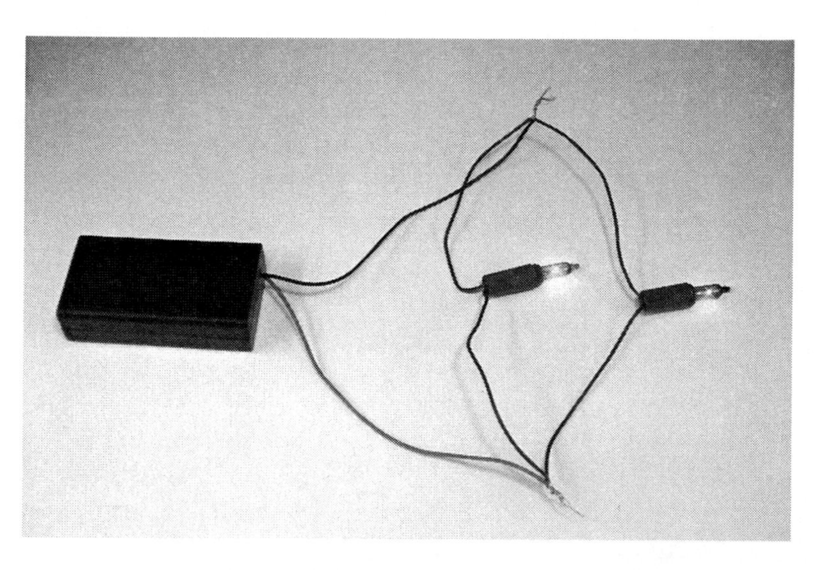

Two one-and-a-half-volt batteries in a battery holder and two bulbs or LEDs wired in parallel work well for most bulbs or LEDs.

Next drill two holes, one into the back of each eye socket. You can drill just about any size hole you want, as long as it is large enough for the wire from your eyes to fit though. A hole a little larger than the wire makes it easier to feed the wire through.

Feed the wire from your eyes through the holes from the front of the skull.

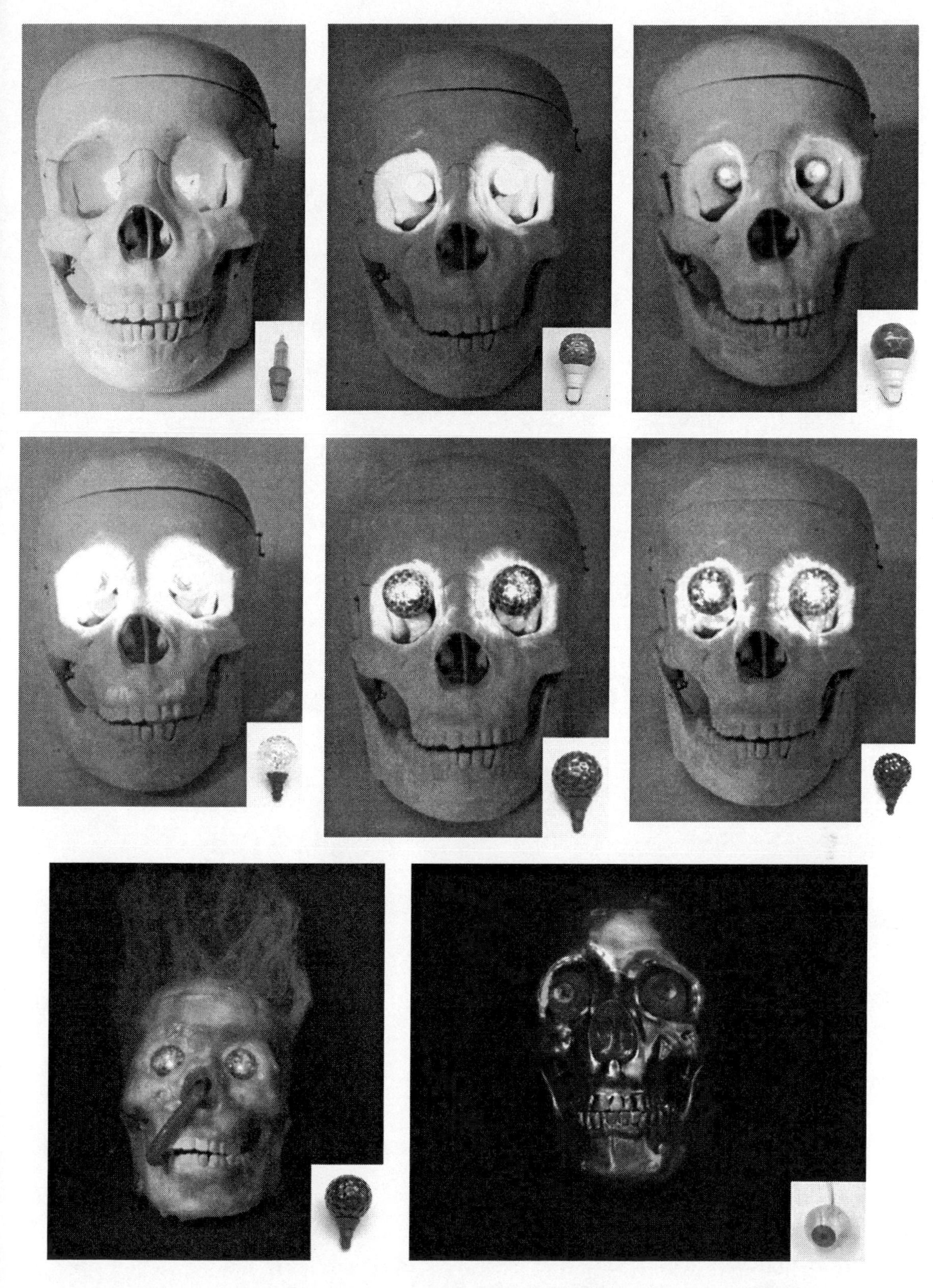

Several examples of props you can build with holiday lights or LEDs.

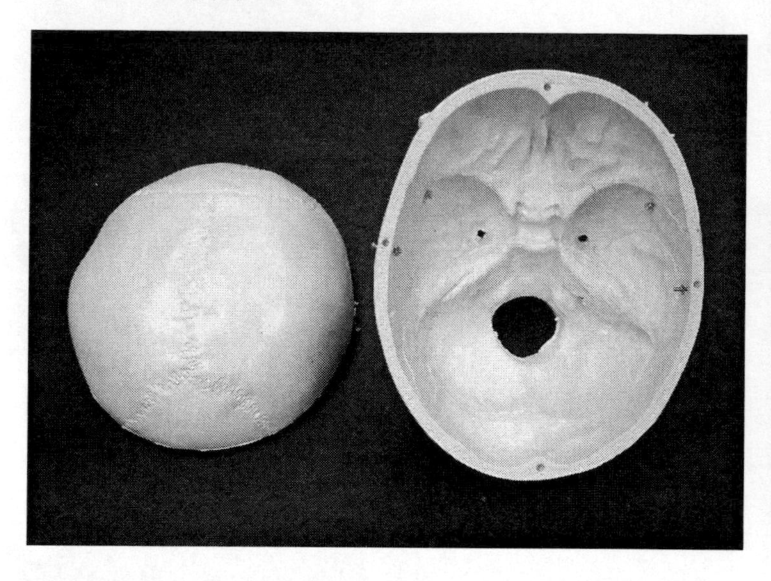

If your skull has a cut calvarium, removing the top of the skull makes it easy to run wires to the eye sockets. It also makes a great place to hide a battery pack.

Use some type of adhesive on the backs of your eyes to hold them into the eye sockets, and insert the eyes into the sockets of the skull. To hold my eyes in place, I like to use one of those pliable adhesives that never dries out. This allows the eyes to be repositioned if needed, or if a bulb burns out it can easily be replaced. You can even use chewed gum for this, but once the gum has set for a long time it can be very hard to remove.

Once you have your adhesive in place, push your eyes into the eye sockets of the skull. It may help to gently pull on the wires from your eyes to help feed them into the inside of the skull.

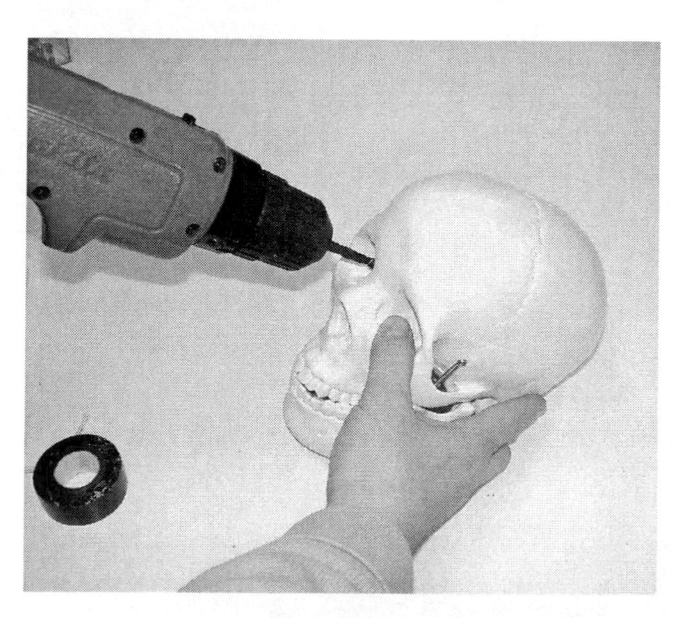

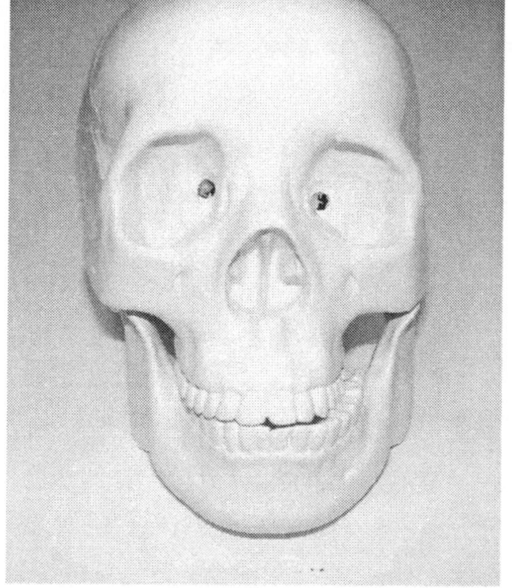

Left: **Drill two holes, one in the back of each eye socket, into the back of the skull.** ***Right:*** **Your hole does not even have to be straight, as long as you can get wire from the eye socket to the back of the skull.**

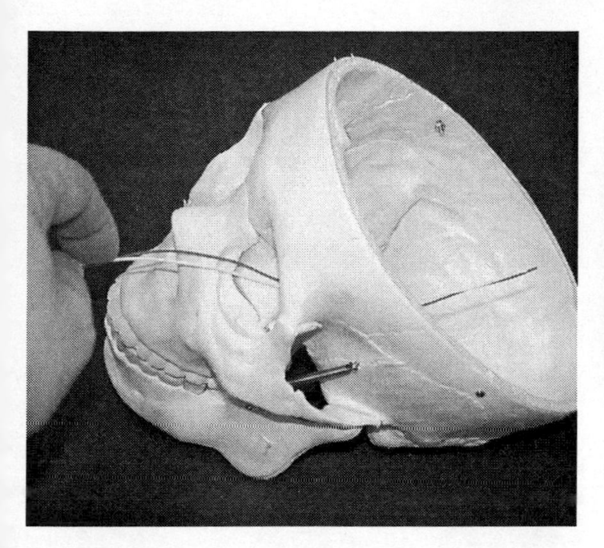

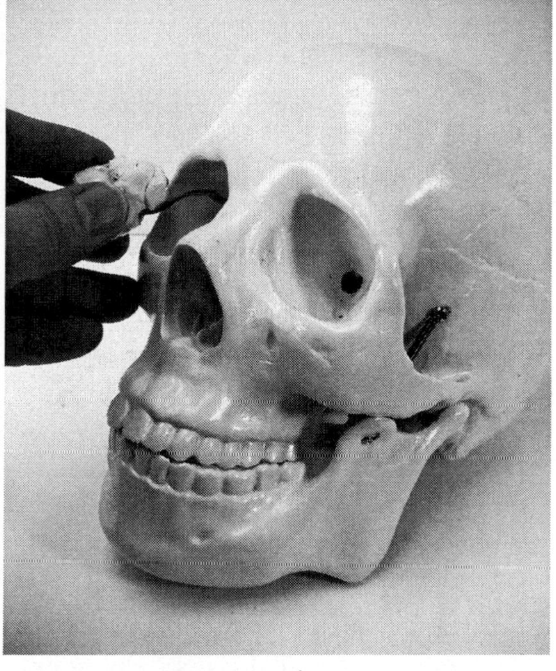

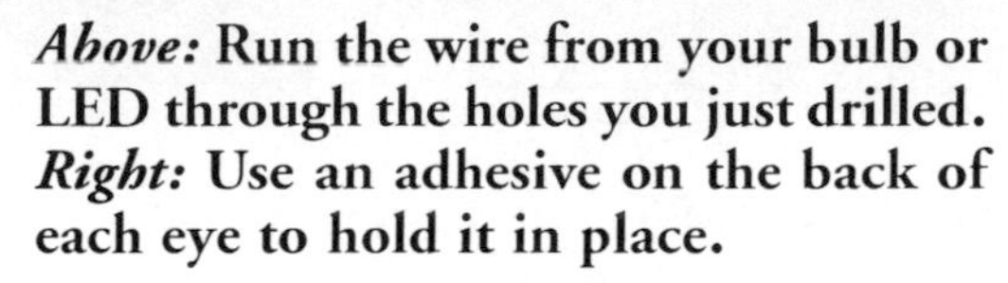

Above: **Run the wire from your bulb or LED through the holes you just drilled.** ***Right:*** **Use an adhesive on the back of each eye to hold it in place.**

Now all you have to do is to wire the eyes to your battery pack. The voltage rating of your eyes and the voltage of your battery pack will determine whether you wire your eyes in series or parallel. In the picture below the eyes were rated at 2.5 volts and the battery pack at three volts. Since the two 2.5-volt eyes in series would require five volts to power them, I chose to run my eyes on a slightly higher voltage and wired them in series and used a three volt battery pack.

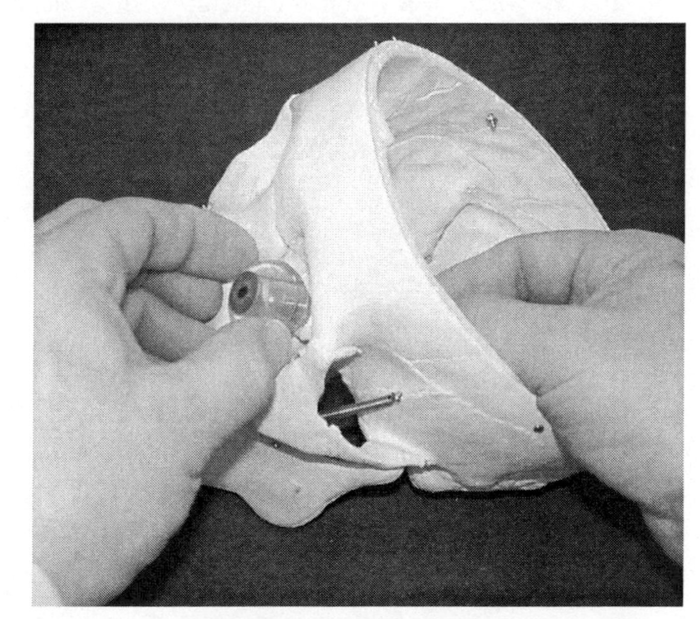

Above: **Once you have your adhesive in place, push your eyes into the eye sockets of the skull.**

As you can see in the picture on the next page, I used a battery pack small enough to fit inside my skull. This is a great way to hide the batteries and make your prop completely portable. With the removable top of the skull, the batteries are easy to replace and yet well hidden from view. Of course if you want to use a larger battery pack or locate the batteries remotely from the prop, you can run the wires from your eyes, through the hole in the bottom of the skull, where the spine would enter, and then to the battery pack. You can locate the battery pack a good distance from your prop. However, if you go too far the resistance of the wire will begin to reduce the number of volts available to your bulb (you should have no problem going 10 feet or more). Thicker wires (lower gauge number) will allow you to go farther with less loss of voltage.

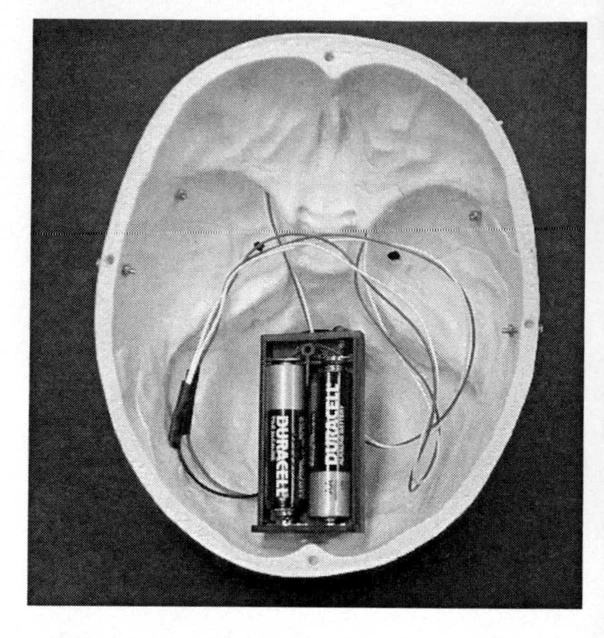

The inside of a skull with a cut calvarium is a great place to hide a battery pack.

If you choose to use a skull which does not have a removable top, see the section in this book entitled Twinkle Eye Skull for instructions on how to run your wires.

Now that you know the basics of how to wire small, low-voltage lights, it is time for you to use your imagination and see what ideas you can come up with. A little light in a dark environment can be a great way to get people to look where you want them to, and can turn a dull, boring prop into one that shines.

TWO-WAY MIRRORS

You have most likely seen two-way mirrors on TV police dramas, where the detectives watch on one side of the mirror, as the suspect is questioned on the other side. The detectives can see the suspect, while the suspect sees only his reflection in a mirror. Such mirrors of course are not just for the police and spies; they can be very helpful to hauntaholics as well. In this section, I will show you not only how you can use two-way mirrors in a haunt, but also how you can make your own inexpensive two-way mirrors.

Let us start by discussing how a two-way mirror works. My apologies to any of you who may be physicists; this explanation will be very simplified, and perhaps not 100 percent accurate from a technical standpoint. It is meant simply to help those with a limited scientific background to be able to better use two-way mirrors in their haunts.

Most mirrors are a piece of glass with a thin silver or aluminum layer on one side, and a dark black layer on top of this. From the mirror side, light strikes the glass, passing through it and hitting the silver layer, where most of the light is reflected back. The dark black layer absorbs what little light makes it through the thin silver layer. The reflected light is the image you see in the mirror. From the back side, light hits the dark black layer and goes no farther.

On a two-way mirror, the black layer is omitted and the silver layer is a little thinner. This allows some light to pass through the mirror while some is reflected.

In order for a two-way mirror to be seen as a

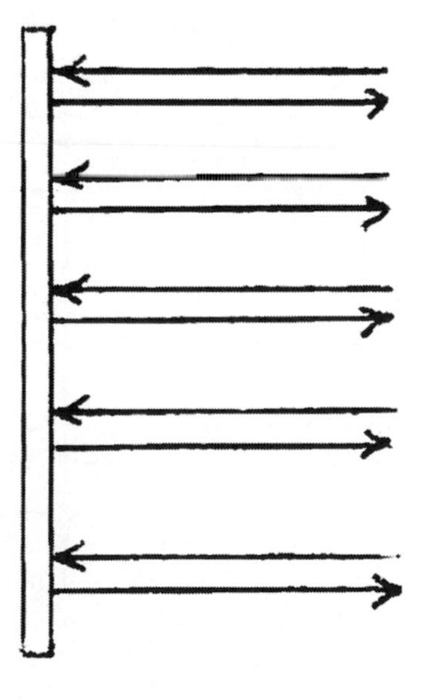

On a mirror light strikes the glass passing through it, hitting the silver layer, where most of the light is reflected back.

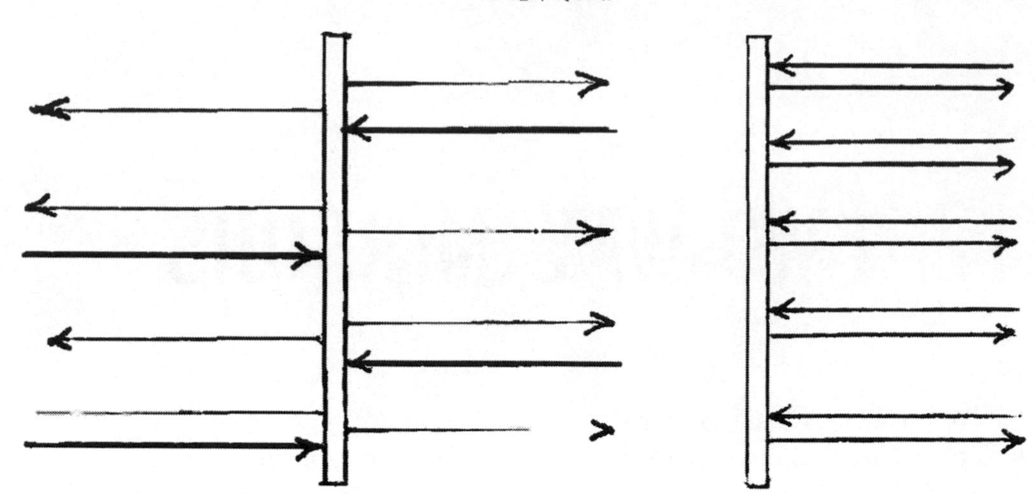

***Left:* On a two-way mirror, the black layer is omitted and the silver layer is a little thinner. This allows some light to pass through the mirror while some is reflected. *Right:* In order for a two-way mirror to be seen as a mirror, the mirror side must be well lit, while the back side is in darkness.**

mirror, the mirror side must be well lit, while the back side is in darkness. The brighter the light on the mirror side and the darker the darkness on the back side, the better the reflected image in the mirror. This is because there is little or no light from the back side to create a second image.

For a two-way mirror to work as a window, you need the same conditions as above, but need to be looking out from the back side. In this case, you have more light passing through the mirror relative to the amount of light reflected back at you. In short, whichever side of a two-way mirror you are on, you will best see what is on the most brightly lit side. Which leads us to a rather interesting little prop you can build.

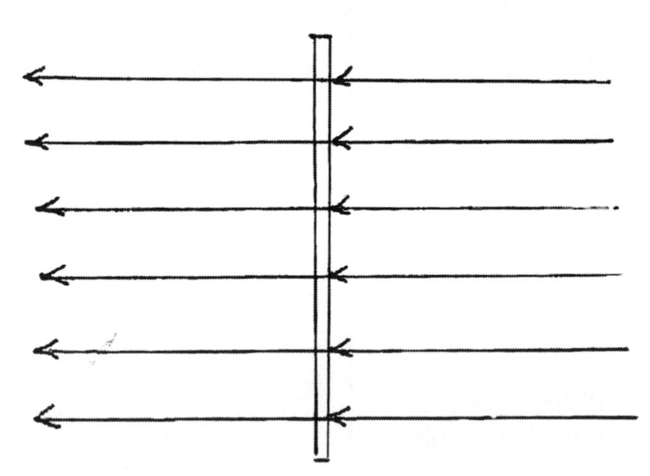

If you are looking from the dark side of a two-way mirror, it acts as a window.

For this prop, we will build our own two-way mirror. This will allow us to customize the size of the mirror and save money over a costly, often hard to find pre-made two-way mirror. On the next page is a picture of the materials needed — with the exception of the secret ingredient that I will tell you about later — and a picture of what the finished prop will look like.

***Left:* Most of the materials needed to make a two-way mirror. *Above:* A finished prop, using a homemade two-way mirror.**

What you end up with is a mirror in which a skull can be made to suddenly appear. As you can see if you look closely, the mirror side is still reflecting the image of the room, or in this case, the author taking the picture.

For this project, I will give you a general idea of how to make the prop. You can modify the steps based upon which materials are easiest for you to find, and how you wish to use the effect. The items I used on the prop shown here were:

- ✓ A picture frame with a wide wooden edges
- ✓ An empty cardboard box with one side slightly smaller than the frame
- ✓ Some packaging tape
- ✓ A sharp knife
- ✓ A staple gun
- ✓ A transparent skull
- ✓ A light from a night light or Christmas house
- ✓ A soft rubber squeegee
- ✓ A pen or pencil
- ✓ A spray bottle
- ✓ Baby shampoo
- ✓ Water

- ✓ Two pieces of tape about three inches long
- ✓ Black spray paint (optional)
- ✓ Rubber gloves (optional)

In addition, you will need our secret ingredient to make the glass from the picture frame into a two-way mirror. This secret ingredient is mirrored window film, which is a thin Mylar film, with an even thinner layer of aluminum fused to it (in short a two-way mirror). This material comes on rolls, in a number of widths, and is pre-pasted so it can easily be applied to any piece of glass or even Plexiglas. This material can be found in many hardware stores and home centers in the window treatment section. Look for it in the section with the window blinds and shades. This product comes in a number of shades (gray, brown, etc.); make sure you buy the mirrored. I mentioned earlier that the window film could be applied to Plexiglas. To me, it is the preferred base for your mirrors in that it is much safer to use. I recommend using Plexiglas whenever possible to reduce the chances of injury from sharp corners or broken glass.

How do you turn this collection of items into a prop? It is surprisingly easy. Start by taking apart your frame. You will need to remove the glass to apply the film, so take this into consideration when selecting the picture frame. I chose an 8 to 10 frame but you may choose whatever size you like. It will make things a lot easier if you choose a frame with a wide area around the glass. I also like to use a wooden frame as it makes it possible to staple the box to the frame, rather than gluing it (this makes it easier to reuse the frame later if you choose).

Start by disassembling your frame. Once you have the glass out you can turn it into a two-way mirror.

Once you have your frame disassembled, you will want to clean the glass. I like to wear rubber gloves for this; it not only keeps from getting fingerprints on the glass but also helps give you a better grip. Of course, you must be careful not to cut yourself, the edges of the glass will be sharp and you must be careful not to break the glass. If you like, you may cut a piece of Plexiglas to replace the glass that comes in the frame.

The following directions for applying the window film are based on the type of film I used. Read the directions on the film you purchase to make sure you apply it correctly.

Once you have cleaned the glass, cut a piece of the mirrored window film a little larger than your piece of glass. An extra inch in each direction will give you enough leeway to position your film easily. Mix a small amount of baby shampoo with water in your spray bottle. Using the baby shampoo water mixture, spray one side of the glass. You will want to make sure it is nice and wet; you really cannot use too much water.

Now take your two pieces of tape, and apply one to each side of one corner of the piece of film you cut earlier. Apply the tape so that about half the length is on the film and the other half extends beyond the film. Press the portion of the tape on the film down firmly, while leaving the portion off the film loose. Now quickly pull the two loose ends of the tape apart. This should remove the backing from the film. Take note of which side the backing comes off of as this is the side you will want to apply to the glass. When handling your film take care not to crease it, as any creases will not come out and will ruin your mirror.

Lay your peeled film on a clean, dry table with the adhesive side down. Lift your film from two sides, letting the center hang down.

Left: **Spray your glass with a mixture of water and a few drops of baby shampoo.** ***Right:*** **Using a couple of pieces of tape, separate the window film from its backing.**

Lift your film from two sides, letting the center hang down.

Position the center of your film over the center of the piece of glass. Carefully lower the film onto the glass, letting the center of the film contact the center of the glass first. Continue to lower the film onto the glass, working from the center out. If you do it right, you should have a nice smooth finish. If you have a few small bubbles, you can still work them out in the next step. If you have a lot of bubbles, or if the film is not properly positioned (if you have any of the glass uncovered); you can still lift the film and try again. Remember to keep the glass wet the whole time.

Once you have the film positioned correctly, it is time to smooth it and press it firmly in place. Spray down the top of the film with your baby shampoo solution; this will lubricate it for the squeegee. Now take your squeegee and work from the center to the edge, removing any small bubbles and pressing the film onto the glass. Repeat this process as often as necessary and in whatever directions needed to give you a nice smooth surface. Remember to keep the film wet while squeegeeing.

Set your mirror aside to dry overnight. While your mirror is drying, you can begin to prepare the skull chamber. Select a cardboard box that has one side with dimensions the same as, or slightly smaller than, the outside dimensions of your frame. The box should be smaller than the outside of the frame, yet larger than the opening of the frame. Try to select a box where the side that most closely fits your frame is one of the sides and not the top or bottom with all the flaps for closing. If your box comes flat rather than pre-folded, close and tape the flaps on the bottom, while leaving the top open.

Place your frame on the side of the box which most closely fits and center the opening of the frame on the box. Take a pen or pencil and mark out the opening of the frame on the box.

Once you have marked the opening, remove the frame and set it aside. Take your sharp knife and cut along the line you just marked. Or, if your frame is like the one I used, where you actually marked where the glass lies, cut just inside the

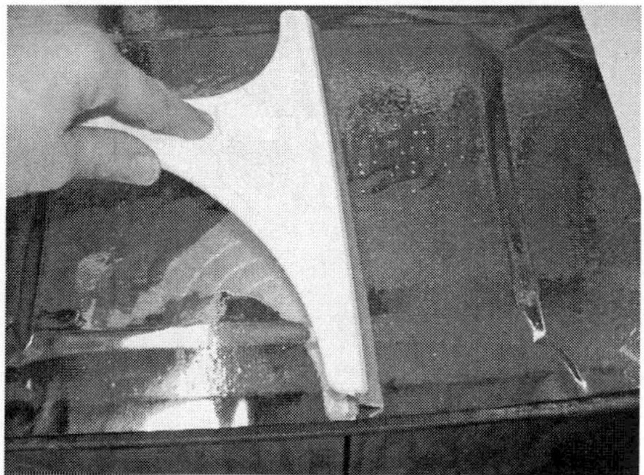

Left: **Spray down the top of the film with your baby shampoo solution; this will lubricate it for the squeegee.** ***Right:*** **Take your squeegee and work from the center to the edge, removing any small bubbles and pressing the film onto the glass.**

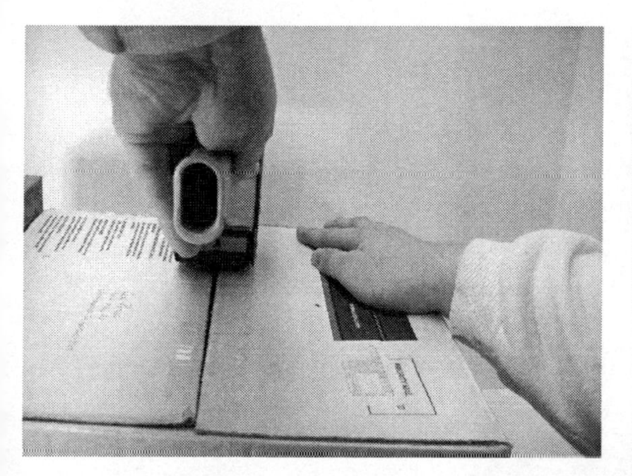

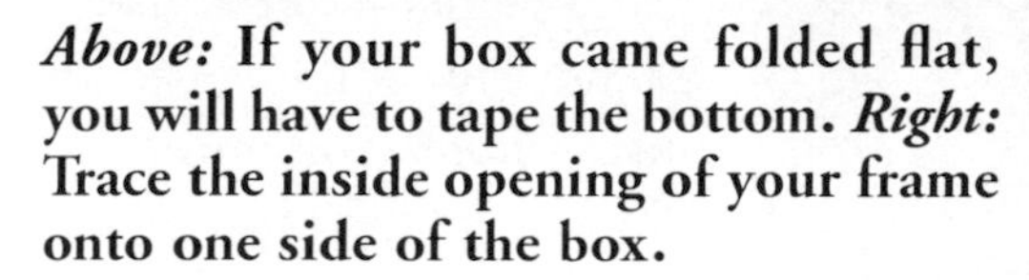

Above: **If your box came folded flat, you will have to tape the bottom.** ***Right:*** **Trace the inside opening of your frame onto one side of the box.**

lines. You are trying to match the size of the opening you are cutting in the box to the size of the smallest opening in the frame.

If you choose, you can paint the inside of the box black (flat black is preferable). This will give you the maximum contrast between the inside of the box and your lighted skull.

After your mirror has dried overnight, it is time to trim off any excess window film. Take your sharp knife and carefully cut along the edge of the glass to remove any film which hangs over. It is a good idea to place some scrap paper or cardboard under your glass to avoid damaging the surface below. If you still have

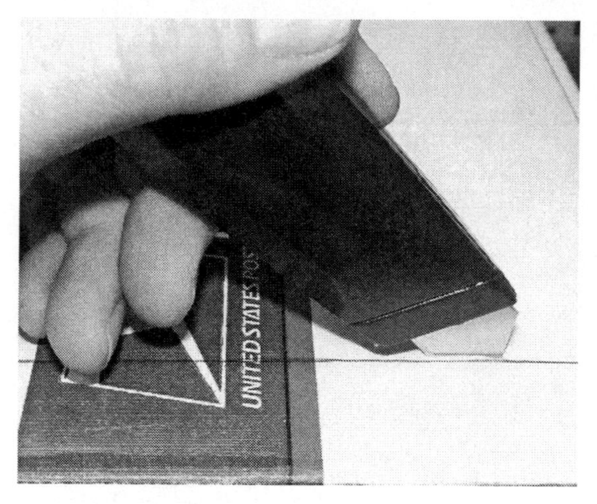

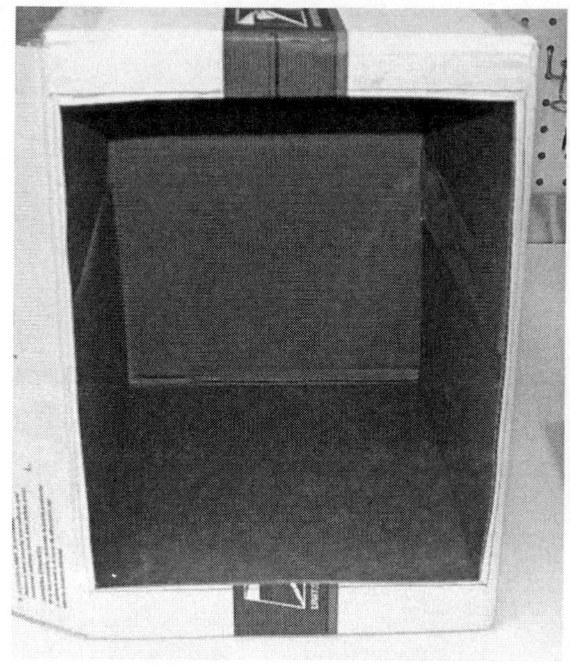

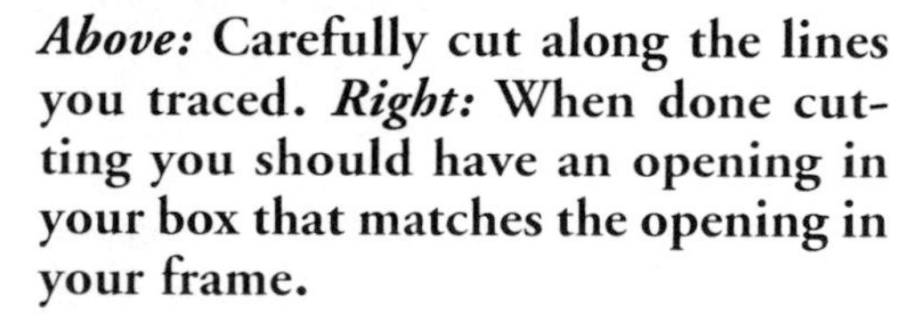

Above: **Carefully cut along the lines you traced.** ***Right:*** **When done cutting you should have an opening in your box that matches the opening in your frame.**

a few tiny imperfections in your mirror, do not worry. These should clear up in a few days. If not, you can always peel the old film off and try again.

Now place your mirror into the frame. It does not matter if you place the film to the front or back of the frame, but I prefer to place it to the back. This avoids having the relatively delicate film exposed to the room, where it can be more easily damaged or soiled (it is easier to clean the glass than the film). We have reached one of those points where I just cannot give you detailed instructions. You must now secure the mirror into the frame without obstructing the view through the mirror. Just how you do this will depend on the frame you are using. You usually cannot use the frame backing which came with your frame as it would not allow you to see

After your mirror has dried overnight, it is time to trim off any excess window film.

through the mirror, so you must find another way. You may be able to use glue or tacks, or do it the way I did. For my frame, I used sticks from frozen treats. These are the small wooden sticks that frozen fudge or fruit-flavored treats come on. Simply wash them off after you have finished the treat, and they can be used for hundreds of things. I simply placed the sticks in the grooves the original frame backing sat in. Mine was tight enough that I did not even need to glue the sticks, although you may need to.

Once your mirror is trimmed, it is ready to be installed back into the frame.

Next, with the front of the frame facing down, place the box over the frame with the cut-out opening centered on the frame. Then attach the box to the frame. If you used a wooden frame, you can use a staple gun to staple the box to the frame. I like this method because the staples can easily be pulled out and the frame reused for another project. If you did not use a wooden frame, you will have to find another way to attach the box to your frame. You may want to try hot melt or some other appropriate glue.

It is now time to add a prop and light to the inside of your box. I like to use a transparent skull with a nightlight bulb

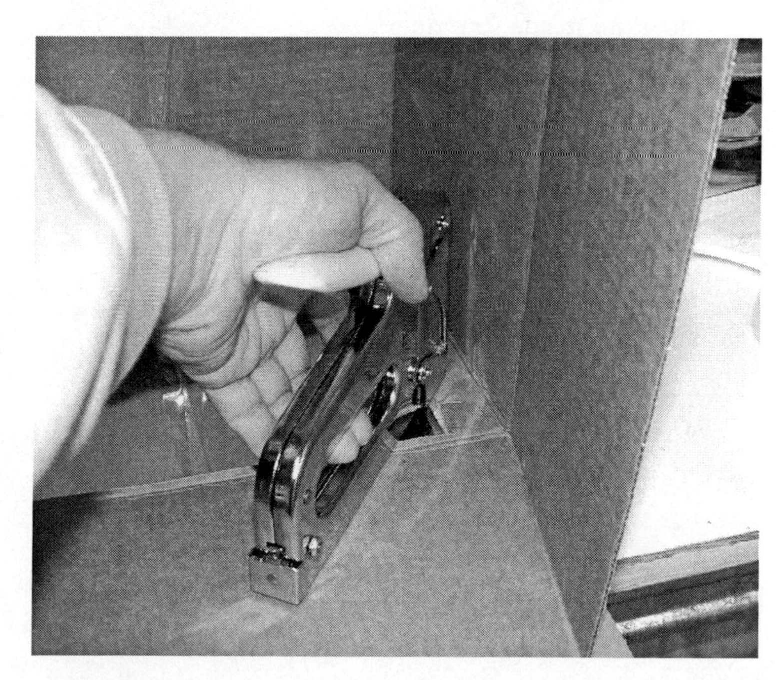

If you used a wooden frame, you can staple the box to the frame.

***Right:* My assistant taking a picture of the finished prop in a room with bright lights and the skull unlighted. *Below:* This is what the prop looks like with the skull lit up.**

inside (see section in this book Skull Light Skull Bright). This is the easiest way to add a prop and light without having to worry about hiding the lights from view. You may need to place another small box or other object below the skull to get the right height. Once you have your skull positioned in the box, close the flaps and tape them shut and your prop is ready. If you plan on moving your prop a lot, you may need to secure the skull inside so it does not shift.

You will find you get your best effect in a room where the lights are a little dimmer. Better yet, in a room where you turn off the lights as you turn on the light in your skull. The effect you will have is a mirror in which a skull suddenly appears. To go from mirror to skull, simply turn on the light in the skull, or turn off the room lights and turn on the skull light.

If you wish to use a prop that does not contain its own

light, you will need to add lights to the box. If you wish to do this, I suggest that you hide the lights behind the frame. You can use the lights which are sold to go inside of the little porcelain houses you sometimes see under Christmas trees, or other similar small lights. The one thing you must be extremely careful about is the heat generated by your lights. Some bulbs can generate enough heat to easily ignite your cardboard box. You must make sure you have enough space between the bulbs and the box, and that your bulbs run cool enough. As a general rule, if anything gets too hot to comfortably leave your hand on, do not use it!

Of course, a box with a mirror on the front will look out of place most anywhere you put it. To use this effect most efficiently, you will need to hide the box. The best way to do this is to build it into a wall. If you do not want to cut a hole into one of your walls at home (and I cannot say I blame you if you do not), you can build a fake wall to hang your mirror on. You can see the section in this book entitled Bucky's Home Remodeling for an idea of how to do this. If you do not want to build a wall, another idea is to place your mirror and box on a table, cover the box portion with black cloth (or plastic) and leave the mirror and frame exposed. Drape the cloth onto the table and add some other props around and on top of the box. This will make your mirror appear as if it is just part of a table arrangement.

There is another little trick you can do with the prop you just built. With a little work and a lot of patience, you can make pictures of an effect where your skull seems to be showing through your head. To do this you will need the skull-in-the-mirror prop shown above, a camera and someone to help you. For the best effect you will want to dress in a black turtleneck and have a black background behind you. Place yourself in front of the mirror with the black background behind you. Turn on the light in the box and have your helper stand off to one side with the camera. Your helper can then look through the viewfinder of the camera and direct you to move until the reflection of your head in the mirror is in line with the

With a little effort, you can use your prop to take a picture of yourself and the skull morphed.

skull showing through from the inside. When everything is lined up right, your helper can then take the picture.

You may have to do a lot of adjusting of the room light and the brightness of the light in the box to get a really good picture. Another tough part is lining up your face and the skull. It will take a lot of moving the camera, and moving your face left and right, up and down and closer and farther until you get the perfect picture. Once you do it a few times, you will have a better feel for just how to line everything up, and it will become easier.

Now that you know how to make a two-way mirror, what else can you do with it? Before I once again tell you to use your imagination and see what you can come up with, let me tell you a few of my ideas. A two-way mirror can be a great way to observe your victim without his seeing you. This is a great way to know when to trigger a prop without the victim seeing you waiting to pounce! To do this most effectively, you must be in complete darkness, with your victim in at least partial light. You would want to build a fake wall between your lair and your victim. Make an opening in the wall just a little smaller than your mirror and hang your mirror over it. If the area you are in is much darker than the other side of the mirror, you will be able to see your victim clearly, yet all he will see is his reflection in the mirror.

The picture at right shows what a two-way mirror looks like, looking in from bright light into darkness.

And on the following page is what it looks like from the other side.

This picture was taken by placing a camera inside the box I showed you how to build above, and taking a picture looking out into the room. You can see what is on the light side of the mirror very easily, while someone on the light side can see nothing of the dark side. The red and green spots on the lower right are lights on the camera (the only light inside the box) being reflected by the two-way mirror.

Here again is what a two-way mirror looks like, looking in from bright light into darkness.

Another rather easy and yet dramatic effect is to make a demonic face suddenly appear in a mirror. To do this, you will need a wall with a hole cut out just a little smaller than your two-way mirror. In the example shown here, I used a Corobuff wall as described in the section Bucky's Remodeling Service. I first attached my mirror to the wall with a staple gun (you must have a wood frame on your mirror to use a staple gun); using plenty of long staples to be sure the mirror was firmly attached. I then cut the cardboard wall on the top, bottom and one

The view from inside the box.

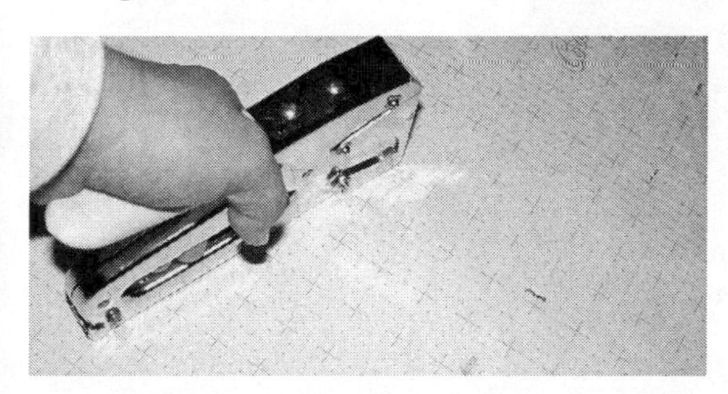

Above: **I first attached my mirror to the wall with a staple gun (you must have a wood frame on your mirror to use a staple gun).** ***Right:*** **Cut the cardboard wall on the top, bottom and one side of the mirror, using the inside of the frame as a guide.**

side of the mirror, using the inside of the frame as a guide.

This created what amounted to a small door on the back of the two-way mirror.

Create a small door at the back of the mirror.

After that, I grabbed a flashlight and my handsome face and was ready for my scare. To pull off this effect, you will need to have your victims passing by your mirror in somewhat dim light. As they approach the mirror, all they will see is a mirror with their reflections in it. You will be waiting on the other side in complete darkness with your flashlight handy.

As the victims approach, open the flap on the dark side of the mirror and shine the flashlight in your face. You should be able to see your reflection well enough in the mirror to position the light just right for the maximum effect. Below you can see what my handsome face looks like when lit this way.

Once the victims are startled, simply close the flap on the back of the

Left: **From the lit side of the mirror passersby will see a mirror.** ***Right:*** **Illuminating your face with a flashlight on the dark side of the mirror will create the illusion of a demonic face suddenly appearing in the mirror.**

mirror. No matter how hard they try to look in the mirror, all they will see is their reflections.

This is about all I have to say about two-way mirrors at this time. Be bold and innovative, and see what new effects you can come up with now that you know how to make your own two-way mirror.

PAPIER-MÂCHÉ, OR, WHAT I LEARNED IN THIRD GRADE

I have always been a firm believer in higher education. It is my belief that no matter how much education you have, you will find it useful some day. As evidence of this, I present the following adaptations of what I learned in the third grade.

You may be very surprised to find out how many great Halloween props can be built simply and inexpensively using simple papier-mâché. For those of you who have not had the benefit of a third-grade education, papier-mâché is a process of using paper and a binding agent to mold an item. This item could be an original sculpture built out of the papier-mâché, or you could use the papier-mâché to duplicate an already-made item.

How do you make this versatile stuff? There are a number of formulas, but they are all basically paper and a binding agent. The most commonly used paper is simple newspaper. The binding agent often varies; I have seen people use flour and water or white glue and water. The one I prefer, however, is liquid laundry starch. This is my preference because it is the most convenient to use. Just shake the bottle, pour out some starch, and it is ready to use — no measuring and no mixing. For the projects presented here, I have used old newspapers and liquid laundry starch.

Let us start with the basics of papier-mâché. For the projects shown here, you start by cutting or tearing old newspapers into strips about ¾" to 1" wide. The exact width is unimportant, but this is the most convenient width for most projects.

For the next step, you will want to put on a pair of rubber gloves. Once you

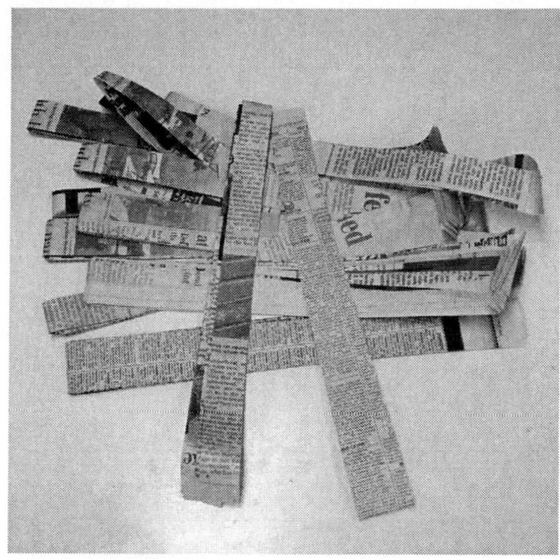

Left: **Starch and newspaper is one of the easiest papier-maché formulas to use, and it yields great results.** ***Right:*** **Strips of old newspaper are the basic building block of papier-mâché.**

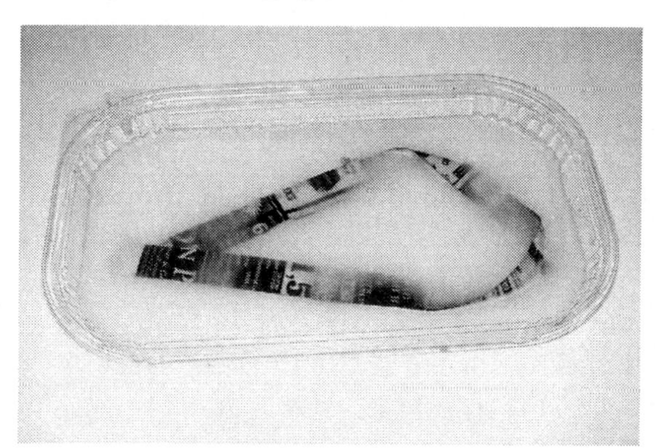

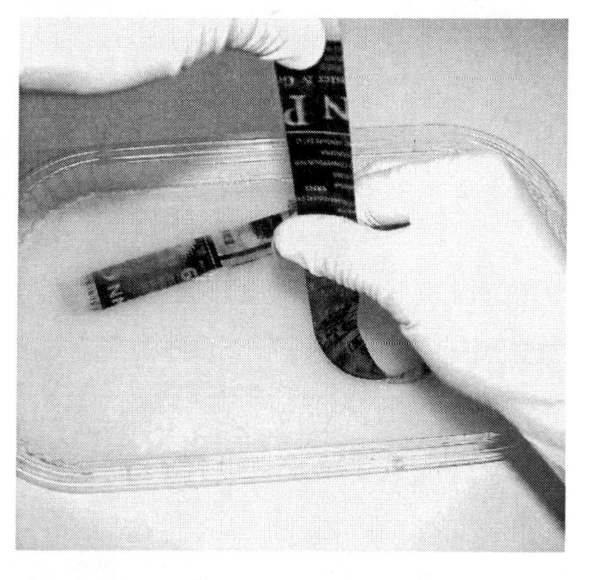

Left: **Soak strips of newspaper in liquid laundry starch.** ***Right:*** **Wipe off the excess starch before applying strips to your project.**

have your gloves on, shake your liquid laundry starch, and pour some into a small, shallow container. Dip one of your strips into the starch and wet it thoroughly. Remove it from the container and remove the excess starch by pulling the strip between two fingers. Your strip is now ready to use.

Now that your strip is ready to use, just what can you do with it? Let me start with one of the simplest yet most versatile techniques: copying an object, in this case a skull.

It is very difficult to copy an object like a skull completely, but it is rather simple to do just the face. While it may not be a full skull, often just the face can be enough, and making it out of papier-mâché will save you a lot of money, especially if you need a lot of them.

To make skull faces you will want to start by fashioning a holder so you can work on your skull without it rolling around. To do this, you simply take a small cardboard box (often the one the skull comes in will work well), cut a hole in one of the sides, and rest the back of the skull you are using as a mold into the hole.

Once your skull is set in the holder, take a moment to look at it. Remember you are using this skull as a form for a skull face which will have to be removed from the skull. Give it a little thought and you will realize that there are several areas you cannot wrap around and still be able to remove the face. Take, for instance, the jaw. If you were to wrap papier-mâché around the back of the jaw, there would be no way you could pull the finished face off the front of the skull without destroying your work. Plan your work so that you cover only those areas from which you can safely remove your finished product.

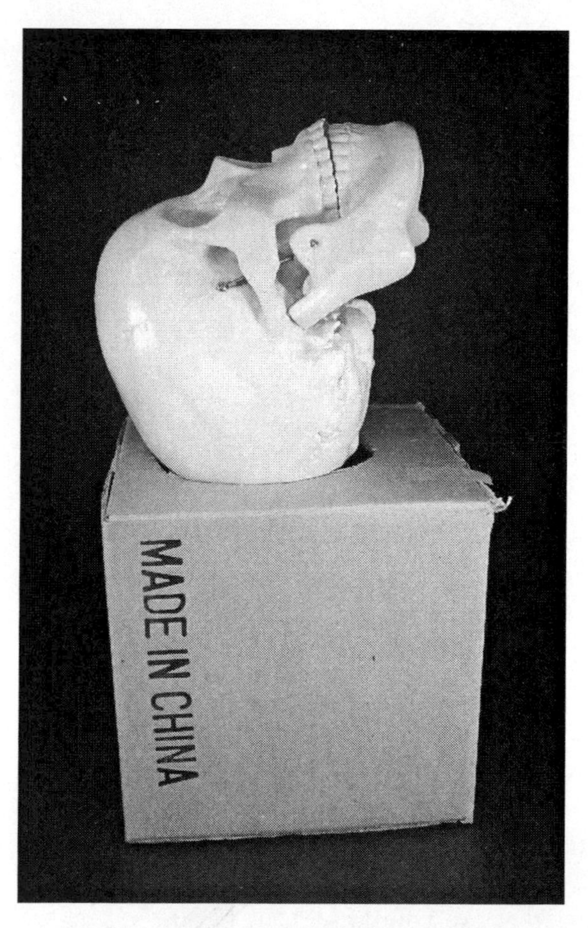

A cardboard box with a hole cut in it makes a handy holder for round objects.

Once you have a pretty good idea as to which sections you would like to cover, it is time to begin applying the paper. You will probably want to have several strips of paper soaking in starch at the same time. This will make things go a little more quickly. Just remember to place them into the starch one at a time, so that you can be certain both sides of the paper get well coated. Once you have a strip in the starch and pushed below the surface, you can add another on top of this with little chance of the two sticking together.

Now, take one of the paper strips out of the starch, pull it between two fingers to remove the excess starch, and you are ready to place it. I recommend you wrap the first strip under the jaw and extend it vertically across the top of the head (see photograph on next page). This strip will define the back of your skull face.

Once you have the first strip in

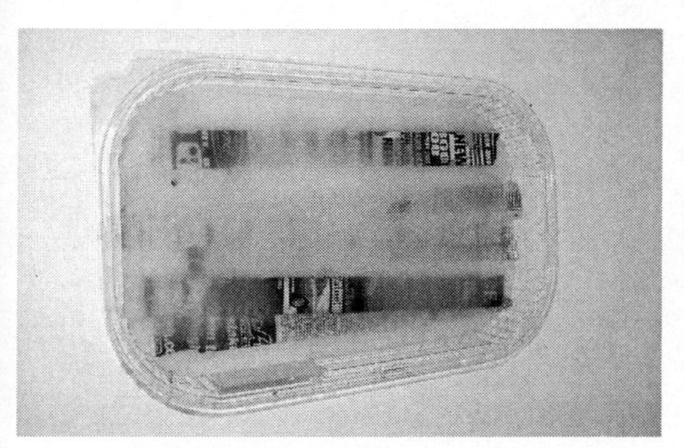

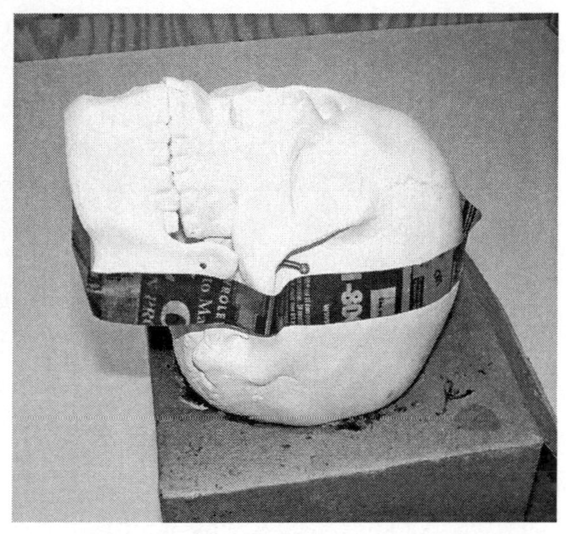

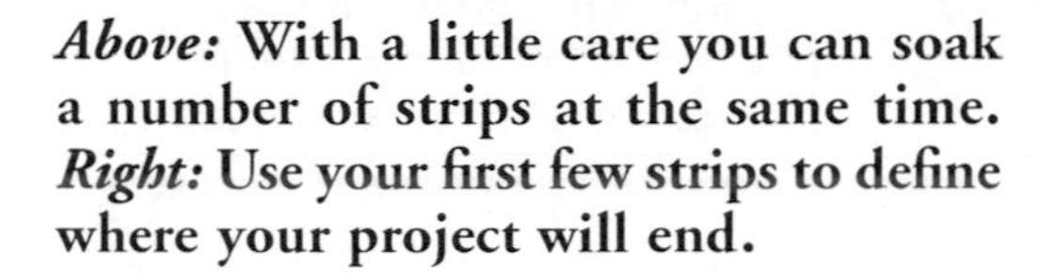

Above: **With a little care you can soak a number of strips at the same time.** ***Right:*** **Use your first few strips to define where your project will end.**

place, it is a good idea to continue adding additional strips along the same line to indicate the end of your face. As you add additional strips, this will serve to mark the point you will not want to go past.

Now it is time to start adding strips in earnest. You may want to start covering the eyes and nose at this point, as they can be a little tricky. For a more realistic look, you will want to make sure you press the paper down to the bottom of the eye sockets and well into the nose.

If somewhere along the line you find a paper strip is too long, just tear it and use the rest somewhere else. Again, I will remind you that you do not want to go past the first few strips you used to mark the end of your face. However, you do want to go all the way to the end of them. Try to come as close as you can to ending exactly at the end of these first strips. If you go a little bit past them occasionally, it does not really matter. You can trim off the excess after your face dries.

With all the curves of a skull, you will notice that as you wrap the paper strips, they will often form puckers.

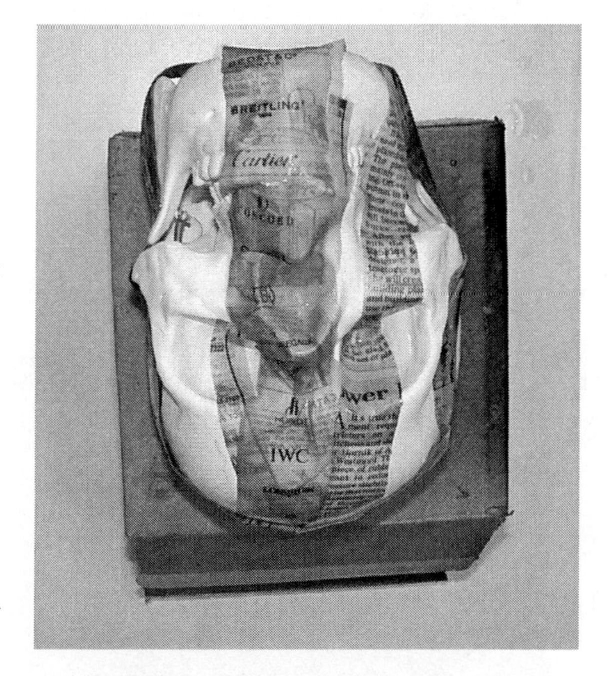

To get the maximum definition on your copy make sure you push your newspaper all the way down into any low spots.

These are best avoided where possible, but they will happen. When they do, it is important to smooth them out. It really is fairly simple to make them blend in. Simply wet them with a little extra starch, and rub over them several times with your thumb or fingers. Now the pucker should lay nice and flat. It is important to keep each layer of paper as smooth as possible so that you do not end up with a lumpy skull.

Continue to add strips until the entire skull is covered. For maximum strength, you will want to place the strips so that they criss-cross one another. The pattern of strips does not really matter as long as they do not all go in the same direction.

Once you have the entire skull covered, go back and do it again. You will want to have a total of three or four layers. Pay particular attention to the back edge of the face, where you placed your first strips. You will be pulling on this to remove your face, so you want it to be solid to hold up to the abuse. Once you have all the layers in place, wet your fingers with liquid starch and go over the entire area you covered with paper. You will want to rub any high spots to smooth them out, and to press all the strips of paper firmly together.

Once you have finished with the rubdown, set your skull aside to dry. This could take a few days. You will likely notice that the eye sockets take much longer to dry. It does not matter if they are still slightly damp when you go to remove your face as long as the rest of the face is dry.

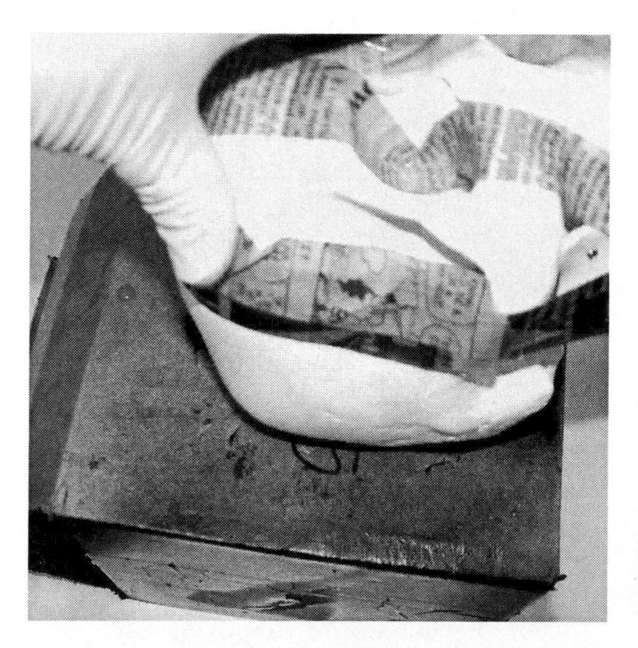

***Left:* It is common for puckers to occur while applying your paper. *Right:* To smooth out a pucker, just wet your fingers in starch and rub the pucker until it lies flat.**

Once your face is dry, it is time to remove it from the skull. This can be a little tricky, but with a little practice it becomes rather easy. Start by taking a dull knife (a sharp one will cut through the face). Work the knife between the skull and the face. It is best to start at the jaw area, where you will find a gap to begin working the knife into. Work all the way around the skull to loosen the face, working the blade in only about a quarter of an inch or so. Once you have made it all the way around, start over again going in a little deeper. Continue doing this until you are as far in as you think you can get. If you make small cuts or cracks, do not worry. Your project is not ruined; we can fix it later.

For maximum strength, you will want to place the strips so that they criss-cross one another.

Now we are ready to peel off your face. A little patience goes a long way at this point. You will want to work slowly and take your time. Starting at the top of the skull, grab the face and pull gently forward. **Be very careful because the edge of the papier-mâché can be surprisingly sharp. Take care not to cut yourself.** Work your way around the skull, loosening the face little by little. When you feel it is ready, pull your face off.

Now is the time to fix any cracks or cuts you may have. This is really very simple. Start by checking your face and finding all the cuts and cracks.

Fixing a crack could not be easier! Just take a

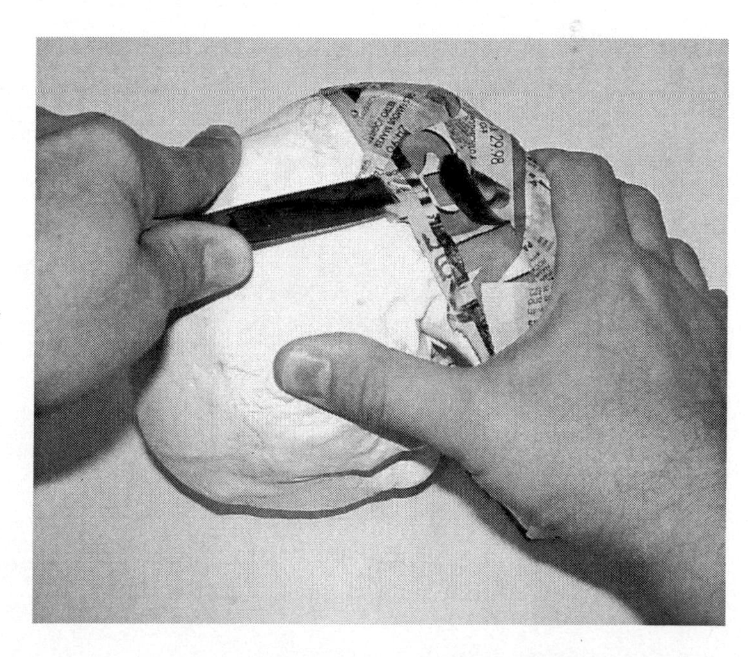

Use a dull knife to start working your copy loose.

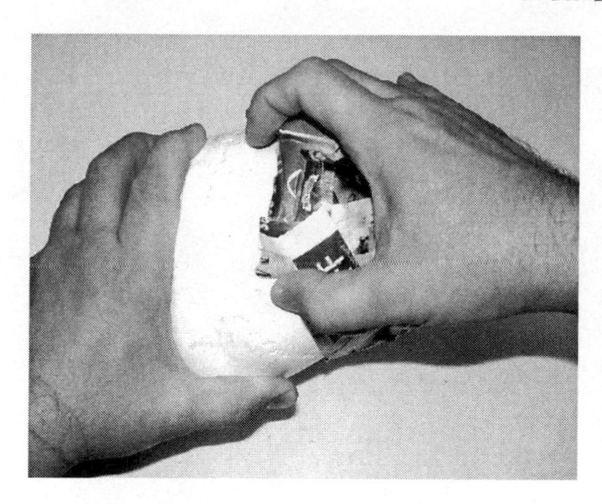

Left: **Carefully peel off your copy. Use caution, as the edges can be very sharp.** ***Right:*** **If your copy cracks while being removed, it can usually be easily repaired.**

strip of paper soaked in starch and place it over the crack, wrapping it around both sides.

You will most likely notice that the inside of your face is still wet in spots. This is not a problem. Just set the face aside to let these dry.

After your face is completely dried, you may now trim off any excess paper to even up the sides. You may also want to trim any high spots on the paper so that your new prop will lie flat.

The final step is to paint your skull face for whatever project you plan to use it. I painted mine as a crackle skull (see section on skull painting). Once it was painted, I simply placed my skull face on the ground. The result was what looked like a

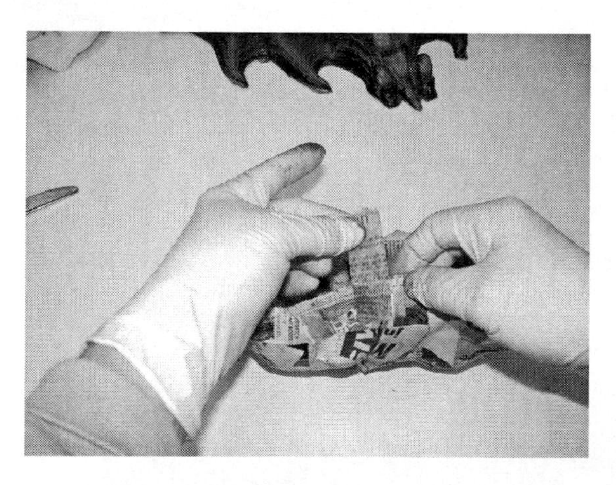

Left: **Fixing a crack could not be easier! Just take a strip of paper soaked in starch and place it over the crack, wrapping it around both sides.** ***Right:*** **Trim off any excess paper.**

The final step is to paint your project.

skull, half buried in the ground (a little dirt rubbed into the face would probably help the effect, but I just couldn't bear to get my new face dirty).

Another thing to keep in mind when painting your face is that it is a good idea to also paint the inside. This will help make the papier-mâché a little stronger, not to mention much more water-resistant.

While I am on the subject of making your finished papier-mâché stronger, there is another technique you can use to make it very strong. You can use an expanding polyurethane foam to fill your prop. This is quite easy and quick, yet it affords a great deal of increased durability. This material is available in most hardware and home stores; the most recognized brand name is probably Great Stuff.

To fill your prop with foam really takes no time at all. Start by reading and following all directions on the product label. When you are ready to begin, start by filling your prop a little less than half full of foam.

You will want to make certain that you fill all the little nooks and crannies in your prop, so work the tip of the foam straw around the mold, aiming it at all the corners. When the prop is about half full, stop, take a piece of cardboard, and press down on the foam, forcing it to fill in all the hard to reach spots.

Once the foam has been well patted down, continue to fill the prop to where it is nearly full.

Now set your filled prop aside overnight to cure. When you come back the next day, you will notice that the foam has overflowed your prop. This is exactly what you want. It will ensure that your prop is completely filled.

It is a simple matter to trim off the excess foam and finish your prop. Just take a saw or sharp knife and trim away the foam even with the bottom of your prop.

You can now paint your prop.

Left: **You can fill your prop with foam for greater strength.** ***Right:*** **Using a piece of scrap cardboard to gently pat your foam can help insure all the little cracks and crevices are filled.**

Left: **Once the foam has been well patted down, continue to fill the prop to where it is nearly full.** ***Right:*** **After setting for a while the foam will expand over the top of your prop.**

Another handy little trick is to add a little UV dye to the starch, making your face black light reactive. For the best effect under black light, you will want to substitute plain white paper for newspaper in the final layer. The dark ink in the newspaper interferes with the glow, and gives the skull a rather unpleasant look. For the last layer of paper, I used ordinary computer paper (often called copier paper). Any white paper should work well. You may find you need to let the white paper soak a little longer than the newspaper; it does not absorb the starch as quickly. Your strips are ready to use when they are limp and fold over on themselves when lifted out of the starch. The UV dye I was a dye used for locating radiator leaks (I was able to buy it at my local auto parts store).

You may be wondering if there any more intricate shapes you can copy with

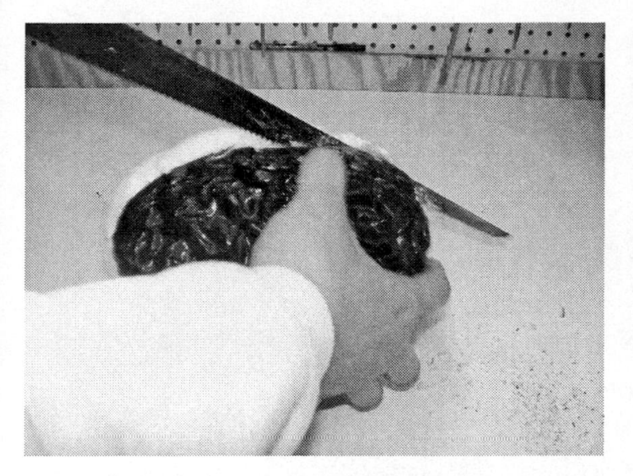

Left: **Take a saw or sharp knife and trim off the excess foam.** ***Right:*** **Once trimmed your project is ready to paint.**

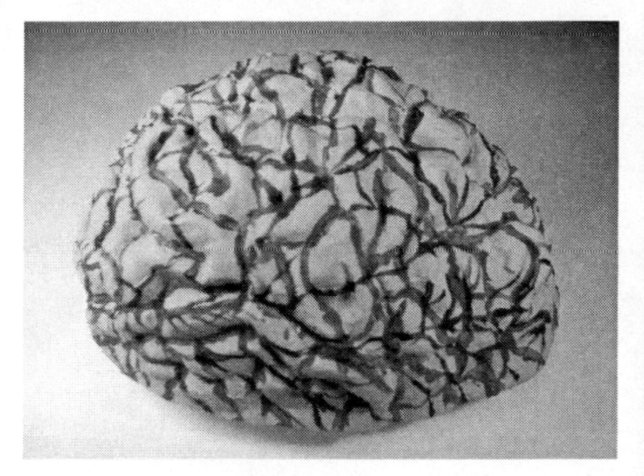

Above: **A little paint and your prop is done.** ***Right:*** **UV skull face photographed under black light.**

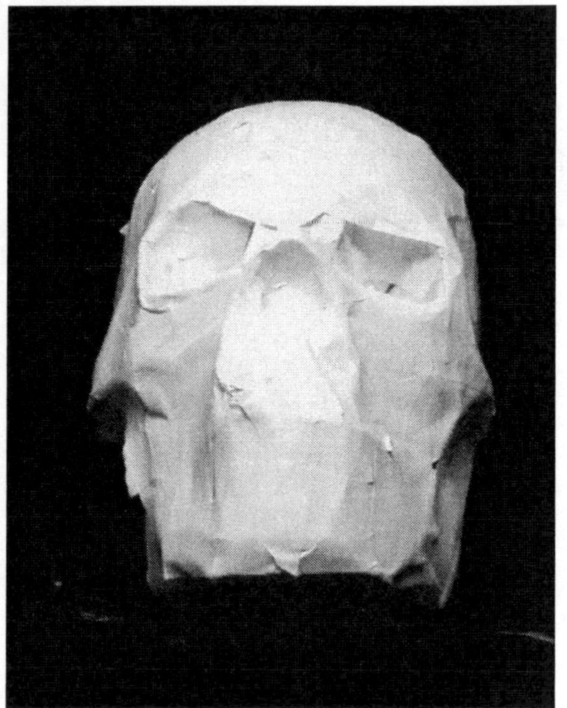

papier-mâché. There most certainly are. In fact, you can copy most any shape you like. Take, for example, the many vacuum formed plastic signs and sculptures you can find at your local Halloween store. Many of them are quite detailed, and can be rather easily and inexpensively copied with papier-mâché. I will show you how to do this with a rather large and intricate gargoyle.

If you have already tried a skull, you will realize how difficult it can be to reproduce detail when covering something with papier-mâché. For larger, more intricate items, like the gargoyle, you will find it best to work from the inside when possible.

A close look at our gargoyle will show that it does indeed have some rather fine detail in several sections, such as the face.

This detail would be very difficult to reproduce using wide strips of paper, so we must use a somewhat different technique. Start by cutting or tearing paper into very small pieces, about ⅛" square. These small pieces can more easily be forced into the fine details.

Next, soak the small pieces in liquid starch. It is a good idea to let them sit until they get good and soft, about thirty minutes or so.

When you have finished soaking your small pieces of paper, put on your rubber gloves and knead the pieces together in the starch. You will want to try to mush them into one mass. Now take the mush, squeeze out the excess starch, and push it firmly into the small, fine details of your mold. In the case of the gargoyle shown, you would want to use this technique on the face, while the muscles in the chest and arms can more easily be done with strips of paper. Use the paper mush only where the detail is very fine. For lesser detail, strips will give you greater strength and save a lot of time.

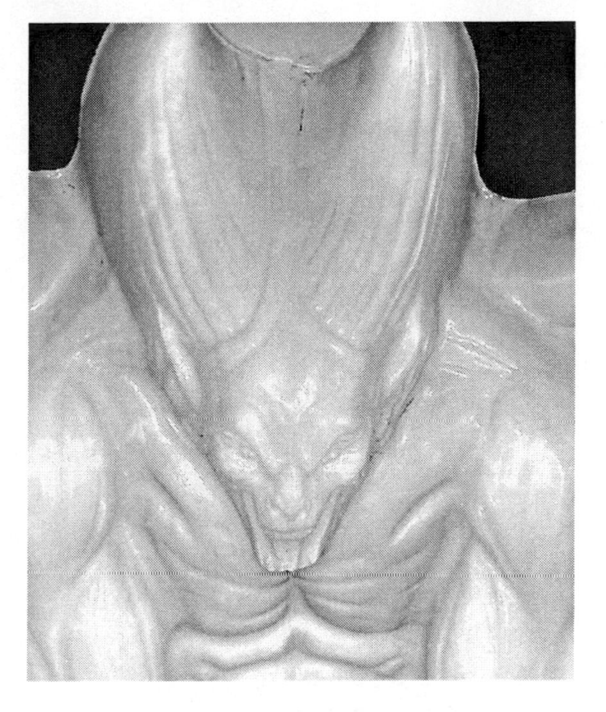

This close-up of a commercially manufactured gargoyle shows fine detail, which can be hard to reproduce with papier-mâché.

Make certain you press the mush all the way down into the details; work it several times to force out any air and make the mush fill in the details. Keep the layer of mush as thin as possible; you will be adding strips of paper over this for strength and the mush takes a very long time to dry. In fact, if your mush layer is too thick, it will seemingly never dry. As you work the mush into the mold, you will notice that you work a lot of starch out of the paper. To the extent possible, tip your mold and drain off this excess. When you are satisfied that you have filled all the fine details, set your project aside and let it dry completely. Once you notice that the exposed paper appears dry, still let your mold set for several days. The mush below will still be wet, and it takes a very long time to dry.

Opposite, top: **There are many items that can be copied using papier-mâché.** ***Opposite, bottom:*** **For larger, more intricate items, like the gargoyle, you will find it best to work from the inside, when possible.**

Left: **Start by cutting or tearing paper into very small pieces, about ⅛" square.**
Right: **Next, soak the small pieces in liquid starch.**

Now it is time to start filling in the rest of your mold. Start by placing strips along the outside edges of the mold. Where necessary, tear the paper to make it level or nearly level with the edge. In very tight spots, I find it better to just fold the paper back into the mold.

Next, look at the inside of your mold. Find any long, straight depressions and run a strip of paper into these low spots. This will give you a smoother edge on the finished project.

You can continue to add strips until the entire mold is filled to a depth of three or four layers. Remember to always work the strips into the low spots. Work them until they are smooth in the mold and fill all the detail. Remember also that you want to cover any areas that you filled with the mush. Work the wet strips onto the surface of the dried mush to make sure they will stick.

Again, set your project aside to dry for several days. Once it dries, it is time to remove your project from the mold.

Now take the mush, squeeze out the excess starch, and push it firmly into the small, fine details of your mold.

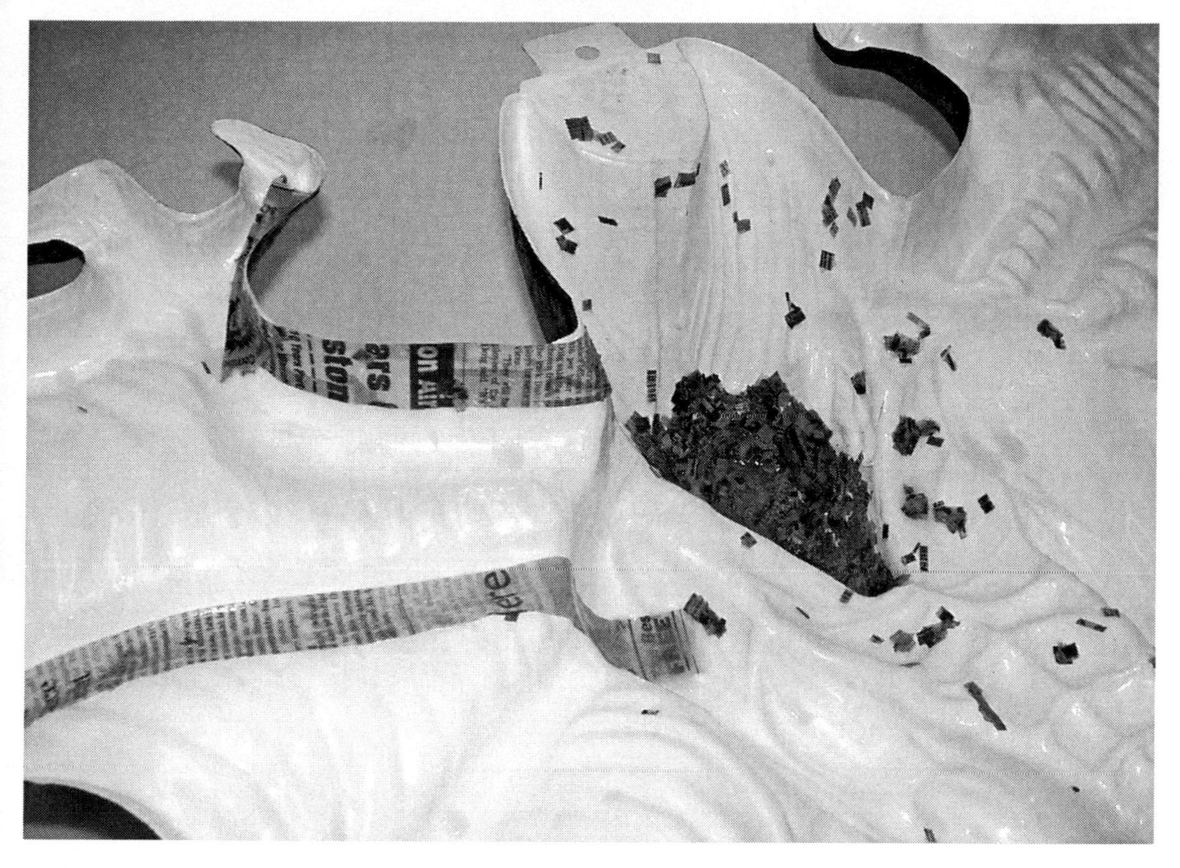

Place strips along the outside edges of the mold.

Start at one corner or point and gently work the papier-mâché out of the mold about an eighth of an inch. Continue doing this around the entire mold, then start around again, pulling the project out just a little farther. Continue working around the mold, pulling the project out a little farther each time until the project is completely free of the mold.

If you find that some of the detail you filled with the mush was not actually dry and stays behind in the mold, you can still fix it. Remove the rest of the project from the mold and leave the still-wet mush in the mold until it dries (again, this may take days). Once the mush that was left in the mold has dried, remove it and attach it to the rest of the project by wetting it with starch and attaching it to the part of the project it broke off of. Set aside to dry.

If the papier-mâché that was still in contact with the mold is still wet, set it aside to dry. Even if you think it is not still wet, it does not hurt to let your project sit overnight before painting, to make sure.

It is now time to trim off any paper which is protruding beyond the mold. Simply take a sharp pair of scissors and cut away anything that does not belong on your finished project.

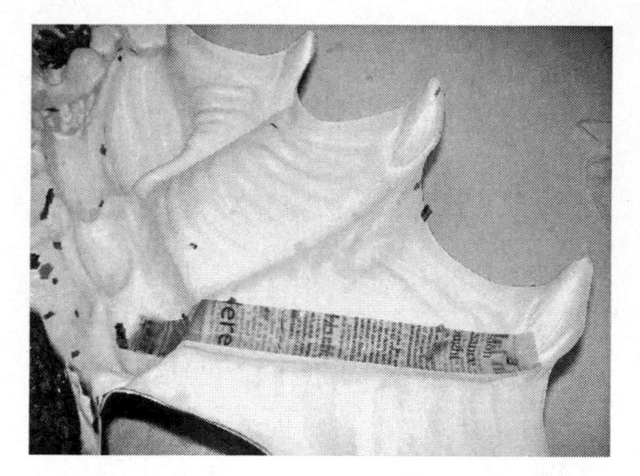

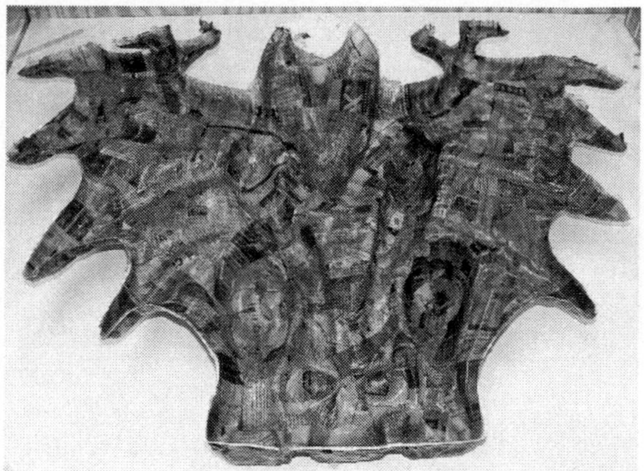

***Left:* Find any long, straight depressions and run a strip of paper into these low spots. *Right:* A mold completely filled with papier-mâché.**

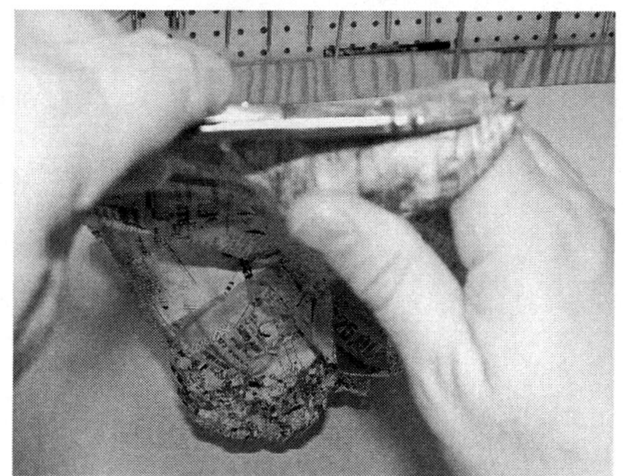

***Left:* A copy removed from the mold. *Right:* Take a sharp pair of scissors and cut away anything that does not belong on your finished project.**

Finally, you can paint your prop for the look you would like. For my gargoyle, I used stone paint.

I also molded a bat. I had to rely on my wife to do the paint job, because she has all the artistic ability.

Or, how about a brain, made in a brain-shaped gelatin mold? The possibilities are endless.

There is one other use for papier-mâché I would like to mention, and that is making your own custom mask. For this, all you need is some aluminum foil, some paints, a paintbrush, and of course, papier-mâché.

To make your mask, start by choosing a face to copy (I wanted an extremely good-looking mask so I chose to copy my own face). Take your roll of aluminum foil and cut off a piece about four feet long, fold it in half the long way and then

A completed copy of a gargoyle.

fold it in half again the same way. What you end up with is a piece of foil about one foot by the width of your roll.

Now take the foil and mold it to the face you wish to copy. Take extreme care around the eyes and nose. You must use a very light pressure around the eyes; it is best for the person whose face is being copied to do this area. He will be able to control how much pressure is being exerted on his eyes. Make sure your model has his eyes closed!

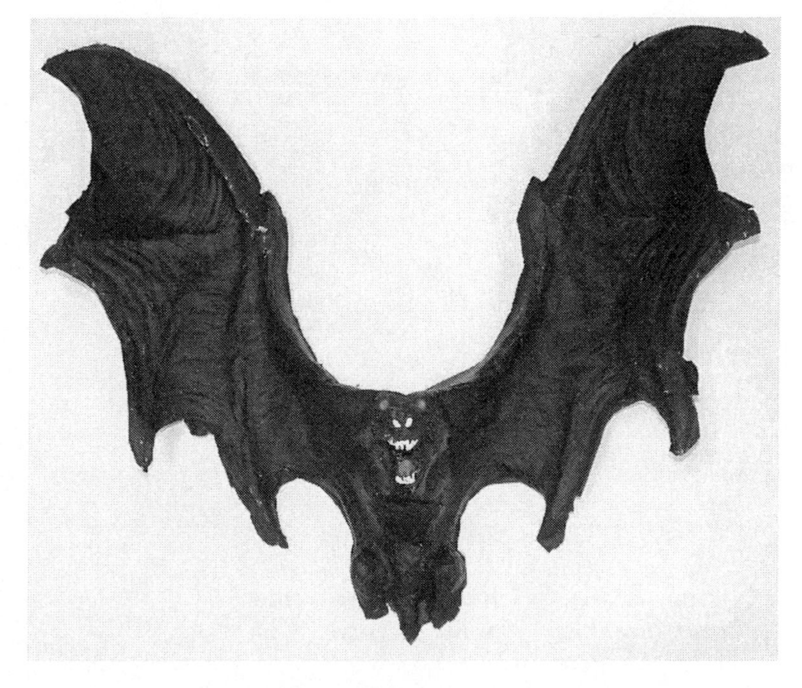

A copy of a bat.

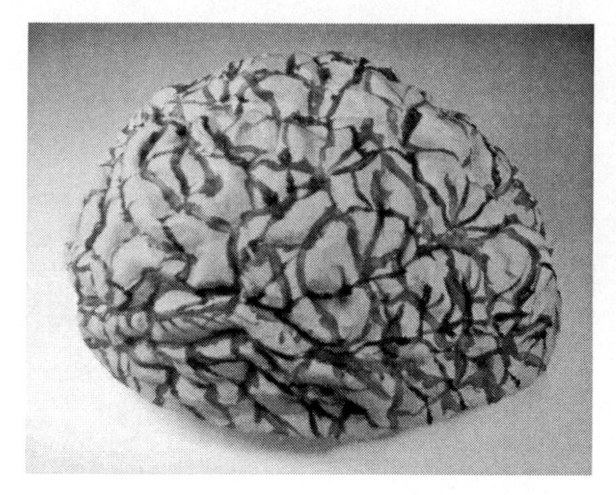

Left: **A papier-mâché brain made by copying a gelatin mold.** ***Right:*** **Folding over a piece of foil is the first step in making your own mask.**

You must also take care not to seal the nose area so tightly as to cut off the air supply! On all other areas, press the foil down somewhat firmly, and try to smooth it as much as possible.

Remove the foil from the face, and you now have a mold to form your papier-mâché in.

Now begin placing your paper strips soaked in starch on the inside of your mold.

Continue adding strips until the entire inside of your mold is covered.

Set your mask aside overnight to dry and then remove it from your mold. If

Above: **Take the foil and mold it to the face you wish to copy.** ***Right:*** **Remove the foil from the face, and you now have a mold to form your papier-mâché in.**

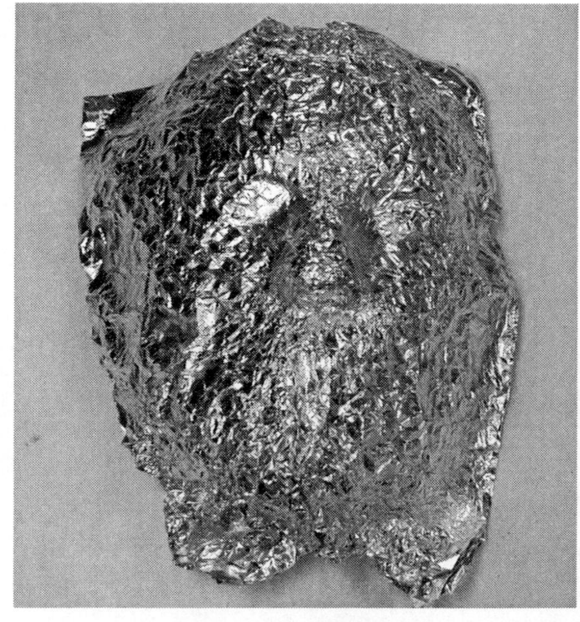

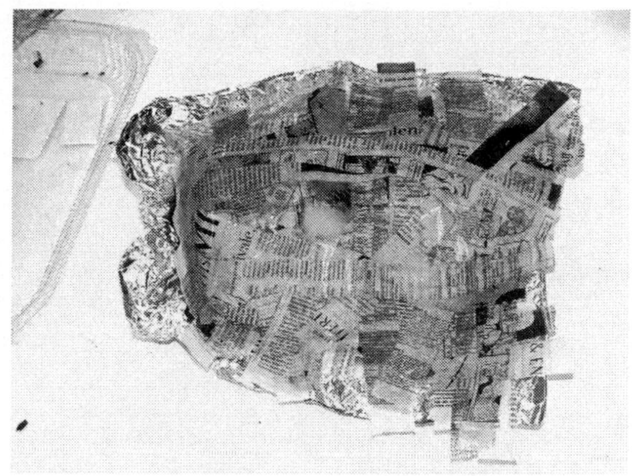

Left: **Begin placing your paper strips soaked in starch on the inside of your mold.** ***Right:*** **Continue adding strips until the entire inside of your mold is covered.**

the side that was in contact with the foil is still wet, set your mask aside to dry before proceeding.

Once you have your mask nice and dry, you can trim off any excess papier-mâché and paint it or decorate it any way you like. If you plan to wear your mask this is a good time to cut out the eyeholes and another hole under the nose so that you can breathe. Remember that any mask you wear will obstruct your vision, so be very careful when and where you wear mask. Smaller eyeholes may make the mask seem scarier, but you must cut them large enough to provide adequate vision for what you will be doing while wearing your mask.

After your mask is trimmed and you have cut any holes you need to cut, break out your paints and let your imagination run wild. It is usually not necessary to paint the inside of the mask, as no one will see this side of it. Of course if you want to, go for it.

If you would like to wear your mask, you can cut or poke two small holes in the sides near the ears. You can then put pieces of string through the holes so the mask can be tied to your head. Or, if you prefer, you can take a

Set your mask aside overnight to dry, and then remove it from your mold.

Above: **Once you have your mask nice and dry, you can trim off any excess papier-mâché.** ***Right:*** **Once trimmed your mask is ready to paint.**

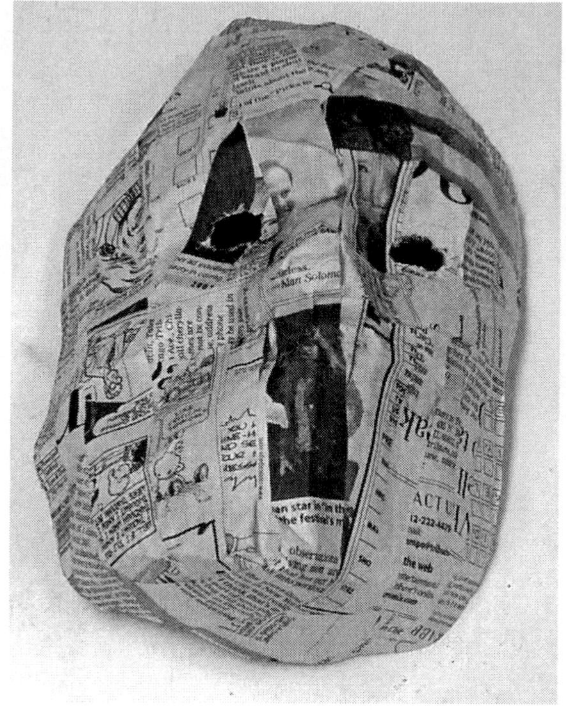

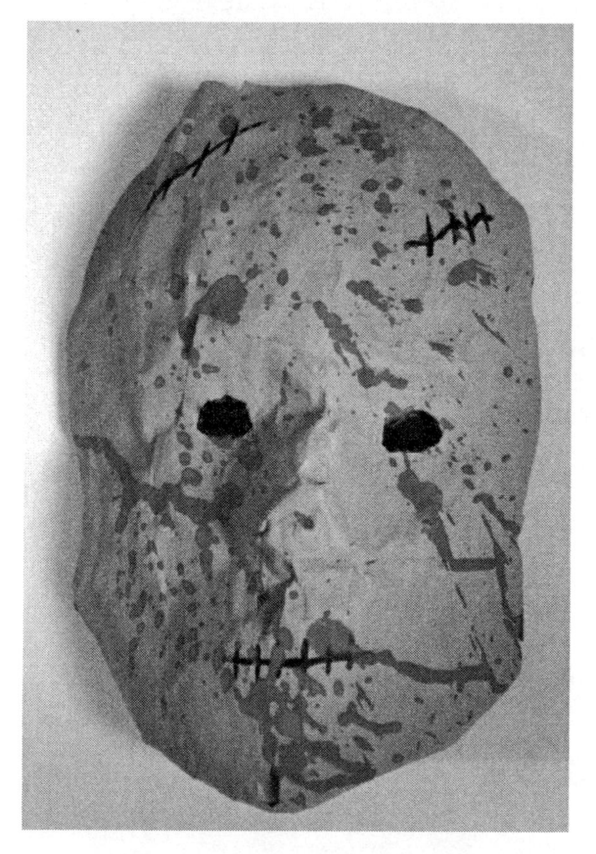

After trimming you can paint your mask.

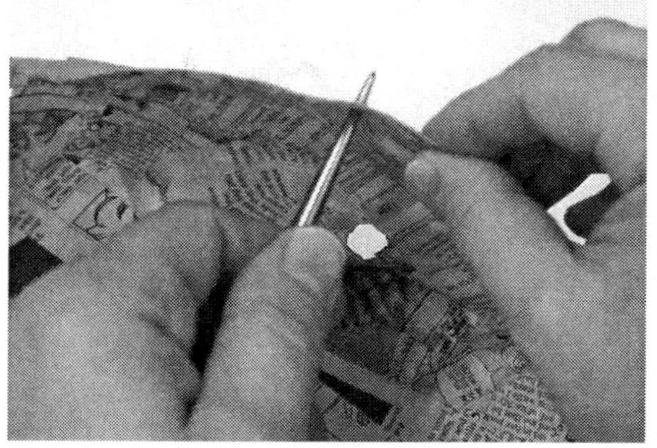

Cut or poke two small holes in the sides near the ears.

large rubber band, cut it and tie each end to the holes in the mask (adjust the length of the rubber band so it will hold the mask securely on your head).

And now that you know the basics of papier-mâché, you can come up with your own ideas and develop new ways to use it in your own haunt!

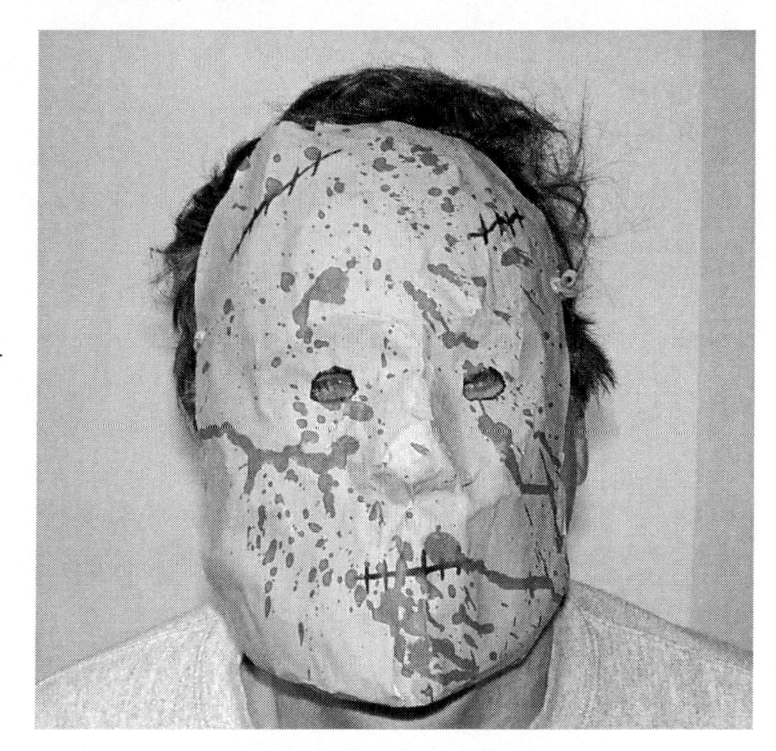

The author wearing his finished mask.

PART II
PROJECTS

TERROR EYE SKULL

OK, let's start out with a really easy one.

For this project you will need:

- ✓ One skull (your choice)
- ✓ Two pieces Eyes of Terror gum
- ✓ A pliable adhesive (chewed gum will work)

Step One: Take two pieces of your adhesive and roll them into cigar shapes about 1½" × ¼".

Step Two: Take these pieces of adhesive and press them to the back of the Eyes of Terror.

These are materials you will need to create a terror eye skull.

Left: **Step One: Take two pieces of your adhesive and roll them into cigar shapes.** ***Right:*** **Step Two: Take these pieces of adhesive and press them to the back of the eyes.**

Step Three: Place the gumballs into the eye sockets of the skull and you're done.

This project shows how some of the simplest ideas can make a rather impressive prop. The skull I used for this project came from The Anatomical Chart Company. The Eyes of Terror gum is available at most grocery stores around Halloween, and for the adhesive most anything will do. I prefer the temporary type so that the eyes can be removed for repositioning or to reuse the skull. As stated earlier, even chewed gum works for this.

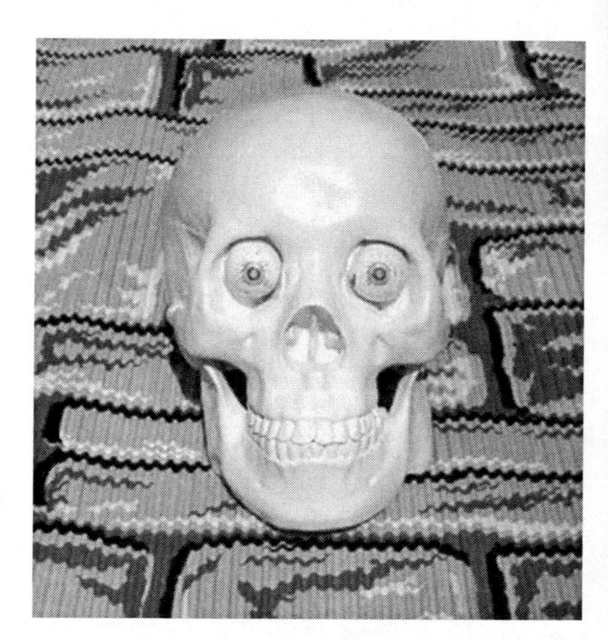

Step Three: Place the eyes into the eye sockets of the skull.

TWINKLE EYE SKULL

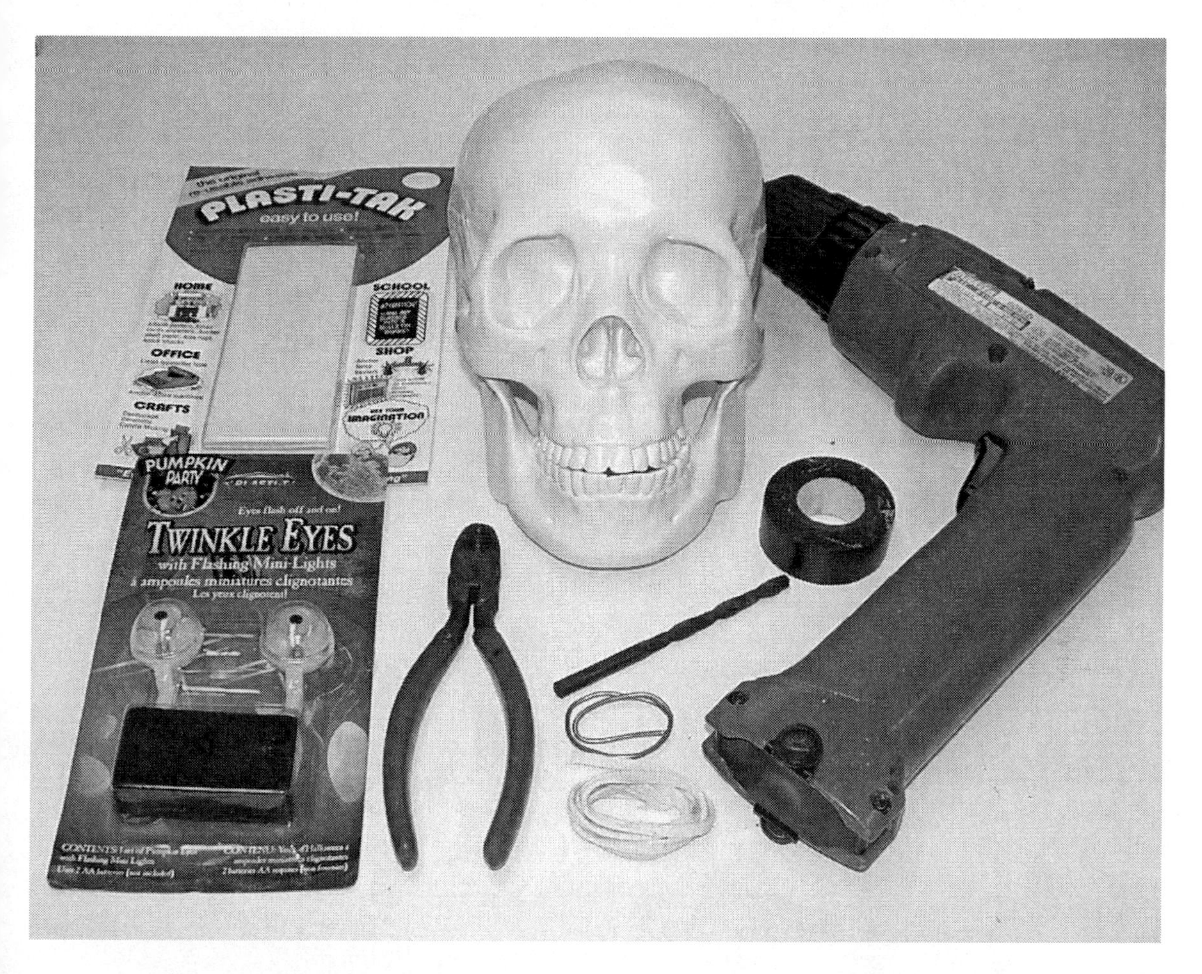

These are the materials you will need to create a twinkle eye skull.

For this project you will need:

- ✓ One skull, your choice as long as it is hollow
- ✓ One set of twinkle eyes

- ✓ Two AA batteries
- ✓ Some pliable adhesive (chewed gum will work)
- ✓ A short piece of string
- ✓ A small piece of solder, or a small nut or similar small weight (optional)
- ✓ Electrical tape
- ✓ Wire cutters
- ✓ Long-nose pliers (optional)
- ✓ A drill, with drill bit
- ✓ Safety glasses (mandatory)

Step One: Using your drill and drill bit, drill two holes, one in the back of each eye socket of your skull. The size of these holes does not matter, as long as they are large enough to pass your string through when it is tied to the twinkle eye wires. Drilling the hole a little larger will make things easier than drilling it too small. The location of the holes is not critical as long as they are in the very back of the eye socket. If one hole is a little higher or lower than the other or a little more to the right or left, this will not present a problem.

Step Two: Remove your twinkle eyes from the package. Twinkle eyes can be found in many stores that carry Halloween items. You can often find them in grocery stores near the pumpkins at Halloween time. These eyes are meant to be put in pumpkins, but I think they look much better in a skull.

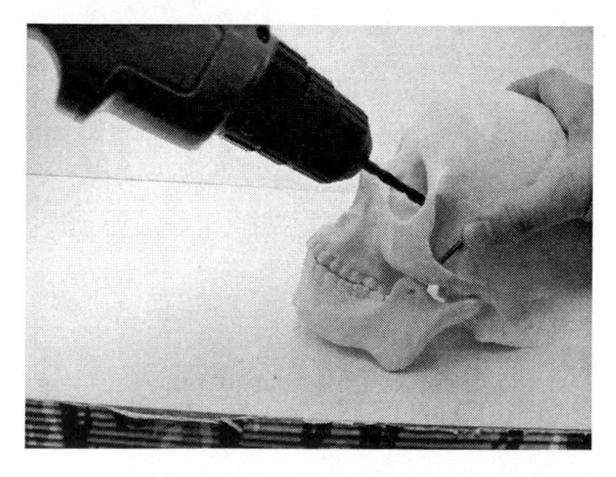

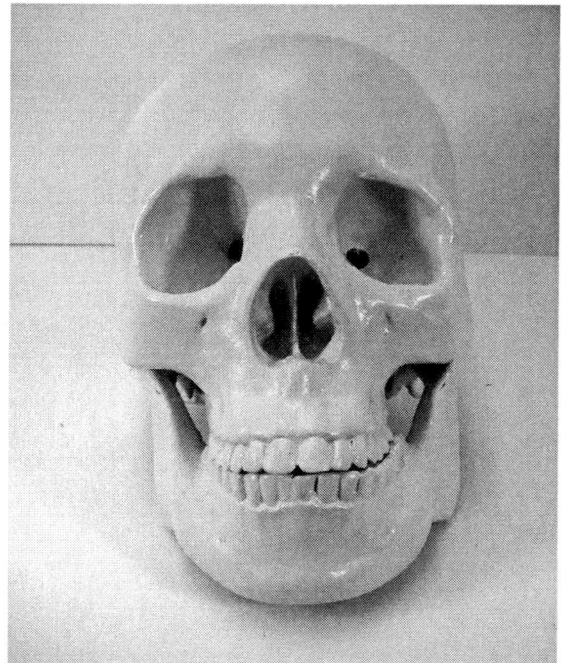

Left: **Step one: Using your drill and drill bit, drill two holes, one in the back of each eye socket of your skull.** ***Right:*** **If one hole is a little higher or lower than the other or a little more to the right or left, this will not present a problem.**

Once you have the twinkle eyes out of the package, you will need to cut the wires between the eyes and the battery pack so that you can run the wires through the skull. This is one point where you need to be a little careful. You want to cut the wires so that you have enough length on the eyes to make it through the skull, and enough left on the battery pack to reconnect the wires. I have found that on most skulls cutting about 1.5 inches away from the battery pack works well. If your wires are too short, you can always splice in a short piece of wire to increase the length. Take note of how the eyes are wired to the battery pack; you will need to reattach them later in the same way.

Step Three: You should be wearing your safety glasses anytime you are working on a project. If you do not have them on yet please put them on now! This part can be a little tricky, but if you take your time you should get through

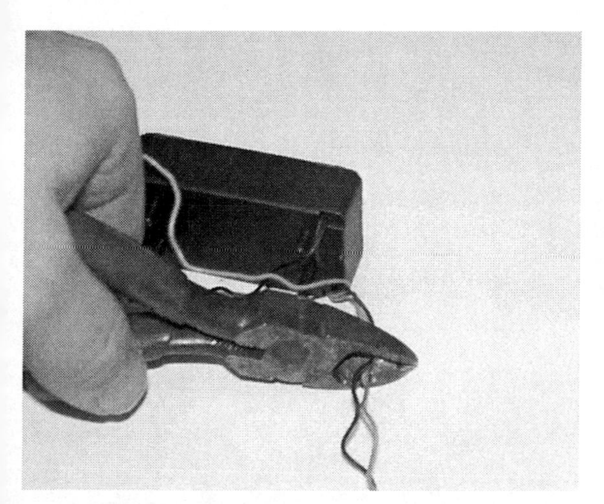

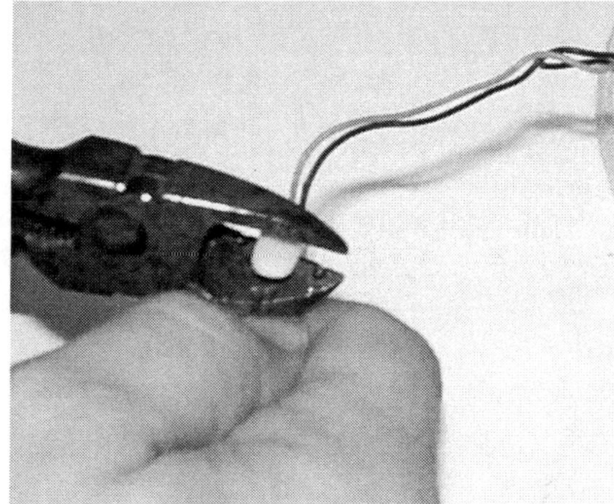

Left: **Cut the wires between the eyes and the battery pack.** ***Right:*** **Using your wire cutters, carefully cut and break the plastic away from the wires, up to the back of the eyeball.**

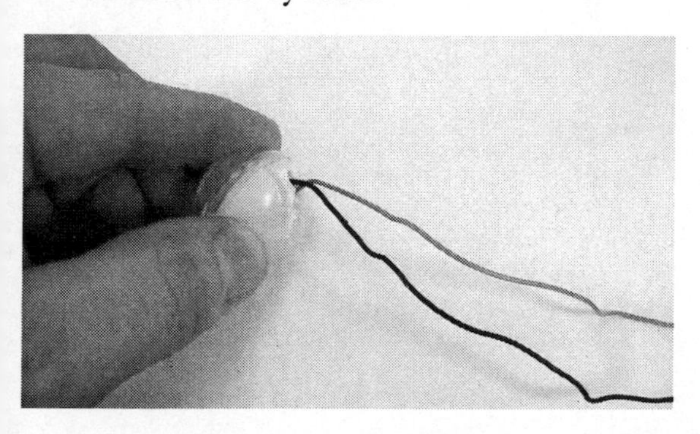

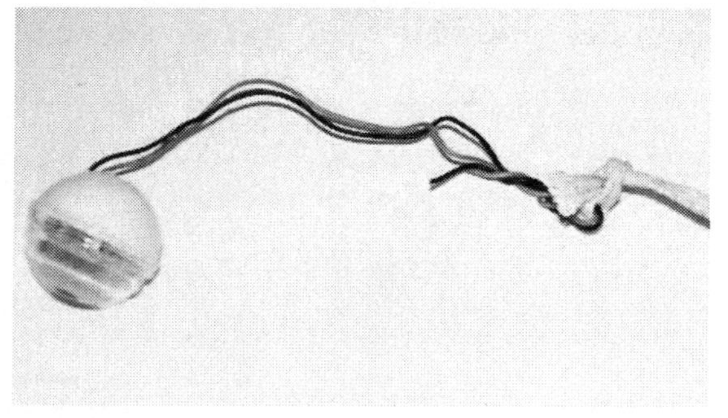

Left: **The eyes trimmed and ready to place in the skull.** ***Right:*** **Tie the end of the wires from one of your eyes to your piece of string.**

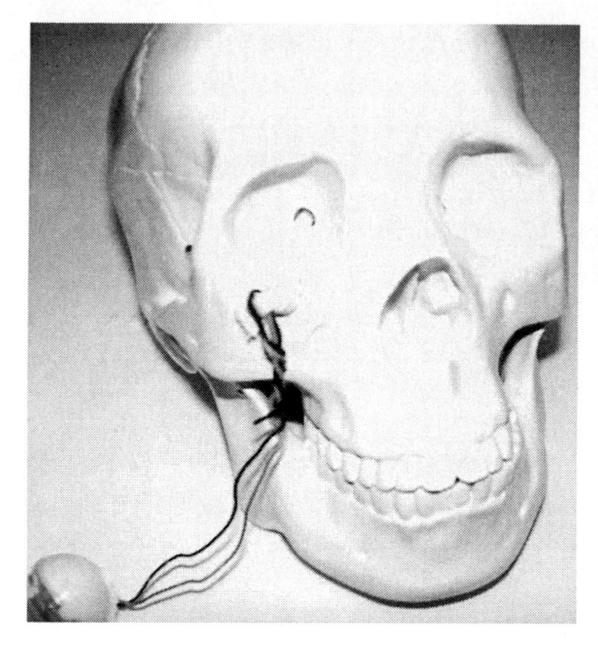

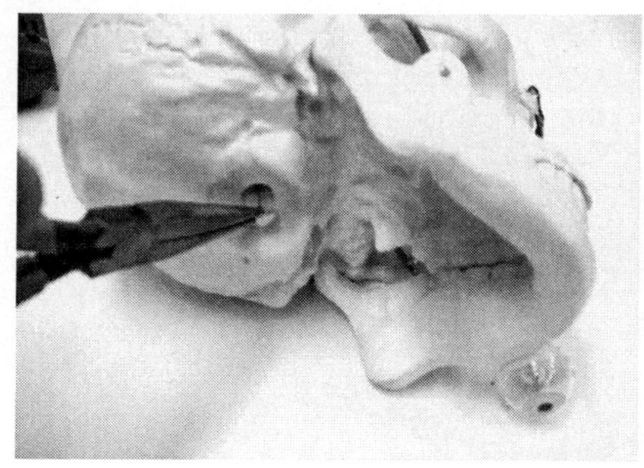

Left: **Take the free end of the string (or the end with the weight) and place it into one of the holes you drilled into one of the eye sockets.** ***Right:*** **Reach up the hole with long nosed pliers and pull the string out.**

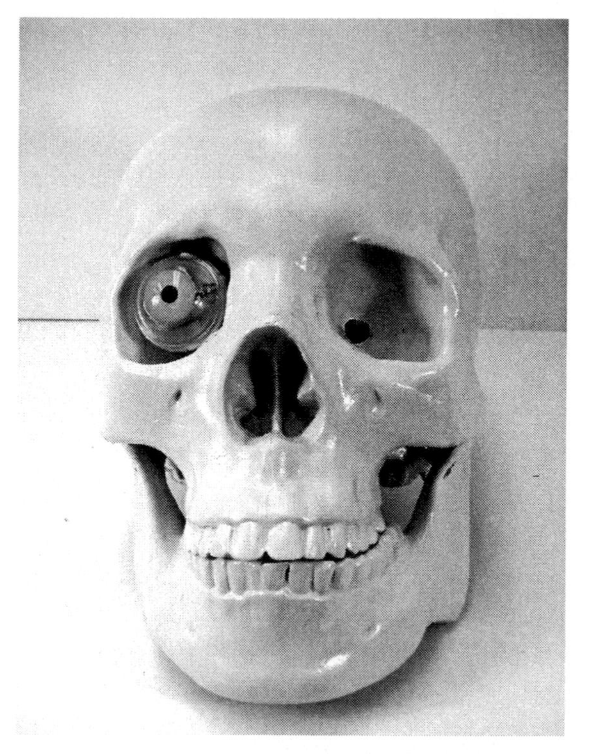

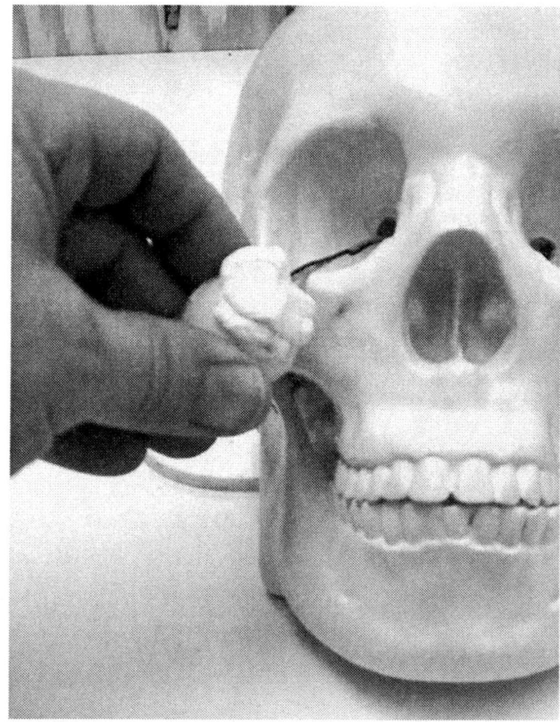

Left: **Test your eye for correct fit.** ***Right:*** **Apply the pliable adhesive to the back of the eye.**

it just fine. You will notice that your twinkle eyes have a plastic stem coming down from the back of the eyeball. This stem is meant to be pushed into a pumpkin; we will have to remove this stem to place the eyes in a skull. Using your wire cutters, carefully cut and break the plastic away from the wires, up to the back of the eyeball. You will want to try to pull and hold the wires to the

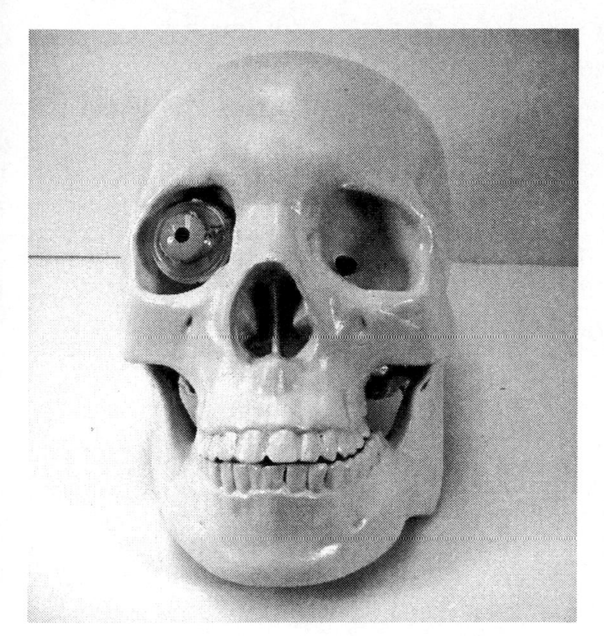

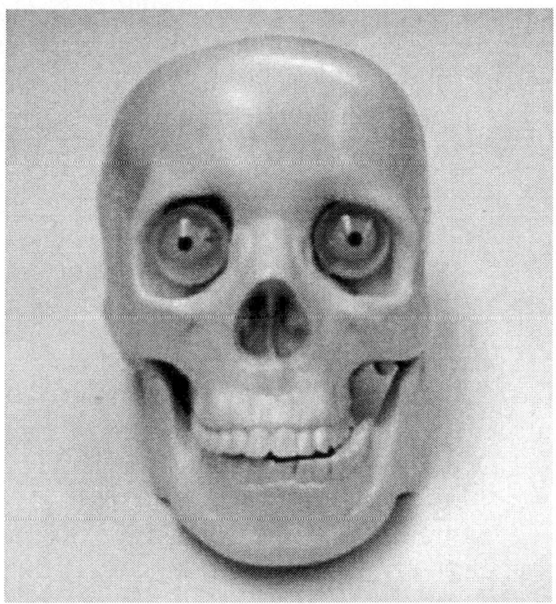

Left: **The first eye in place.** ***Right:*** **The twinkle eye skull with both eyes in place.**

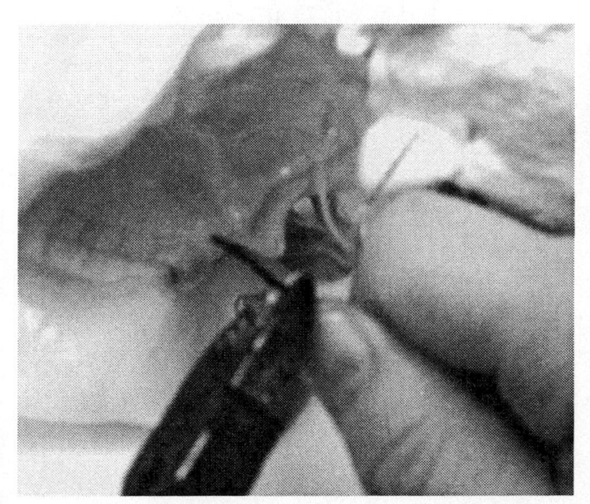

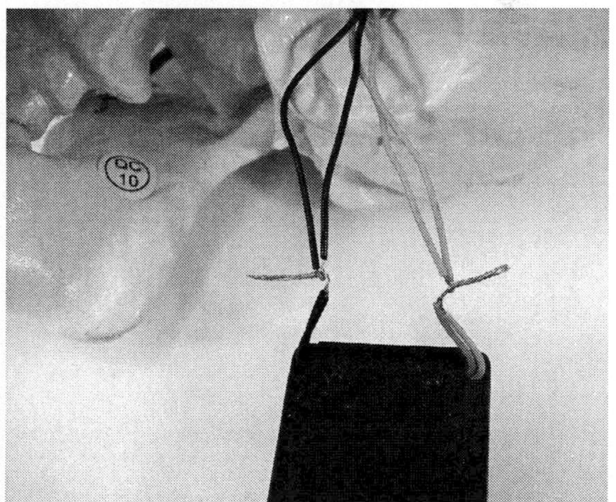

Left: **Carefully strip off about ¾" of the insulation on all the wire ends from the eyes and battery pack.** ***Right:*** **To connect them, simply twist the wires together.**

side opposite the side you are cutting. Work slowly and take care that pieces do not fly off in such a way as to endanger anyone. Everyone in the room should be wearing safety glasses! When you reach the back of the eyeball, it is next to impossible to remove all the plastic. Leaving a little will not matter. If you have not trimmed off enough, you will have a chance to fix this later.

Step Four: Take a piece of string about a foot long. Tie the end of the wires from one of your eyes to your piece of string. Try to keep the knot small; it need not be a very strong knot. It is more important to be able to untie the knot later than to have it hold. If the knot should let go while you try to pull the wires though the skull, it is a simple matter to retie the knot and try again.

Step Five: You may want to tie a small piece of solder or some other small weight to the end of the string opposite the eye. If you choose to do this, make certain the weight will pass through the hole in the bottom of the skull. I usually find this unnecessary, using long-nosed pliers to pull the string out instead of relying on the weight to pull the string down to the hole.

Take the free end of the string (or the end with the weight) and place it into one of the holes you drilled into one of the eye sockets. Feed all of the string up to the wires into the skull.

Step Six: With the skull in an upright position, and the hole in the bottom of the skull facing down, shake the skull until the string can be seen over the hole in the bottom of the skull (or if you are using a weight, until the weight falls out bringing the string with it). You should now be able to reach up the hole with long-nosed pliers and pull the string out.

Continue to pull on the string until the wires on the eye begin to pull into the skull. Try to fit your eye into the eye socket of the skull. If it does not fit you may need to trim a little more plastic off the back. The eye most likely will not

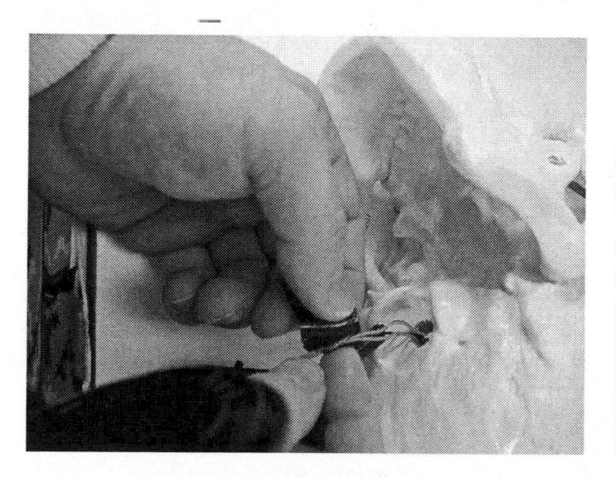

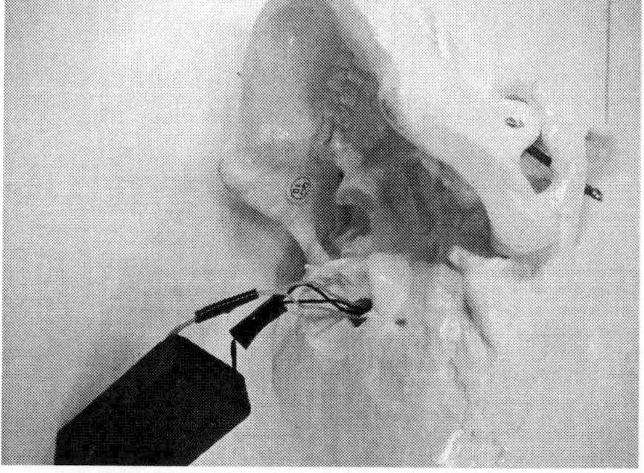

Left: **Use electrical tape to cover your spliced wires.** ***Right:*** **Make certain that your tape covers all exposed copper and extends over the insulation of the wire.**

fit all the way to the back of the eye socket. This does not matter as long as you can position the eye so it looks straightforward and most of the eye is well within the skull. This is your prop, and the eye is in the right position when it is where you want it.

Step Seven: Apply the pliable adhesive to the back of the eye. What you use to stick your eye into the skull does not matter much. I like to use an adhesive which is pliable and does not set up hard. This allows you to reposition the eyes at any time, and if you get tired of the twinkle eye skull, you can easily pull the eyes out and reuse the skull. I have even used chewed gum as my adhesive. This works well, but after a while the eyes can be a little tough to remove.

Now insert your eye into your skull and position it as you like, pulling on the string to pull the wires into the skull as you set the eye. Pull the wires through the bottom of the skull and untie the string.

Step Eight: Repeat steps three through seven for the other eye.

Step Nine: Carefully strip off about ¾" of the insulation on all the wire ends from the eyes and battery pack.

Step Ten: Connect the wires from the eyes to the wires from the battery pack in the same way they were connected before you cut them. This should be very easy, as they are color coded; it does not matter which orange and which black goes to which eye as long as one of each color goes to each eye. In fact, you can twist all the orange and all the black together if you like, and the eyes will work just fine. To connect them, simply twist the wires together.

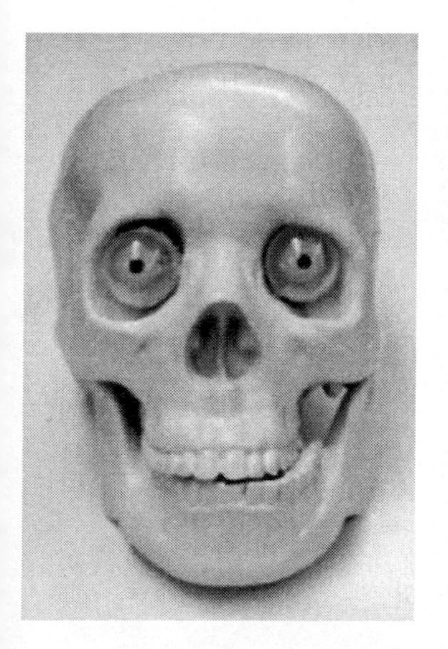

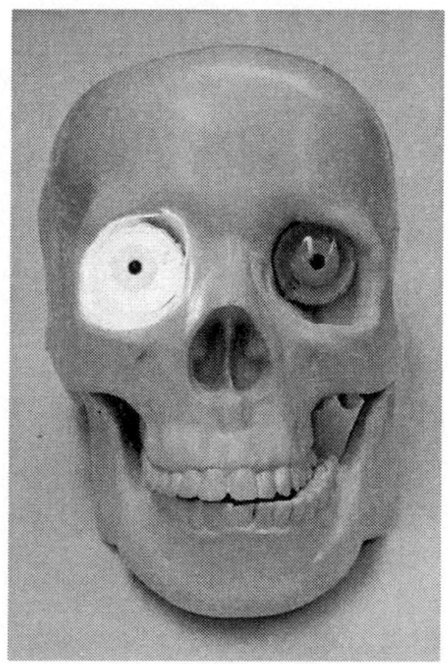

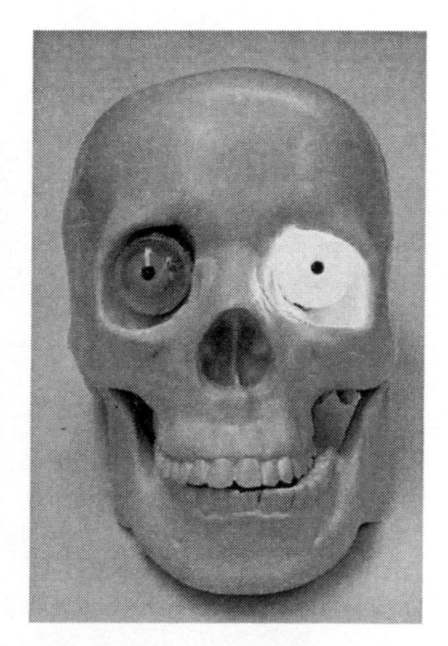

Left: **Your twinkle eye skull is now done.** ***Middle:*** **When the batteries are installed the eyes will flash randomly. Sometimes the left eye will be on.** ***Right:*** **Sometimes the right eye will be on.**

Step Eleven: Tape all the exposed copper with electrical tape. Use a piece of tape about one inch long and wrap it tightly around the bare copper and continue to cover at least ⅛" of the insulation on either side. If needed, add another layer of tape over the first to ensure all the bare copper is covered. If you do not properly cover the bare copper and the orange and black touch, copper to copper, your lights will not work. You may also run the risk of the wires overheating and starting a fire. Just make sure you never have exposed bare wire and you will be fine.

Your twinkle eye skull is now done.

Put the two AA batteries into the battery pack and the eyes should begin to flash in a somewhat random pattern, usually one side first and then the other.

Of course, twinkle eyes are not the only lights you can put into a skull this way. You could use the Demon Eyes (from this book) or other lights for a myriad of different looks (see section Put a Light In It).

UNEARTHED SKULL METHOD ONE

For this project you will need:

- ✓ One skull, your choice
- ✓ One can of brown paste shoe polish
- ✓ One toothbrush (used and worn out is fine)
- ✓ A few cotton swabs
- ✓ A shoe brush or rag

Step One: Select your skull. For this project, I prefer the fourth quality skulls from The Anatomical Chart Company. The plastic they are made of seems to be somewhat rough, and maybe even a little porous, which allows them to take color better than a glossy skull. I have tried different skulls with varying levels of success; you may want to test your skull in an inconspicuous spot before doing the whole thing.

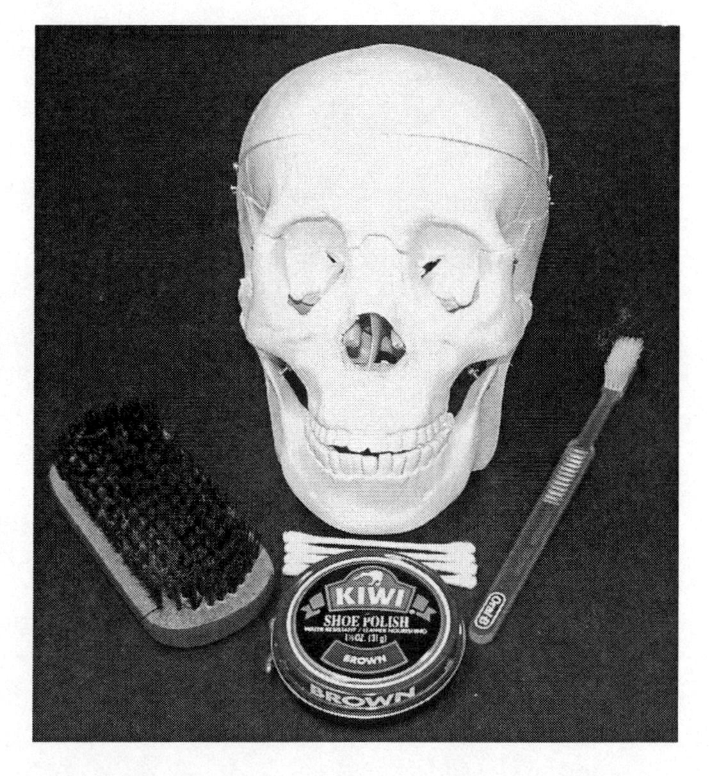

These are the materials you will need to create an unearthed skull using method one.

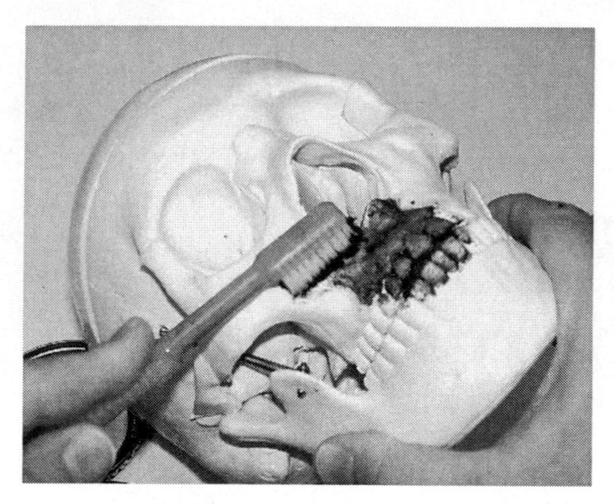

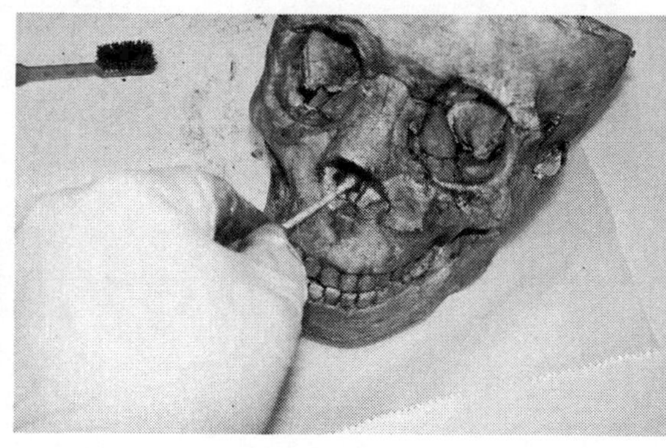

Left: **An old toothbrush is a good way to apply polish to your skull.** ***Right:*** **Use cotton swabs to get into some of the tighter spots such as the nasal cavity and the eye sockets.**

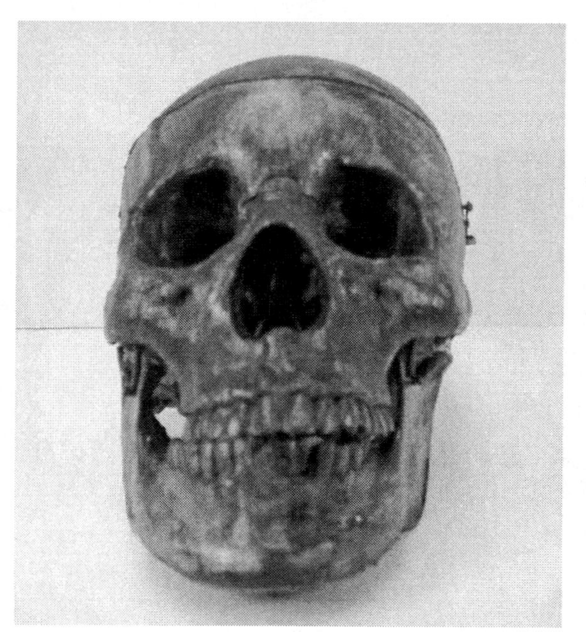

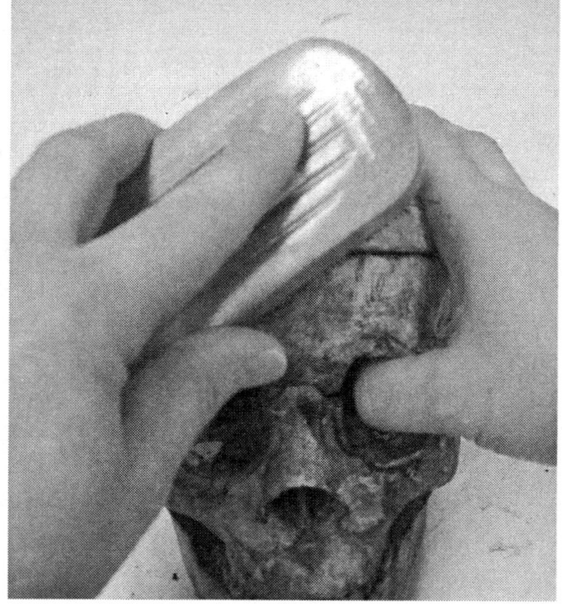

Left: **When you have finished applying the polish, let your skull sit overnight.** ***Right:*** **Buff off the excess shoe polish.**

Step Two: Using your toothbrush, apply brown shoe polish to your skull. **Do not use the toothbrush on your teeth after doing this project!**

Try to work the polish into the skull, applying a somewhat uneven layer. Use cotton swabs to get into some of the tighter spots such as the nasal cavity and the eye sockets.

When you have finished applying the polish, let your skull sit overnight.

Step Three: Using your shoe brush or rag, buff off the excess shoe polish.

Your skull is now done, and should look like it has been buried in the ground for years.

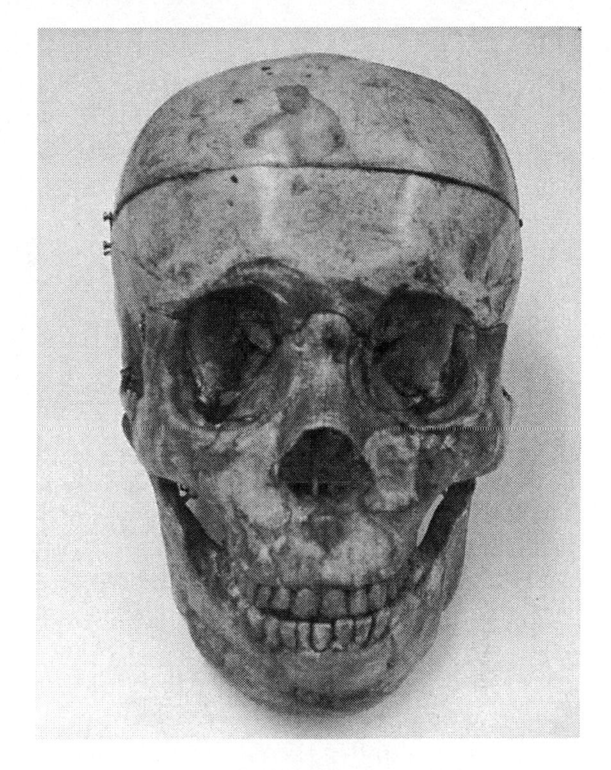

When done your skull should look like it has been buried in the ground for years.

UNEARTHED SKULL METHOD TWO

For this project you will need:

- ✓ One skull, your choice
- ✓ Some wood stain (for the skull I did here I used a shade called provincial)
- ✓ One brush or a small soft cloth
- ✓ A few cotton swabs
- ✓ Rubber gloves

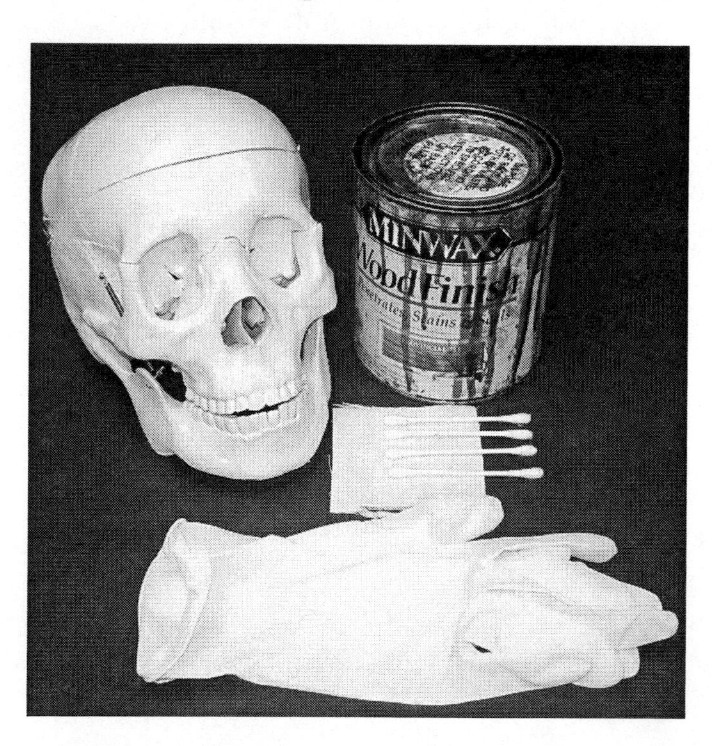

Step One: Select your skull. For this project, I prefer the fourth quality skulls from The Anatomical Chart Company. The plastic they are made of seems to be somewhat rough and maybe even a little porous, which allows them to take color better than a glossy skull. I have tried different skulls with varying levels of success; you may want to test your skull in an inconspicuous spot before doing the whole thing.

These are the materials you will need to create an unearthed skull using method two.

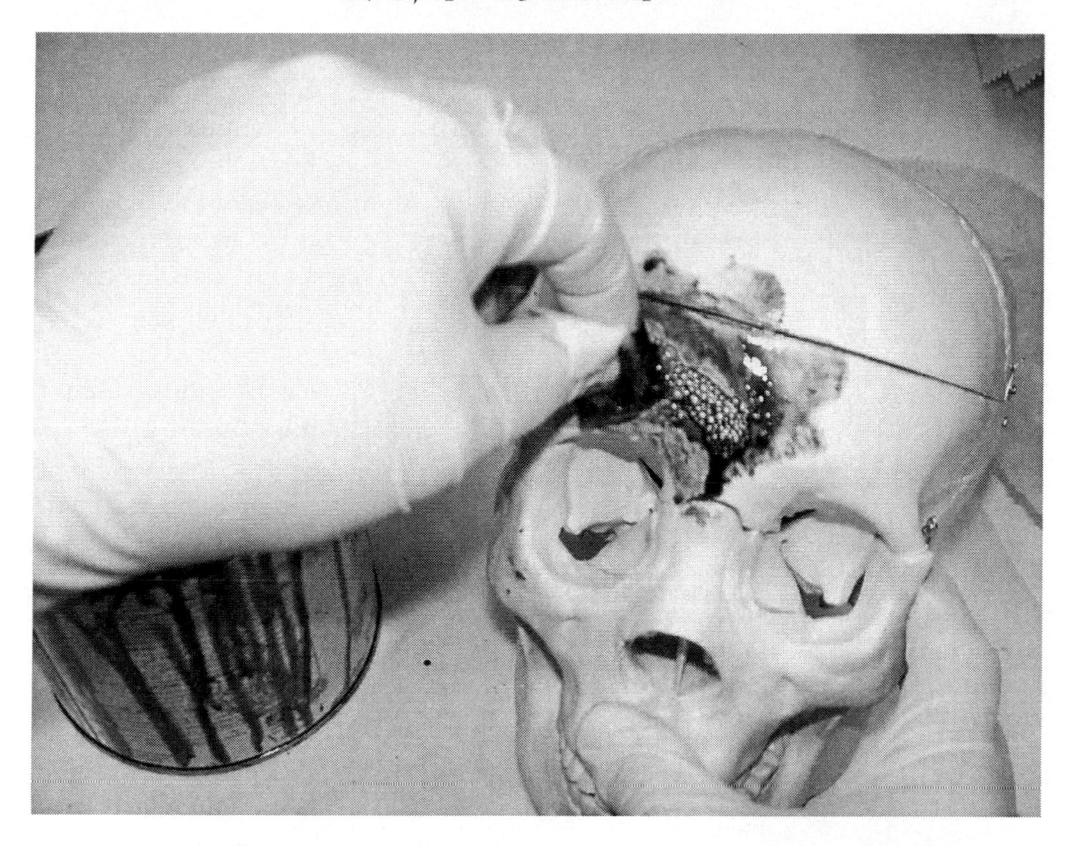

Using your brush or soft cloth, apply stain to your skull.

Step Two: Using your brush or soft cloth apply stain to your skull.

Try to work the stain into the skull, applying a somewhat uneven layer. Use cotton swabs to get into some of the tighter spots such as the nasal cavity and the eye sockets.

If you have a glossy skull, or if you find that for some other reason the stain tends to wipe off and not cover well, you will have to dab on the stain. To do this, apply a thin layer of stain to your skull and let

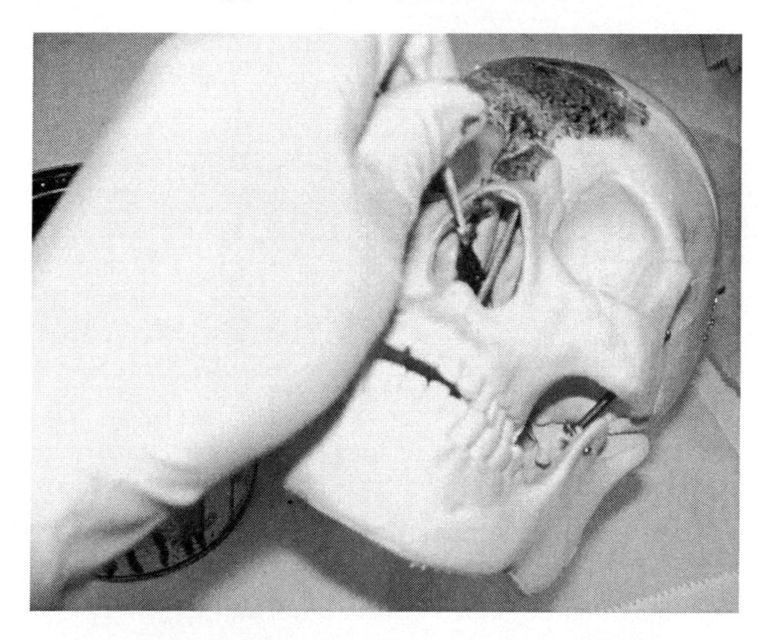

Use cotton swabs to get into some of the tighter spots such as the nasal cavity and the eye sockets.

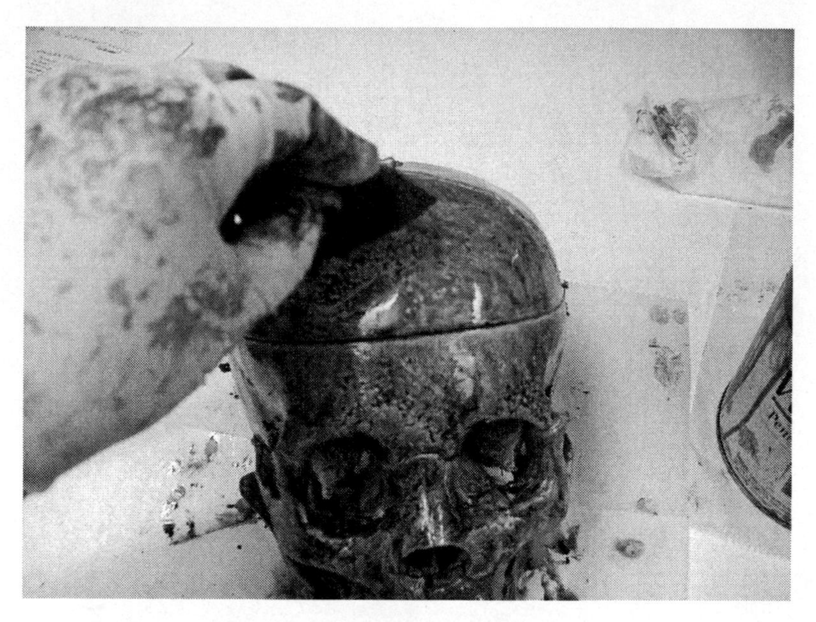

If you have a glossy skull, or find that for some other reason the stain tends to wipe off and not cover well, you will have to dab on the stain.

it sit until tacky. Now apply a heavier layer of stain on top of the first. Allow this layer to begin to dry, and then take your cloth and repeatedly dab your skull. Continue doing this every couple of minutes, until the stain turns very tacky. This dabbing will give you a thicker, more uneven, somewhat mottled look.

When you have finished applying the stain, let your skull sit overnight. Your skull is now done and should look like it has been buried in the ground for years.

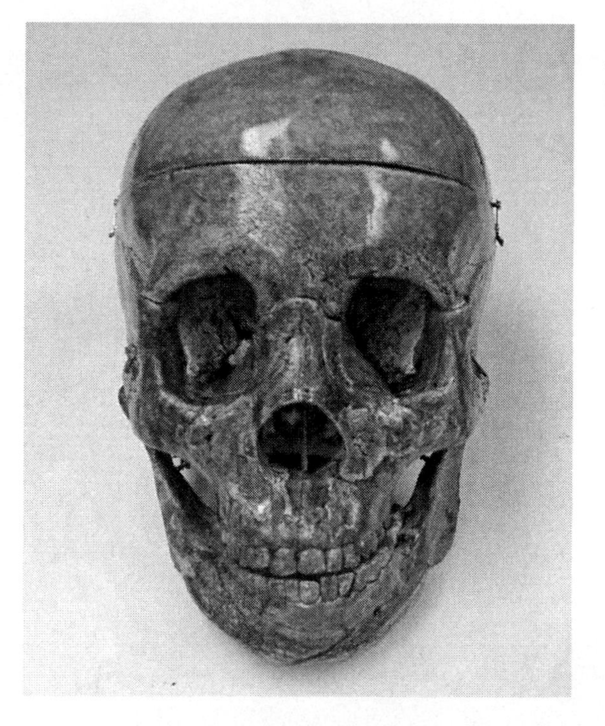

When done your skull should look like it has been buried in the ground for years.

AGED SKULL

For this project you will need:

- ✓ One skull
- ✓ One crackle paint kit (white or antique ivory; I prefer ivory as it helps add to the aged look)
- ✓ Some walnut stain (water based preferred; you may, of course, substitute another color if you would like a different look)
- ✓ Some satin finish clear coat (again I prefer water based, but you may use what you like)
- ✓ Some yellow paint tint
- ✓ Several small pieces of cotton cloth
- ✓ Several cotton swabs
- ✓ Several pairs of rubber gloves
- ✓ Safety goggles
- ✓ Face mask or respirator

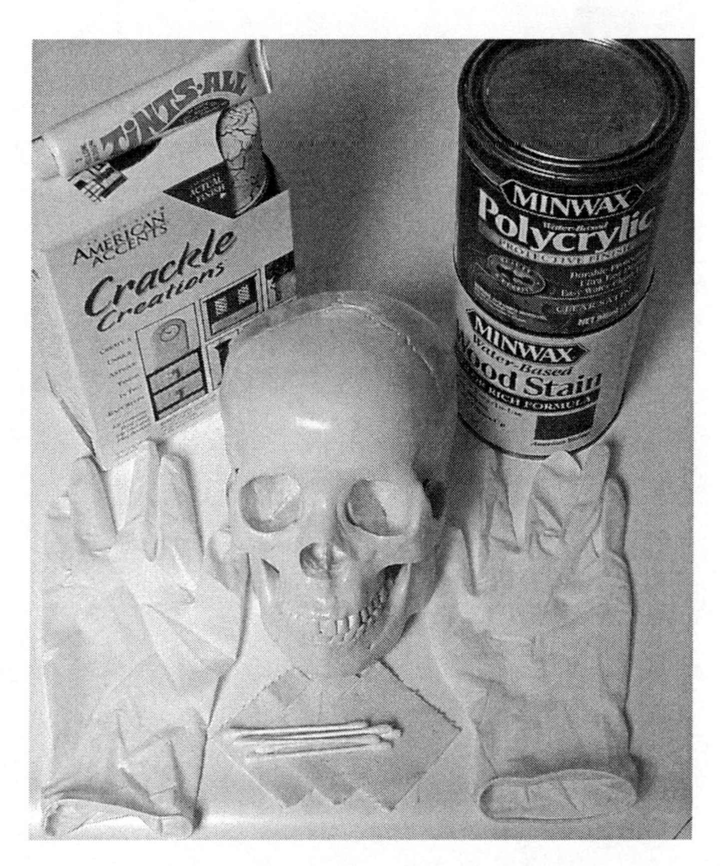

These are the materials you will need to create an aged skull.

Note: As you will need to wait for paint and other finishes to dry this project could take several days to complete.

Step One: Read the section in this book entitled Skull Painting, with special attention to the section on the crackle skull.

Step Two: Read the directions on your crackle paint kit.

Step Three: Prepare a cardboard box holder as described in Skull Painting. Place your skull upside-down in the holder. Following the manufacturer's directions and the tips from the Skull Painting section, apply the base coat from the crackle paint to the bottom of the skull. Let it dry, then turn the skull over and paint the top of the skull with the base coat.

Step Four: Take a close look at your skull as it sits right side up on the holder. You will want to note what parts of it would be impossible to paint with the skull in this position. Once again turn the skull upside-down in the holder.

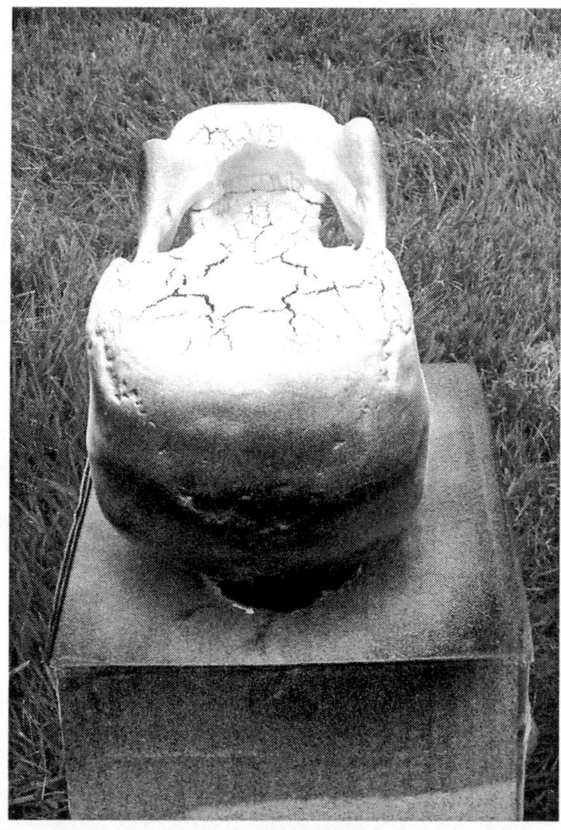

Left: **Apply the base coat for your crackle paint.** ***Right:*** **Following the manufacturer's directions, apply the topcoat of the crackle paint only to those sections of the skull that would be impossible to paint with the skull right side up.**

Following the manufacturer's directions, apply the topcoat of the crackle paint only to those sections of the skull that would be impossible to paint with the skull right side up. Be careful to avoid over-spray onto any other part of the skull. Let the paint dry thoroughly (about one hour) before proceeding.

Step Five: Turn your skull right side up and proceed to paint the upper parts. Work quickly using one good heavy coat. Once a section has begun to crackle, do not go back over it, as this will have a tendency to cover the crackle effect and leave you with a very small crackle pattern or none at all. Now just sit back and watch as your skull crackles, you will see fine and large cracks appear as if by magic. Now set your skull aside overnight to dry.

Step Six: Using a small piece of cotton cloth, apply a very light layer of stain to the skull (be sure you are wearing gloves for this or you will end up staining your hands better than the skull). You are better off using too light a coat than too heavy of one; you can always add another coat if you want a darker look. Try to avoid too many streaks or lines in the finish; however, you may wish to make some sections darker than others (this will add to the realism). For the

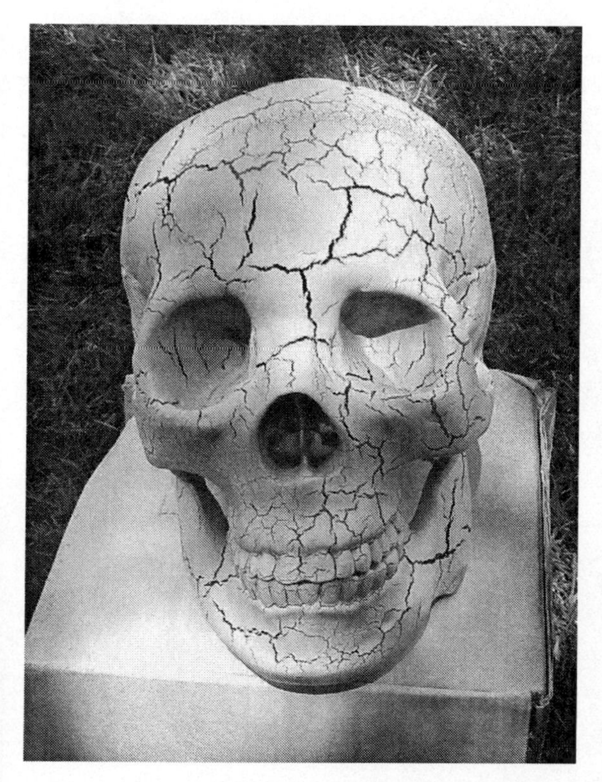

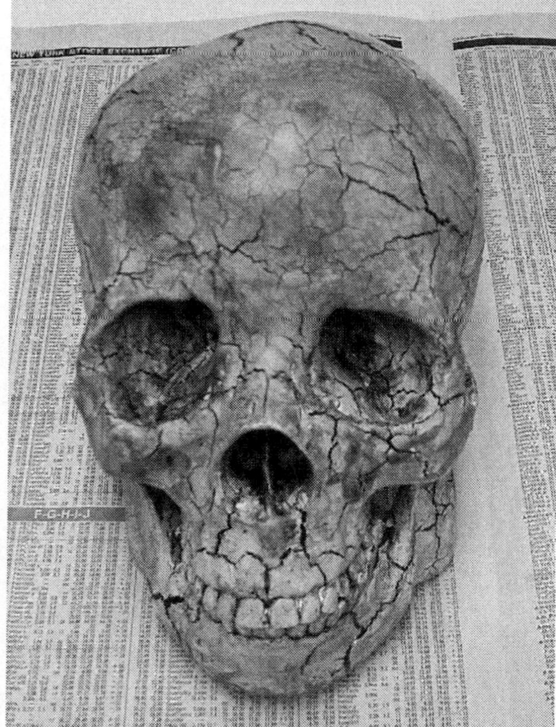

Left: Turn your skull right side up and proceed to paint the upper parts. Work quickly using one good heavy coat. _Right:_ Using a small piece of cotton cloth, apply a very light layer of stain to the skull.

hard to reach spots, like the eye sockets or inside the nose, use a cotton swab lightly coated with stain.

Again, if you simply must know what stain I used, it was Minwax Water-Based Color Rich Formula, in American walnut. I chose the water-based formula for its ease of cleanup, and also because it seems a little thinner than the oil-based stains, allowing me to get a nice light brown color. Of course, most any stain should work well. If you would like your finished skull to look just like mine, use a walnut stain. If you would like to experiment, try different colored stains for a very different look. This is an opportunity to experiment; try to improve on my basic design and come up with your own unique, one-of-a kind props.

If you have the equipment to do so, this step may be done with a spray gun, which I feel gives a better look with fewer streaks. If not, the method described above can give very satisfactory results. The skulls shown here were done using a cloth, not a spray gun.

When you have a color you like, once again, set the skull aside overnight to dry.

Step Seven: Add a small amount of the yellow paint tint to some of the clear coat and mix well. One note on choosing your tint: some tints will work only in oil-based clear coats, and some will work only in water-based clear coats, while still others will work in either. Make sure the one you use is right for the clear coat you have chosen. You will want more of a pale straw color than a canary yellow. It is better to go too light than too dark.

Add a small amount of the yellow paint tint to some of the clear coat and mix well.

If you simply must know, the tint I used was Tint-All, number two yellow medium. Again, most any tint should work. The clear coat I used was Minwax Polycrylic clear satin water-based (I chose the water-based again for the ease of cleanup). Not surprisingly, most any clear coat you use should work well.

Step Eight: Apply the tinted clear coat, using the cotton cloth and cotton swabs to reach the tight spots (or, if you prefer, a spray gun). Apply a thin, light coat and let it dry. If you would like a more yellowed look, keep adding additional coats until you get the look you want. Each additional coat will give more of a yellow hue to the finished prop. Here is the one point at which I deviated from the package directions. I did not sand between coats. I felt that due to the intricate shape of the skull, I would run too much of a risk of removing the layers of color below. Instead of sanding I just let the finish dry to the touch, but did not allow the full cure time recommended on the label. Once you have applied the number of coats of clear coat you want, set your skull aside overnight to dry, and admire your finished prop the next day.

Once you have the skull with the yellowed appearance you like, you may add additional layers of non-tinted clear coat if you like. On the skull I did for this book, I simply used two coats of tinted clear coat with no additional coats of untinted. What you do on your skull will depend on how much tint you added to your clear coat and the finished look you like.

The technique described above allows for a myriad of variations. Try experimenting with different base colors, different stain colors and coat thicknesses, or

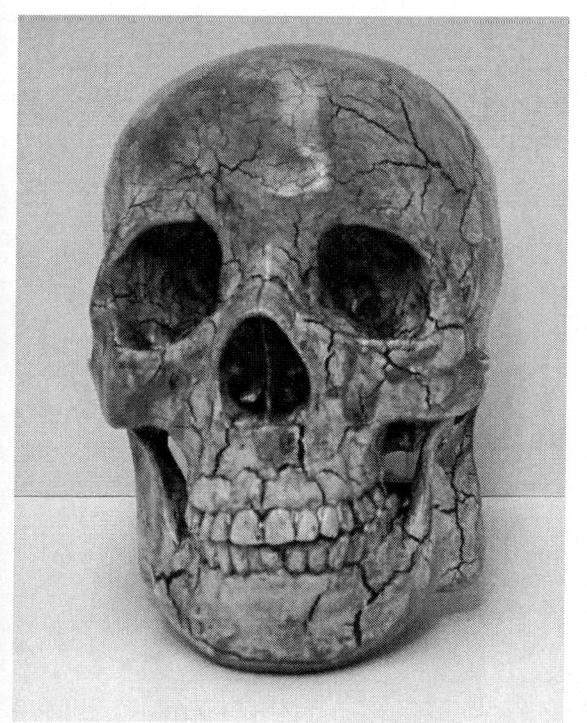

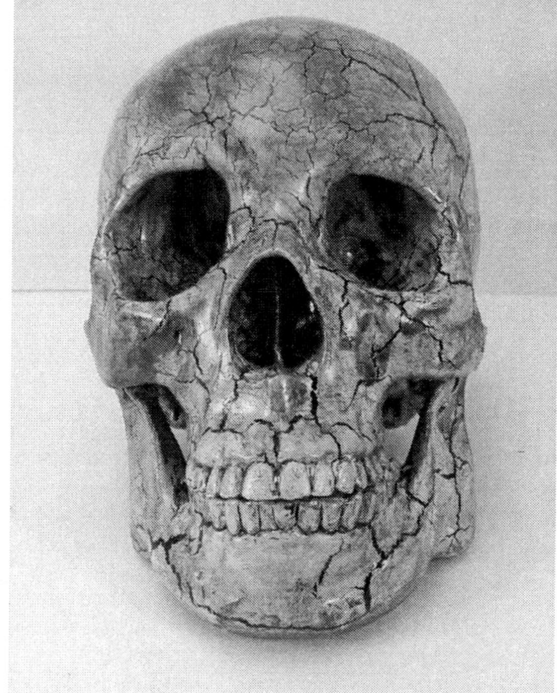

Left: **A finished aged skull using ivory crackle paint.** ***Right:*** **A finished aged skull using white crackle paint.**

even different colors of tint in the clear coat, not to mention the number of coats of clear coat. You may want to try preparing several small cardboard squares with crackle paint, and then try different stains and clear coats on these rather than risk ruining a skull if you do not like the end product.

Of course, this technique is not limited to skulls. Why not try it on femur bones, or any bone for that matter? Or, once you have mastered the technique, even a full skeleton.

***Opposite:* These are the materials you will need to create a barbecued skull.**

BARBECUED SKULL

For this project you will need:

✓ One skull, your choice
✓ One can of expanding polyurethane foam sealant

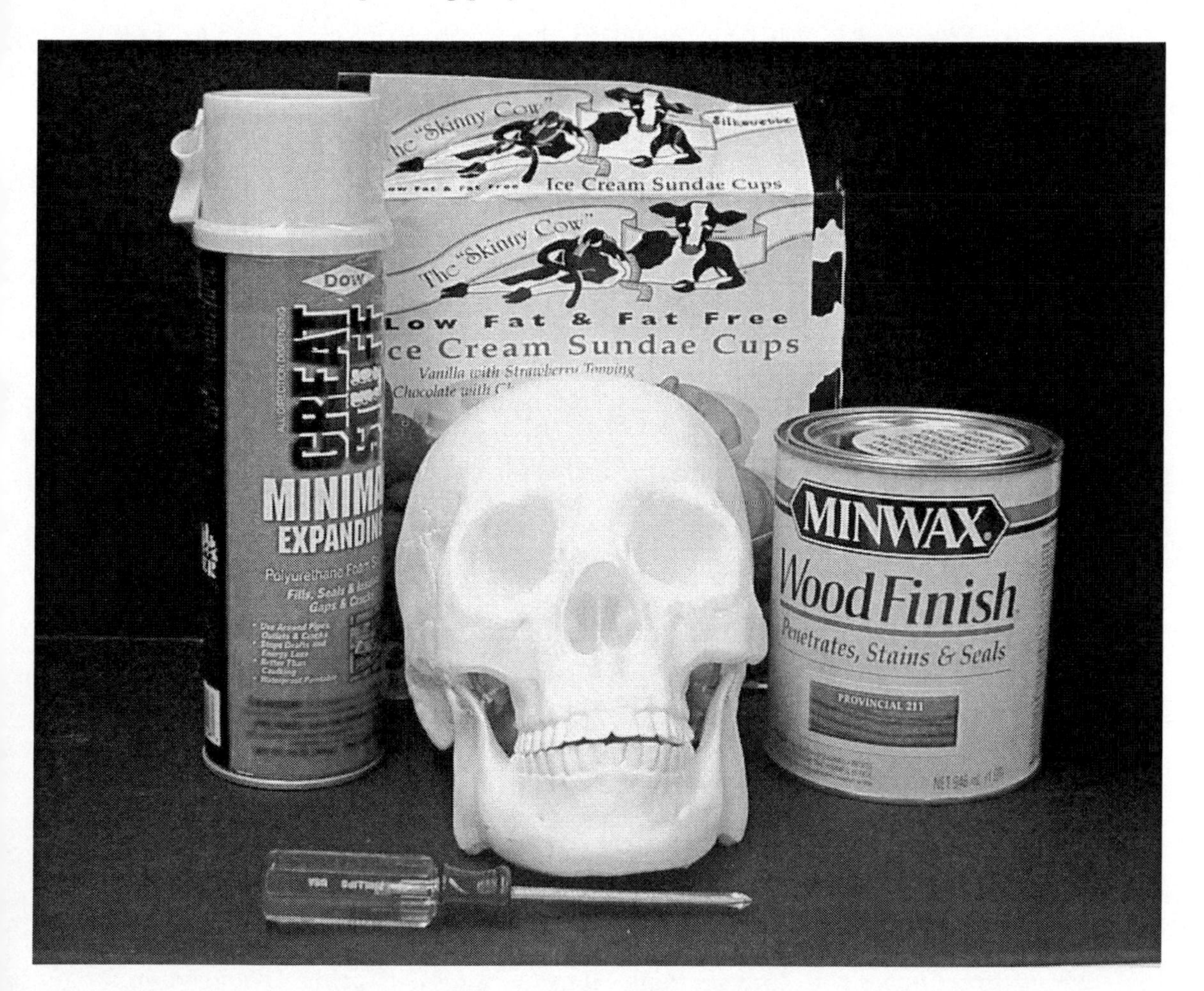

- ✓ Several pieces of thin cardboard
- ✓ Blood red paint (optional)
- ✓ Gel stain, mahogany or your choice
- ✓ Second color of gel stain, chestnut or your choice (optional)
- ✓ Rubber gloves (you may need several pairs)
- ✓ One small nail
- ✓ One piece of string or wire
- ✓ A paintbrush or small piece of soft cloth
- ✓ A screwdriver (optional)
- ✓ Glue gun with glue (optional)
- ✓ A small paintbrush (optional)
- ✓ Petroleum jelly (optional)
- ✓ Cotton swabs (optional)

Step One: Cut or tear your cardboard into several strips about two or three inches wide and six inches long; you need not be exact. You will want to use a thin cardboard, not corrugated cardboard from a heavy-duty box. If you can get some nice shiny, slippery cardboard, so much the better, but any thin cardboard will do.

Step Two: Select your skull. I prefer one without a cut calvarium, that is to say, one on which the top of the skull is not removable. If you do use a skull with a removable top, you will have to be very careful later, when applying the foam. You will need to make certain to cover the seam well between the top of the skull and the rest of the skull.

You may want to remove the springs that hold the jaw to the rest of the skull. Once you have finished your prop, the jaw will not be moveable, so why have the hardware showing? If you do decide to remove the springs, I suggest you save them, in case you

Cut or tear your cardboard into several strips about two or three inches wide and six inches long; you need not be exact.

ever need to repair another skull. If you choose not to remove the springs, skip to step five.

Step Three: Apply a small amount of hot melt glue to the top back of the jaw, where the jaw meets the skull. Avoid gluing the teeth. You can be as neat or as sloppy as you like here, because you will soon cover any mess you make. **Caution: Hot melt glue and the glue gun are hot! Be very careful not to burn yourself!**

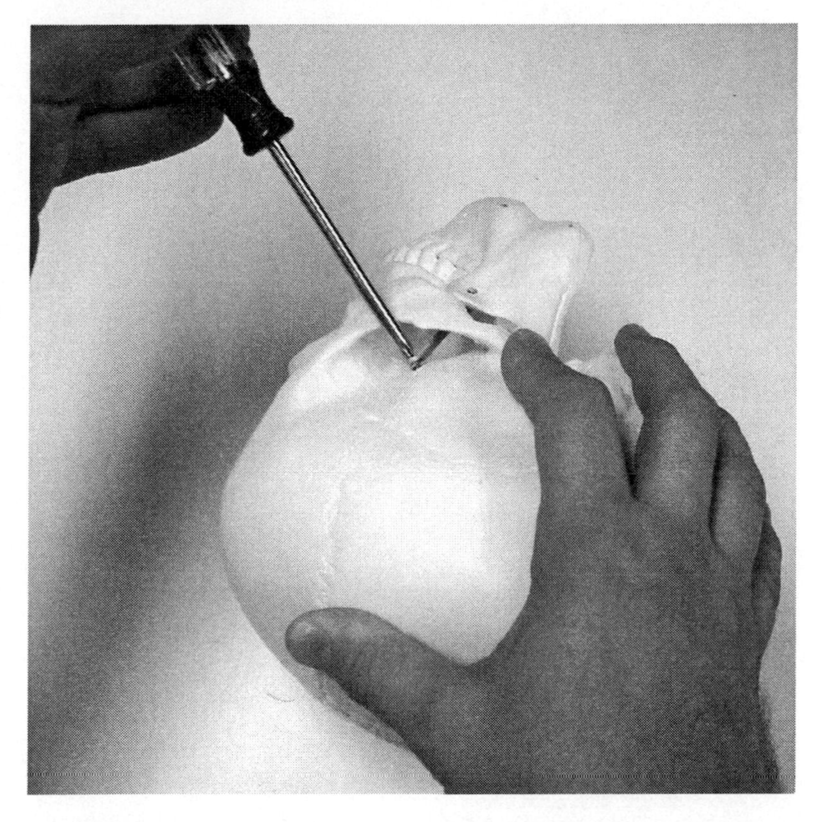

You may want to remove the springs that hold the jaw to the rest of the skull.

Step Four: Quickly, before the glue cools, replace the jaw on the skull and hold until the glue sets (about one minute). **Caution: Hot melt glue and the glue gun are hot! Be very careful not to burn yourself!**

Step Five: Take a small nail; tie it to a piece of string or wire, and then tie the other end off to a convenient overhead location.

Step Six: Now take one end of the nail and place it into the hole in the bottom of the skull. Continue to push the rest of the nail into the skull, taking a few inches of the string in with it. Now pull back on the string and the nail should hold your skull in a comfortable working location. If your skull does not have a hole, you may need to drill one. Or, instead of hanging your skull, you can just work on your skull in sections, waiting for one section to dry before moving on to the next.

Step Seven: Now it is time to start adding foam to the skull. You will want to put on rubber gloves for this operation. The foam is very sticky when wet and will stick to just about anything, including your skin.

I have found two types of expanding foams: polyurethane and latex. I strongly recommend the polyurethane; it is harder and makes for a much more durable prop. Polyurethane foam is available at most hardware stores; it is used for sealing cracks around windows, doors, etc.

Before you begin using your foam, you may want to have several items ready to be foamed. Once you start to use the can, it cannot be put away and reused another day. Read all directions and warnings on the can before you start. Make sure you follow these as you work.

Where you start to apply the foam really does not matter; I find it easier to start at the top and work down. Start applying foam a little at a time, moving the can to more or less evenly distribute foam over one section of the skull.

Where necessary use your cardboard strips to push your foam where you want it. You will want to leave a series of high and low spots to give a rough texture to the skull.

Continue adding and shaping the foam until your entire skull is covered.

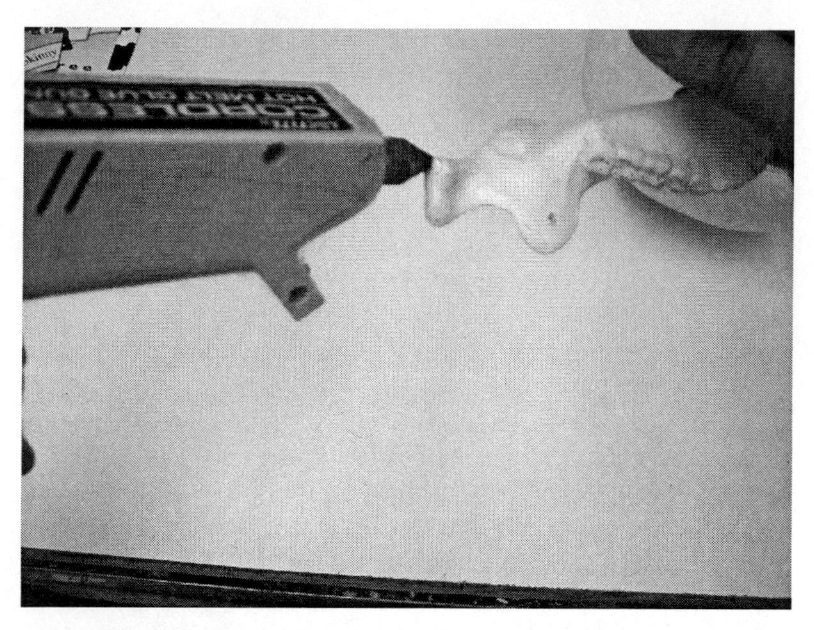

Apply a small amount of hot melt glue to the top back of the jaw, where the jaw meets the skull; avoid gluing the teeth.

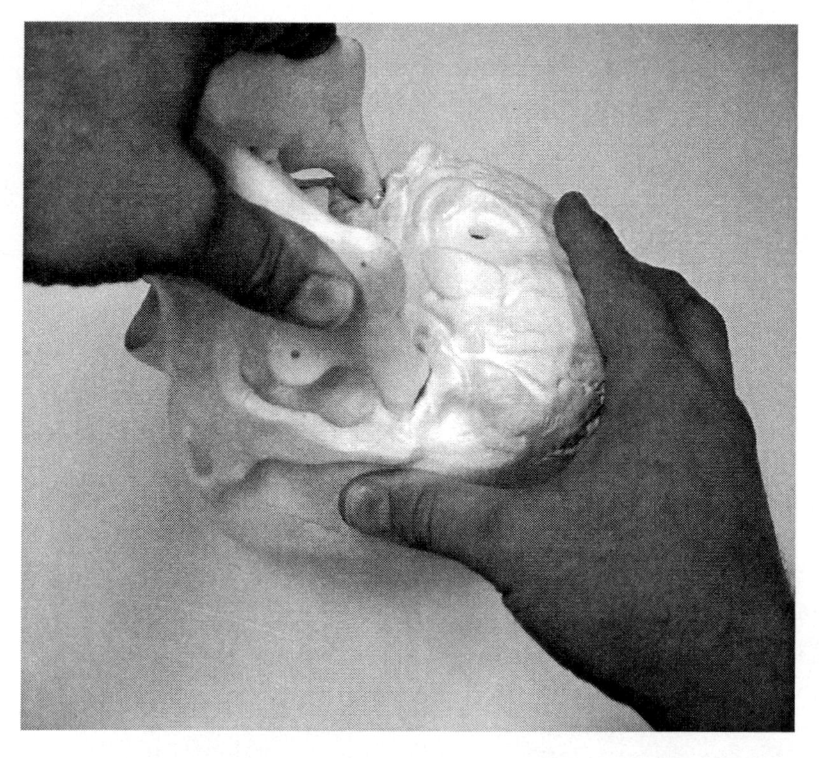

Quickly, before the glue cools, replace the jaw on the skull and hold until set.

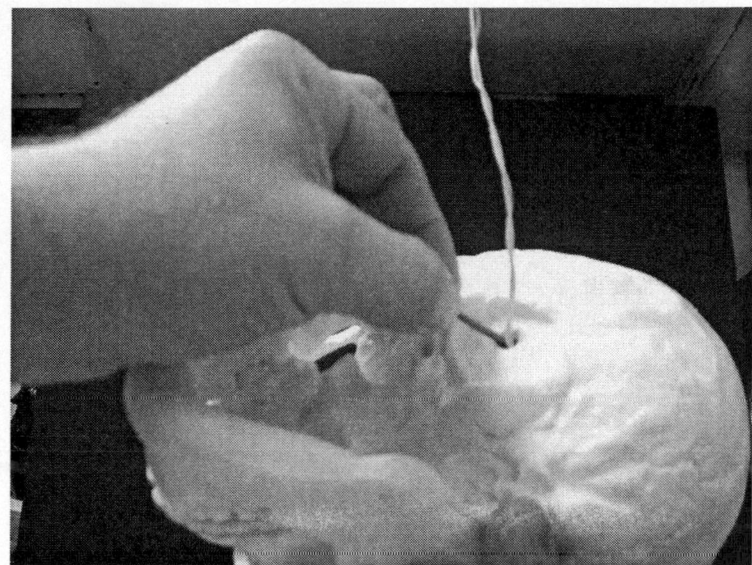

Left: **Take a small nail, tie it to a piece of string or wire, and then tie the other end off to a convenient overhead location.** ***Right:*** **Take one end of the nail and place it into the hole in the bottom of the skull; continue to push the rest of the nail into the skull, taking a few inches of the string in with it.**

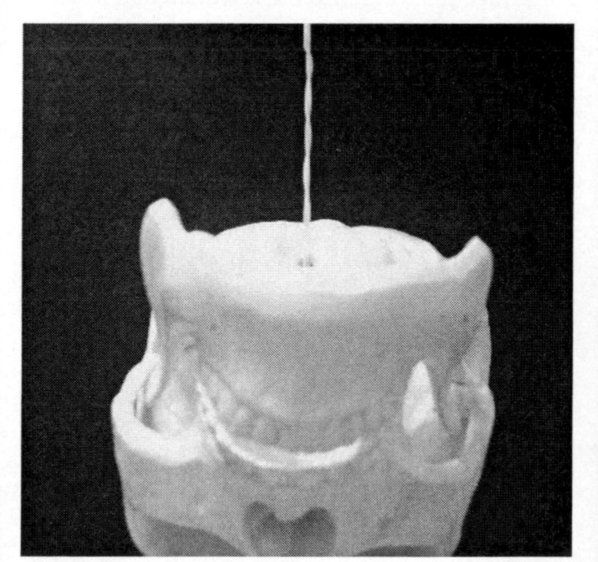

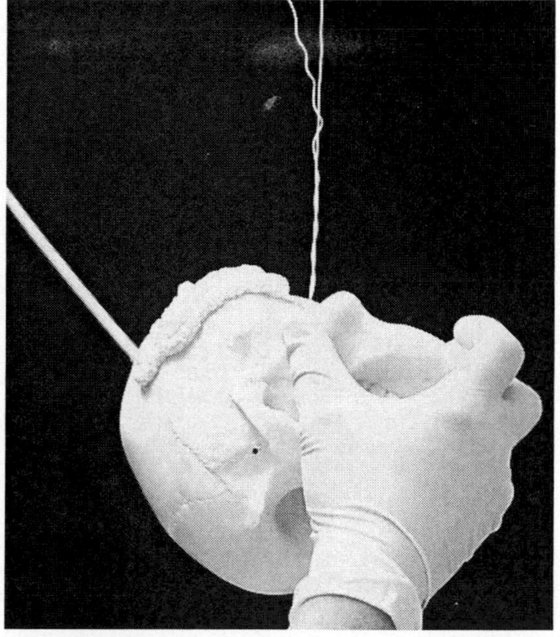

Left: **Pull back on the string and the nail should hold your skull in a comfortable working location.** ***Right:*** **Start applying foam a little at a time, moving the can to more or less evenly distribute foam over one section of the skull.**

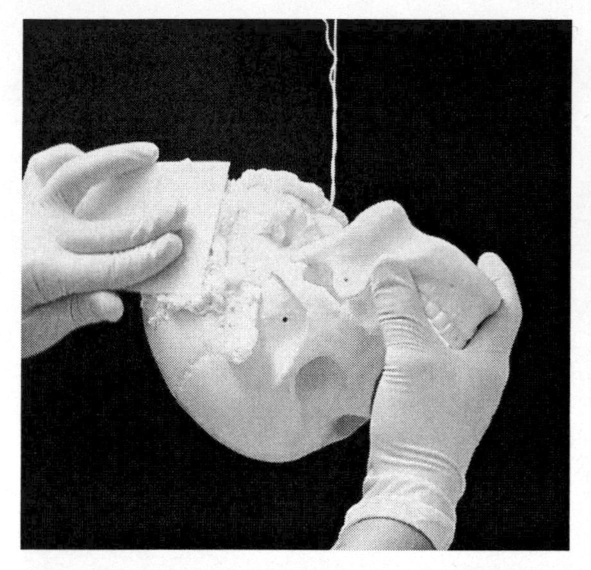

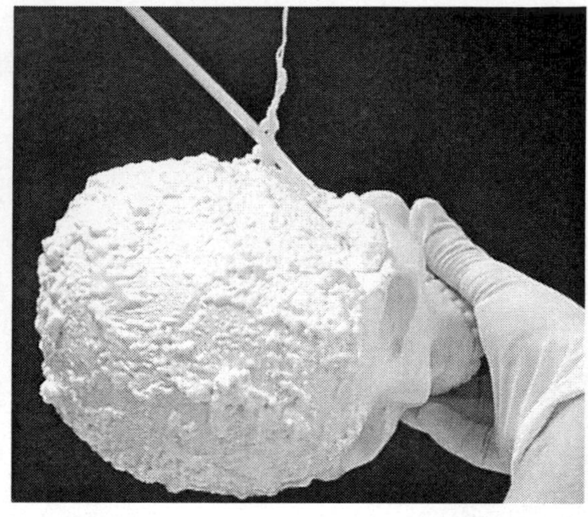

***Left:* Where necessary use your cardboard strips to push your foam where you want it. *Right:* Continue adding and shaping foam until your entire skull is covered.**

The two exceptions to covering the skull are the eye sockets and the teeth. I like to leave the eye sockets empty as it adds a rather menacing look to the finished prop. If you prefer you can easily add eyes or lights to the sockets later. Leaving the teeth uncovered also gives more of a feel of realism. Of course, it is your prop and if you want to fill the eye sockets and cover the teeth go right ahead, if that is the look you want.

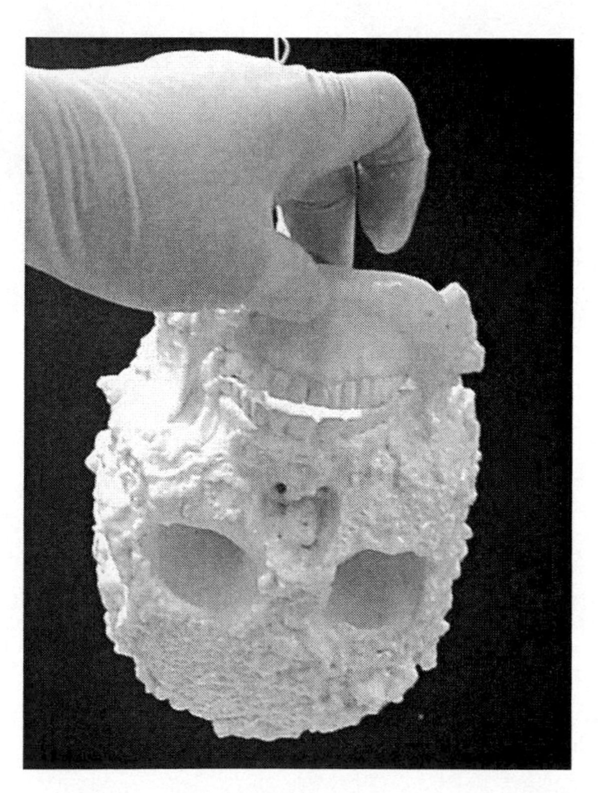

Leaving the eye sockets empty can add a rather menacing look to the finished prop. If you prefer, you can easily add eyes or lights to the sockets later.

You may also want to add enough foam under the jaw to completely fill this area; it will give a more head-like look to the finished prop. Remember the foam will expand as it sets, so try not to overfill this area. If you do apply too much foam it can be trimmed after it sets, but you will find trimmed foam has a very different texture than uncut foam. It is best to avoid trimming foam in any areas that will be easily seen.

If you have any foam left in the can when you are done foaming your props, you may want to make some foam piles on which you can practice your painting techniques. Take some pieces of scrap cardboard and apply foam to the cardboard, the same as you would to the skull. Let the foam on this cardboard expand and set overnight. When set, you can use the foam on the cardboard to test paint and stain combinations without having to waste a good skull. If you have enough foam left in the can, you can make several practice cardboards. I suggest you make them about six by six inches; this will give you a large enough area to get a good feel for how a finished prop would look.

Step Eight: Let your head hang overnight to allow the foam to cure completely.

Step Nine: This step is optional; if you choose not to add red paint to your skull, skip to step 10. In this project, you are trying to turn your skull into what looks like a burned and charred head. Depending on how you like your heads cooked (well done, medium or rare), you may want to add some red paint to the deep crevices of the foam. This will give you more of a rare or medium look by simulating uncooked flesh under the charred outer layers.

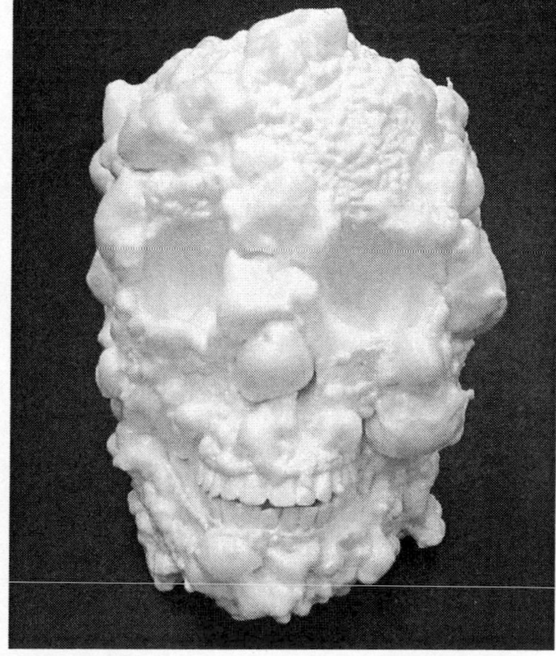

Left: **You may also want to add enough foam under the jaw to completely fill this area, giving a more head-like look to the finished prop.** ***Right:*** **A skull covered in foam.**

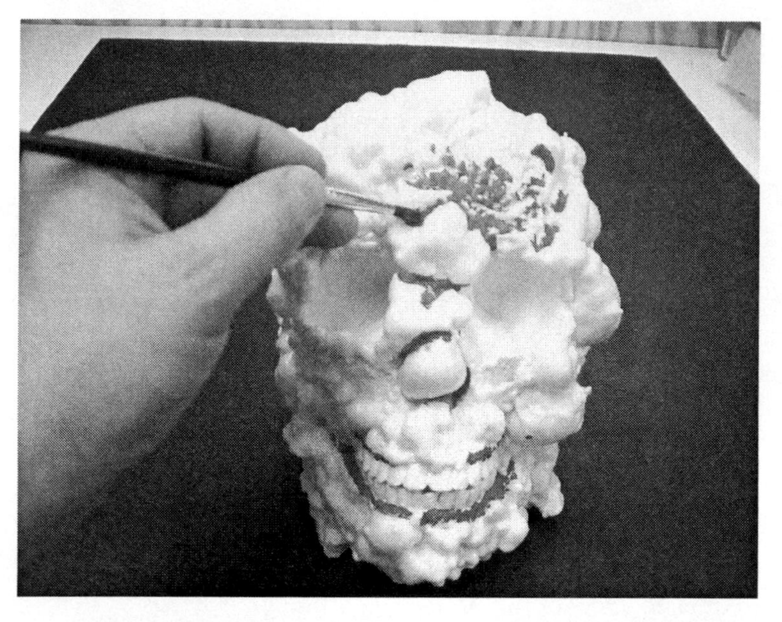

Depending on how you like your heads cooked (well done, medium or rare), you may want to add some red paint to the deep crevices of the foam.

Start by taking your small brush and using it to apply red paint to some of the deepest folds of the foam layer on the skull. You will most likely find you have numerous little holes, nooks and crannies in the foam. These are great spots for an uncooked meat look; just add red paint. Your paint layer does not have to be extremely even as meat does not always cook evenly.

Continue adding red until you have most of the really deep spots filled in (of course you may paint as much or as little as you like since it is your prop). Once you have the deeper grooves filled in, you may want to add some red to areas that are not all that deep — that is, if you are going for a rare look.

Step Ten: This step is also optional. If you would like your teeth to remain white, it is a good idea to cover them with a layer of petroleum jelly. This way if you get a little careless with the stain, the jelly will keep the stain from sticking to the teeth. Just take a cotton swab, dip it into the petroleum jelly and carefully apply it to the teeth. Make sure to cover the whole tooth to the gum line and do not forget to fill the spaces between the teeth. Do not remove this film until you are done applying as many layers of stain as you like, and they are completely dry.

Continue adding red until you have most of the really deep spots filled in (of course you may paint as much or as little as you like; it is your prop).

Step Eleven: If you are using two colors of stain take the lighter or redder looking one and apply it to the foam. For the skull I did here, I used mahogany. You will want to use a gel stain; the more watery stains tend to run off the foam without giving very good coverage.

If you would like your teeth to remain white, it is a good idea to cover them with a layer of petroleum jelly.

You will again want to put on rubber gloves for this step. Take your brush or soft cloth and apply the stain over all of the foam not covered with red paint.

You will also want to cover some of the red paint with a thin layer of stain. Apply just enough stain over the red to darken it, but not enough to completely hide it. You want to try for a look of charred flesh with some red meat underneath. If you have any deep, small, hard to reach areas in the foam, you may want to use a cotton swab soaked in stain to reach these.

Apply the stain in an uneven layer, thicker in some spots than in others. This will simulate a head that has not been evenly cooked. Do not wipe off the stain, just let it sit overnight to dry.

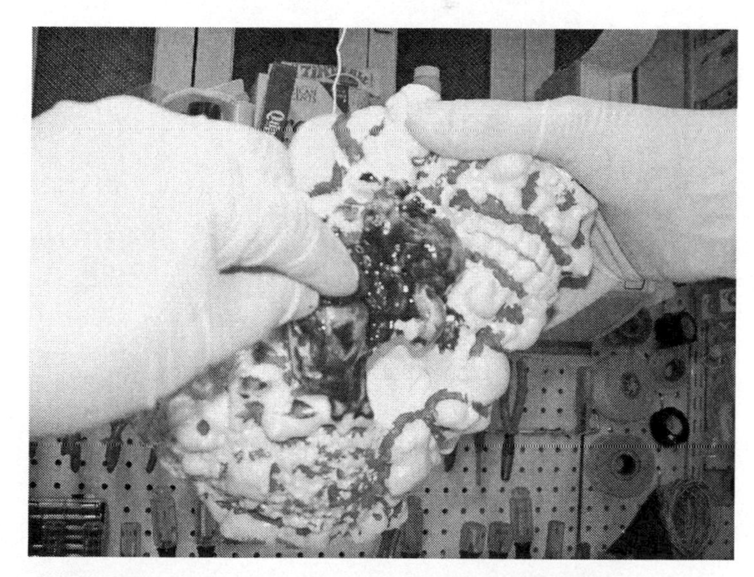

If you are using two colors of stain take the lighter or redder-looking one and apply it to the foam.

Step Twelve: This step is optional. If you have decided to use a second color of stain, now is the time to apply it. I prefer to use the darkest, most brown or black color of stain for this stage. The color I used here was chestnut. Again, you will want

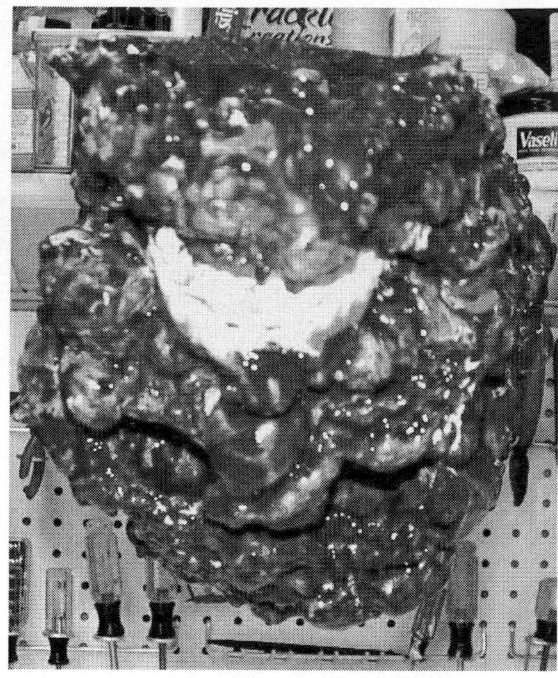

Above: **Apply just enough stain over the red to darken it, but not enough to completely hide it. You want to try for a look of charred flesh with some red meat underneath.** ***Right:*** **Apply the stain in an uneven layer, thicker in some spots than in others.**

to use a gel stain for thicker coverage, and wear rubber gloves to protect your hands. Apply the second color of stain in the same way as the first color, except when applying this layer you will want to stain mainly the high spots of the foam. Apply the thickest layer of stain to the highest spots of the foam, with the coverage getting lighter as you get deeper into the crevices. The look you are trying for is that the outside skin of your head was well burned, with less burning as you get deeper in. This gives added realism, as things generally cook from the outside in (this includes heads).

Again, set your head aside overnight to allow the stain to dry. If you have some very thick areas of stain, you may want to give them two or three days to dry before handling your new prop.

Apply your second color of stain and your head is done.

Step Thirteen: Cut your head down. Cut the string which has been holding your head up as close to the foam as possible. If you do not have enough foam around the string where it enters the skull to keep the string in place, simply push it into the skull. The nail and a small amount of the string will remain inside the prop.

Step Fourteen: If you have applied petroleum jelly to the teeth, now is the time to clean it off. Use clean cotton swabs to remove the jelly. You should find any stain that was inadvertently applied over the jelly wipes right off.

Now that you know all the techniques for barbecuing, let us look at a few variations. I have included the following examples of skulls I barbecued to give you a few ideas of how you may experiment and improve on the basic barbecued skull. With a little practice and imagination, there is no limit to what you can do. If you are an artist, by nature (which I most definitely am not) you can try painting over the foam for almost limitless possibilities.

Let us start with my very first barbecued skull, shown on the next page. It was a fourth class skull, with a cut calvarium; you can see the line of the cut at the top of the skull even after it was done (I did say this was my very first attempt). On this skull, I applied foam, as directed above, and applied a single color of stain. The stain used was a mahogany gel stain; I used two coats and left some foam showing. I also covered the teeth with stain but no foam.

Another variation I have tried is to use the same type of skull as in the last example, with a chestnut gel stain. Again, I left some foam showing under the stain and covered the teeth with stain but not foam. When the stain had dried, I installed a pair of Demon Eyes. Because this picture was taken in bright light,

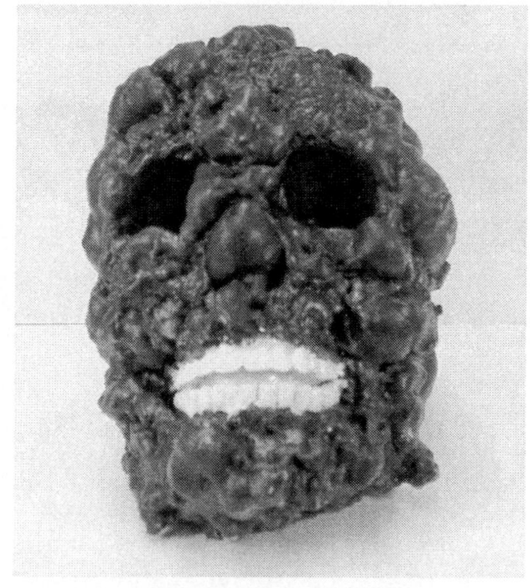

Above: **Remove the petroleum jelly from the teeth.** ***Right:*** **A finished barbecued skull.**

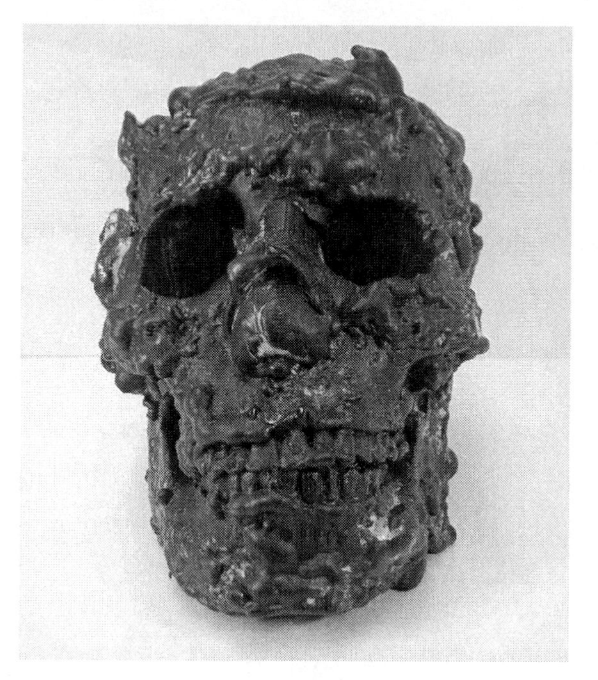

***Left:* My very first barbecued skull. *Right:* A barbecued skull with chestnut stain and Demon Eyes.**

the Demon Eyes were not lit, but I think it looks okay even without the eyes lit. This was my second attempt.

After several attempts with single colors, I hit upon the idea of multiple colors for that true barbecued effect. Of course, you can barbecue more than just a skull. I have barbecued bones, and even a full skeleton. The picture below shows a couple of bones I did.

The last idea that I will leave you with is a bit of a contradiction to what I have said previously. While I feel it generally does not give a good finished product, I have tried regular oil-based stain on a barbecued bone (the color used for the bone pictured was provincial). While I do not think this gave a very realistic look, I do find the look interesting and different.

Of course, you can barbecue more than just a skull. I have barbecued bones, and even a full skeleton.

Perhaps you can use your imagination and come up with a good way to use this look.

On this page is one last picture of another skull I barbecued. In this one I did not fill in the nose and pulled at the foam to give a rather spiky look.

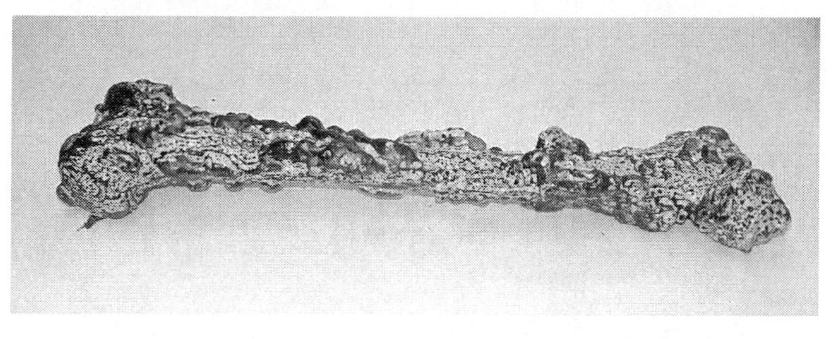

A barbecued bone made with a non-gel stain.

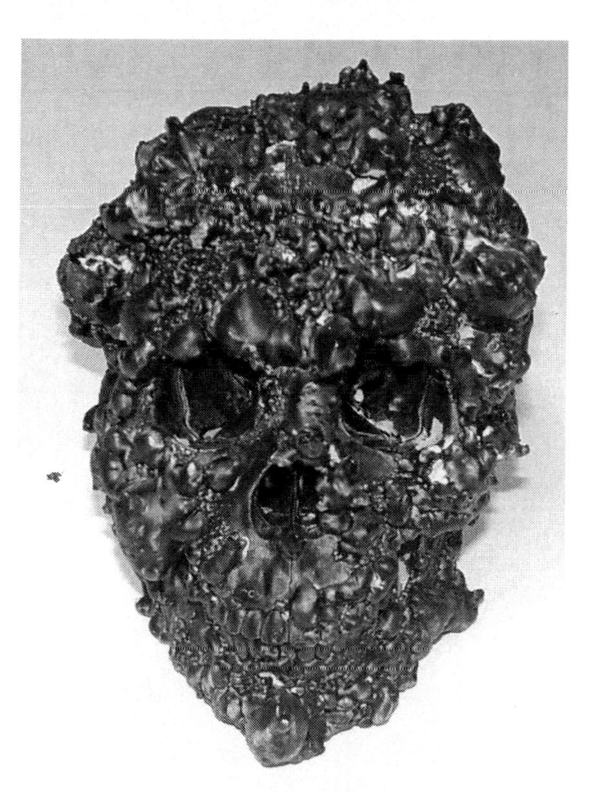

I call this guy Spike.

SUSHI SKULL

For this project you will need:

- ✓ One skull, your choice
- ✓ About ¼ cup glycerin
- ✓ About ½ cup tap water

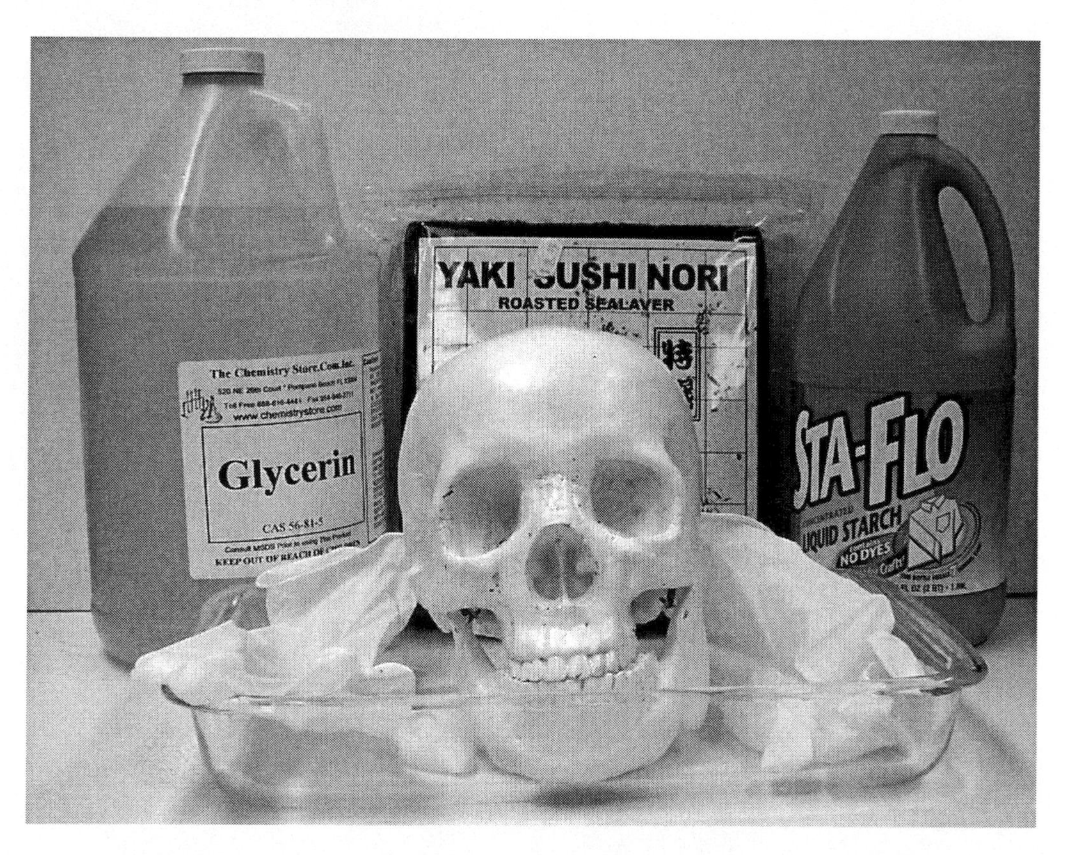

These are the materials you will need to create a sushi skull.

- ✓ About five sheets of roasted sealaver (seaweed sheets)
- ✓ About ½ cup liquid laundry starch
- ✓ One shallow, wide pan
- ✓ One pair of rubber gloves
- ✓ One pair of scissors

Note One: **This project will probably take several attempts to get a decent finished product. Fortunately, the materials, other than the skull, which is reusable, are very inexpensive.**

Note Two: **What the heck is sealaver? It is something I happened upon at a Japanese market one day, while looking for green tea. It is, as far as I can figure, roasted dried seaweed. Those of you who like sushi may recognize it as the outer wrapper on many sushi dishes. I, however, have devised a much more practical use. By the way, it is available in a few colors.**

Step One: Mix the glycerin and water in a shallow pan large enough to hold your seaweed sheets one at a time. In fact, your pan can be just a little smaller than the seaweed sheet, as the seaweed will become soft and pliable when soaked in the solution. Make sure the glycerin and water are well mixed; this could take three or four minutes of stirring.

Step Two: Place the seaweed sheets into the solution one at a time and press down gently to make sure both sides of the sheet get thoroughly wet. Let the sheet soak for thirty seconds to a minute.

Place the seaweed sheets into the solution one at a time; press down gently to make sure both sides of the sheet get thoroughly wet.

Step Three: Gently lift the soaked seaweed by one edge. Hold it over the pan and let the excess solution drip off, then lay the sheet aside (you may want to place it on waxed paper to protect your work surface). Continue soaking the sheets one at a time until all five sheets have been done (you may be able to get by with only four, but I would rather have an extra one than run out in the middle of the project).

Step Four: While wearing rubber gloves, use your

hands to wet the surface of the skull with the starch. You need not be precise; just smear some starch all over the skull, just enough to kind of wet it down a bit. The starch will act as a lubricant to help the seaweed slide as you try to position it on the skull, and later when it dries helps bond the seaweed to the skull.

Gently lift the soaked seaweed by one edge. Hold it over the pan and let the excess solution drip off, then lay the sheet aside.

Optional: You may find it a good idea to make a holder to hold your skull upside down. This can be done in about 30 seconds with just a small cardboard box and a knife. Take a box strong enough to support your skull and cut a hole about 5" × 3". You can now place your skull upside down in the box and it will keep it from rolling around while you work.

Above: **You may find it a good idea to make a holder to hold you skull upside down.** ***Right:*** **Take a box strong enough to support your skull and cut a hole about 5" × 3"; you can now place your skull upside down in the box and it will keep it from rolling around while you work.**

Step Five: Take one sheet of seaweed and position one edge just below the teeth of the lower jaw. Take the sheet and extend it loosely rearward over the back of the skull. Dip your fingers into the starch and work the edge of the seaweed just below the teeth to smooth it down firmly to the skull. Start in the center of the jaw and work to both sides until a fold starts to appear in the sheet.

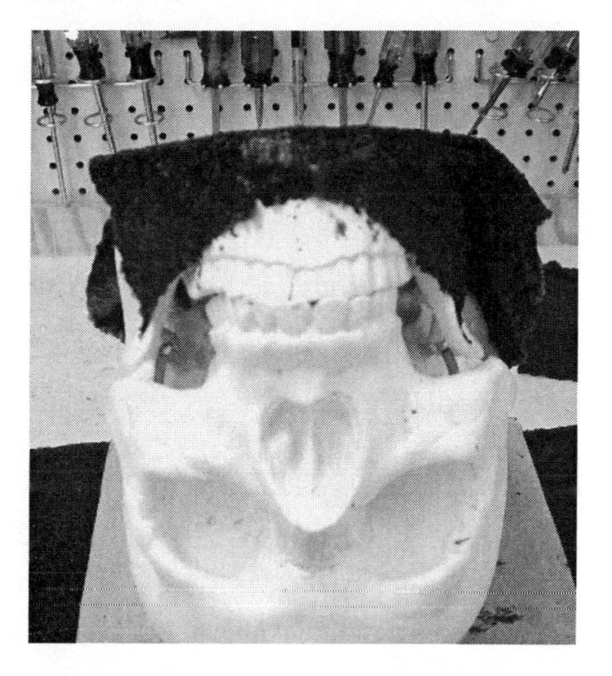

Take one sheet of seaweed and position one edge just below the teeth of the lower jaw.

Step Six: Now it starts to get a bit tricky. You will most likely need to make several skulls to get one that looks really good, but if you make one you do not like you can always strip the seaweed off and start over, or just wash the skull and use it for something else.

Anywhere you get a fold or pucker in the seaweed as you try to mold it to the skull, cut a slit down the center of the fold to the point where the fold seems to end.

Fold back one side of the seaweed from where you just cut. Wet your fingers in starch and smooth down the end of the cut you did not fold back. Work the seaweed down and mold it to the skull. You will be surprised just how much you can work the material. Just remember to keep the fingers of your gloves wet with starch to lubricate them.

Anywhere you get a fold or pucker in the seaweed as you try to mold it to the skull, cut a slit down the center of the fold to the point where the fold seems to end.

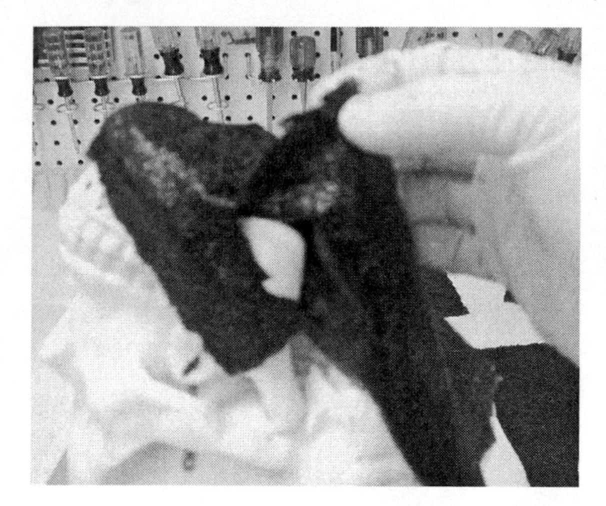

Left: **Fold back one side of the seaweed from where you just cut.** ***Right:*** **Take the flap you had folded back and fold it over the flap you just smoothed down.**

Take the flap you had folded back and fold it over the flap you just smoothed down. Again, keep your gloves wet with starch as you work this flap into place. Keep working any joints until they blend in and seem to disappear. This is the technique you will use throughout the project to add sheets and smooth out folds.

Step Seven: Now lightly stretch the sheet at the back of the skull. Cut the folds and smooth as necessary; keep your fingers wet with starch and smooth the seaweed to the skull.

Step Eight: Use the techniques you have just learned to add sheets to the

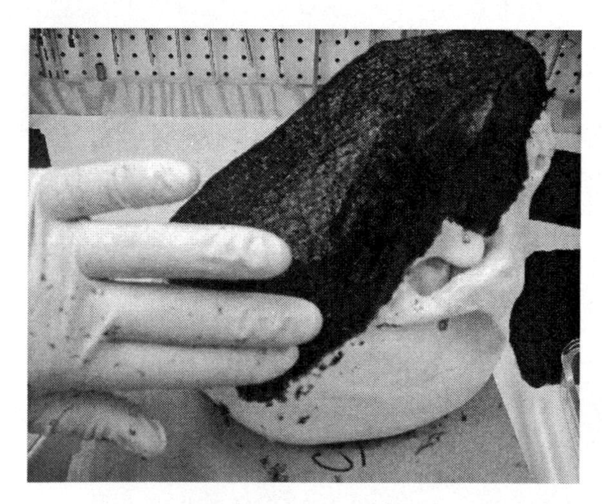

Above: **Keep your fingers wet with starch and smooth the seaweed to the skull.** ***Right:*** **Leave the face for last.**

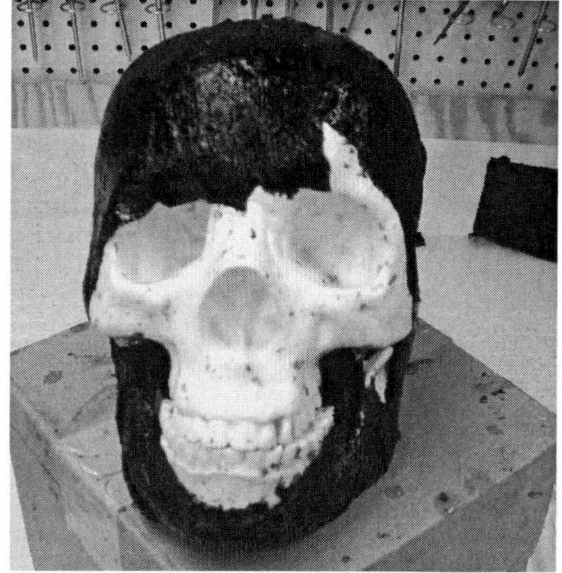

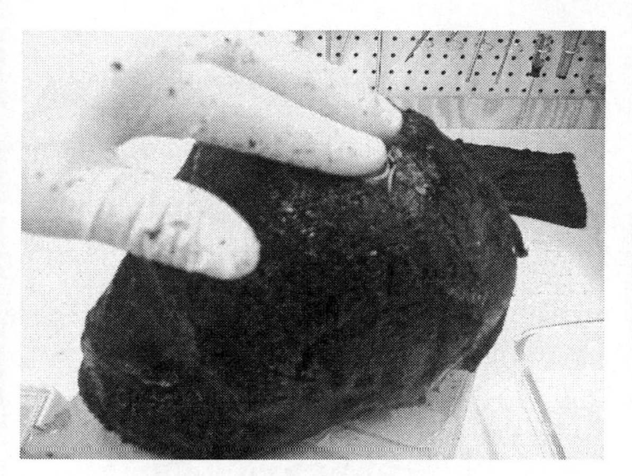

***Left:* Repeatedly wet your fingers with starch and rub all over the head. *Right:* When you are done applying the sheets to your skull it will look like this.**

sides and if necessary to the rear of the skull. Leave the face for last. If a sheet of seaweed is too large or would overlap another sheet excessively, you can use a pair of scissors to trim off the excess.

Step Nine: Add a final sheet of seaweed to the front of the skull. This is done last because while you can work seams in until they almost disappear, they are still slightly visible, more so when you are looking from the bottom sheet to the top sheet. So doing the face last helps hide any little seams.

Be careful when working the face because the eyes and nose offer little support to the covering and it is quite easy to poke a hole at these points.

Step Ten: Repeatedly wet your fingers with starch and rub all over the head. Wet any high spots or bulges and work them smooth. When well wet with starch, the seaweed becomes rather soft and can be worked into place.

When you are done, your skull will look something like the one above. The skin will tighten up somewhat as the head dries.

Set your skull aside to dry at least overnight. When dried your sushi skull will have an oily, almost skin-like feel and will resemble the one at right.

There is also a variation of the

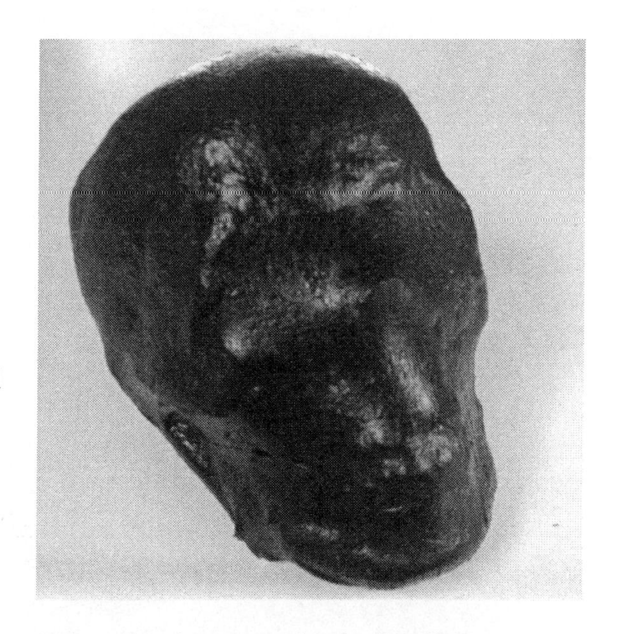

When dried your sushi skull will have an oily, almost skin-like feel and will look like this.

sushi skull you can try. In my first attempt to use sushi wrap to cover a skull, I did not use glycerin and water to treat the seaweed first. The result is what you see following; as the covering dried it shrank and cracked. If you like this look it is easy to do. Instead of soaking the seaweed in the glycerin and water mix, soak it in starch. Once it is wet with the liquid starch just apply following the steps above. I, myself, like this look, as it looks rather like an aged mummy with its skin dried and peeling away from the skull.

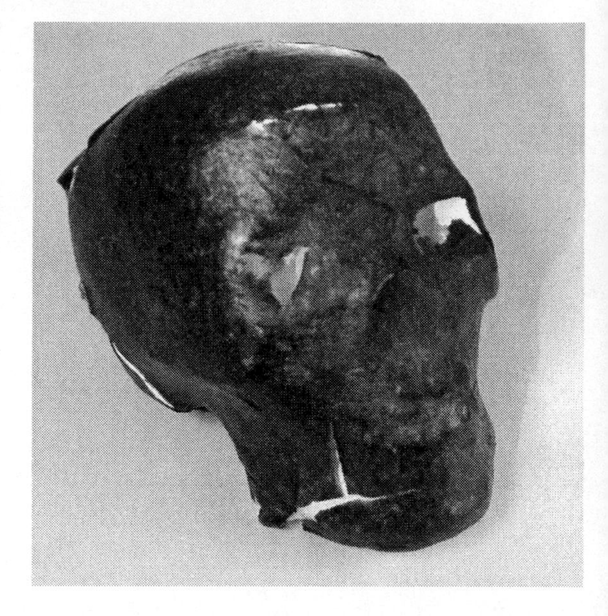

A sushi skull made by soaking the sheets in starch, rather than glycerin and water.

SKULL LIGHT SKULL BRIGHT

For this project you will need:

✓ One transparent or glow-in-the-dark skull
✓ One Christmas house light with bulb (for safety, check to make sure this item is UL listed)

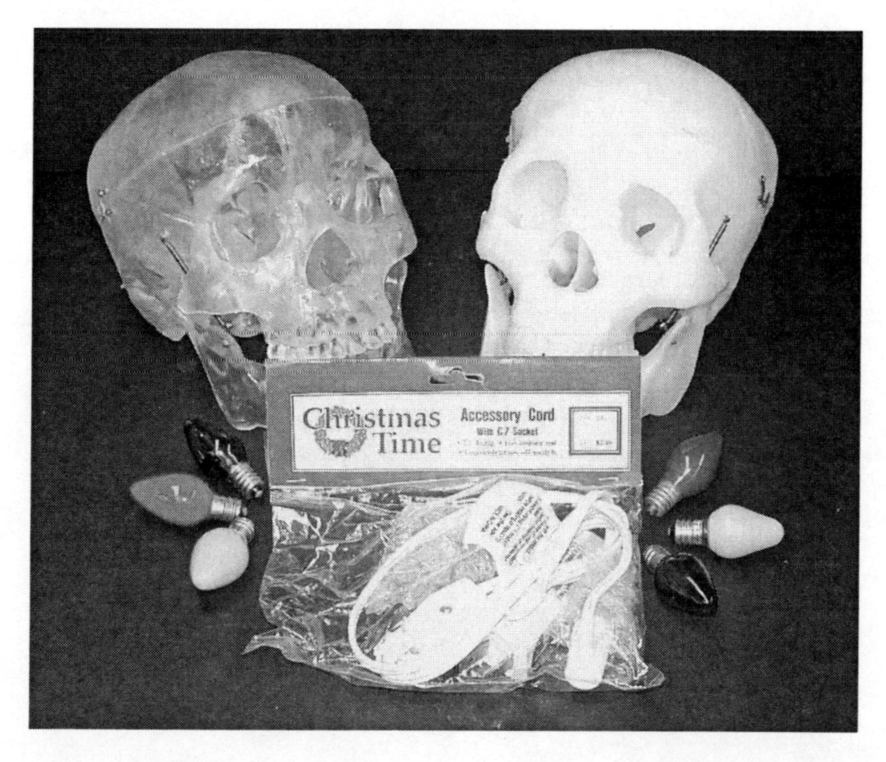

These are the materials you will need to create a skull light.

Note: **This is without a doubt one of the easiest projects to make. The effect, however, is really quite dramatic.**

Step One: Select your skull and light. You will want to select a skull that is completely transparent or at least very translucent (you cannot see through it; however, it lets light through). I have used some glow-in-the-dark skulls, which have worked out very well. The skulls I used were the transparent and glow-in-the-dark skulls from The Anatomical Chart Company.

The lights I use are the bulb-on-a-cord type you see in many night lights or in the little ceramic houses at Christmastime. These most often come with a clear bulb; however, you can find a variety of colored bulbs in stores around Christmastime. I have even found twinkle bulbs, which give a strobe-like effect.

Step Two: Screw your bulb into the socket.

Step Three: Bend the tabs on the socket slightly outward. Start with just a slight bend; you can always go back and bend a little more if your socket does not fit when you install it in the next step.

Step Four: Insert the socket, bulb first, into the hole in the bottom of the skull where the spine would normally enter. The little notches in the tabs should engage the plastic of the skull.

Step Five: Plug the cord from your light into a wall socket and turn on the switch, if so equipped. Your skull should now light brightly. Besides being a great Halloween prop, these skull lights make great night lights.

Step Six: This step is important to insure safety. Because there are many types of lights out there, you must check to insure the bulb you used will not

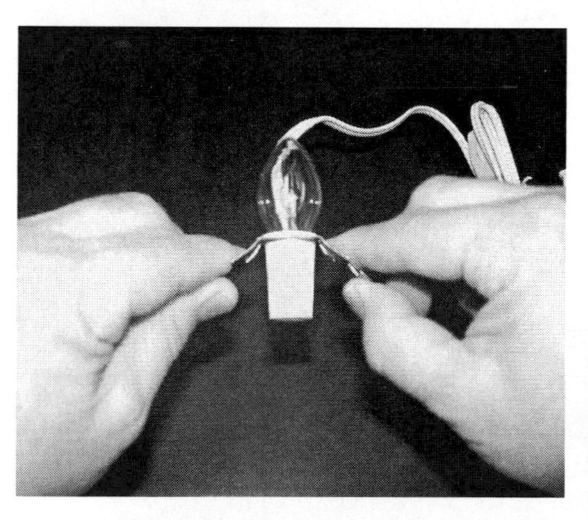

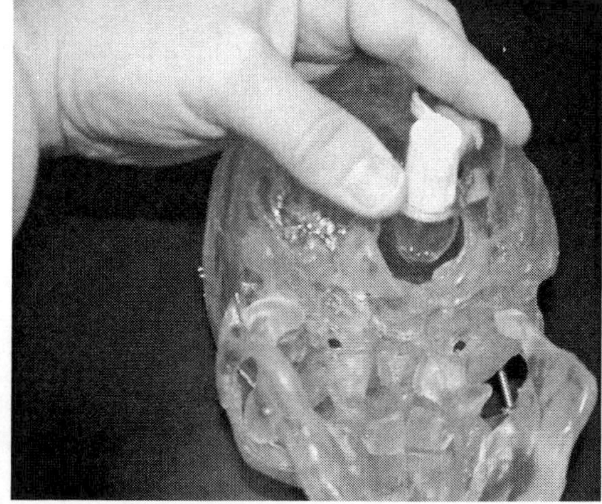

Left: **Bend the tabs on the socket slightly outward.** ***Right:*** **Insert the socket, bulb first, into the hole in the bottom of the skull.**

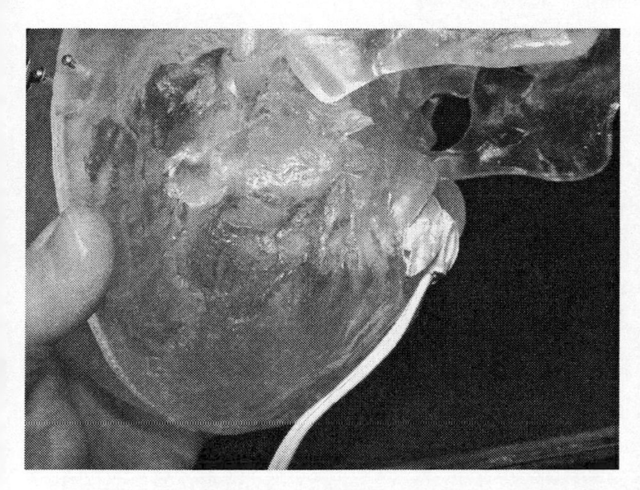

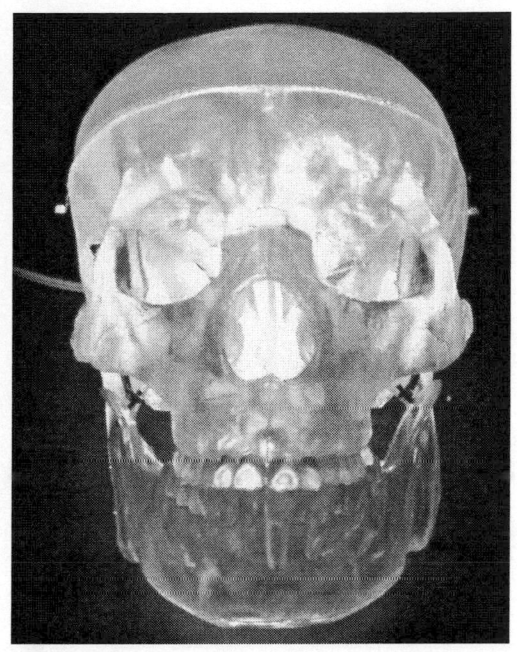

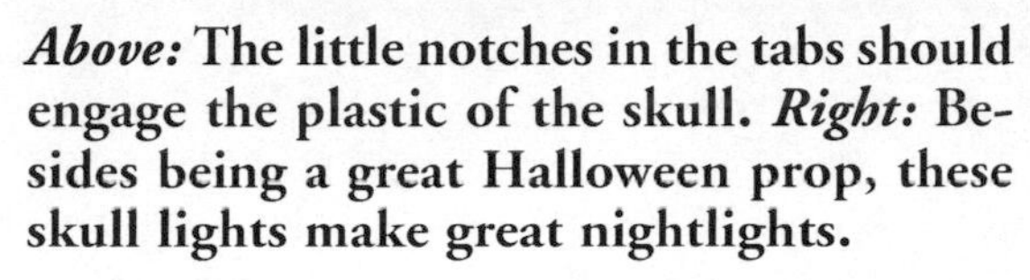
***Above:* The little notches in the tabs should engage the plastic of the skull. *Right:* Besides being a great Halloween prop, these skull lights make great nightlights.**

overheat the skull, causing a risk of fire. Immediately after turning on your light for the first time, place your hand on top of the skull to check for overheating.

Leave your hand on top of the skull for about one minute. The skull should begin to feel a little warm from the heat of the bulb. **If the skull begins to feel hot, immediately turn off the light.** If you find the temperature of the skull ever gets to be more than comfortably warm, shut it off. Leave the light on for about one hour, coming back to check about every five minutes for signs of overheating. These signs would include smoking, softening of the plastic or a temperature too hot to comfortably leave your hand on top of the skull. **If you ever observe any signs of overheating, immediately turn off your light. It should never get more than slightly warm.**

I have built and used a number of these lights using transparent and glow-in-the-dark skulls from The Anatomical

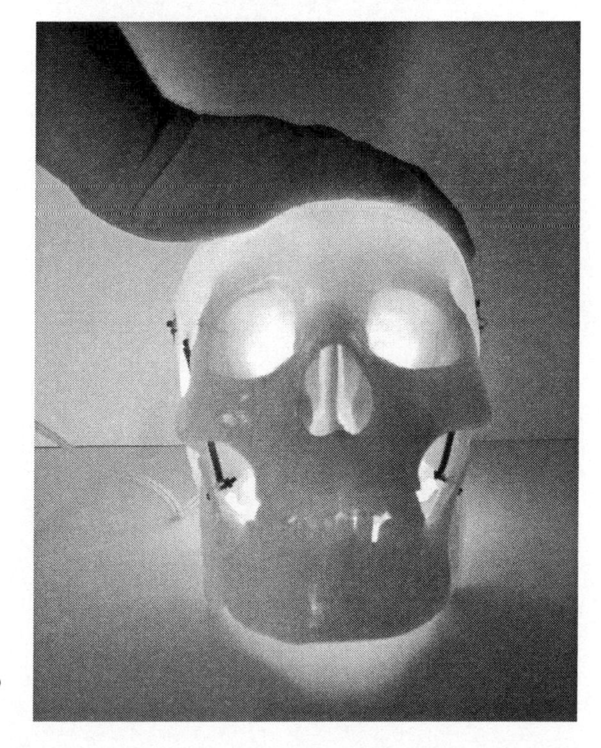

Place your hand on top of the skull to check for overheating.

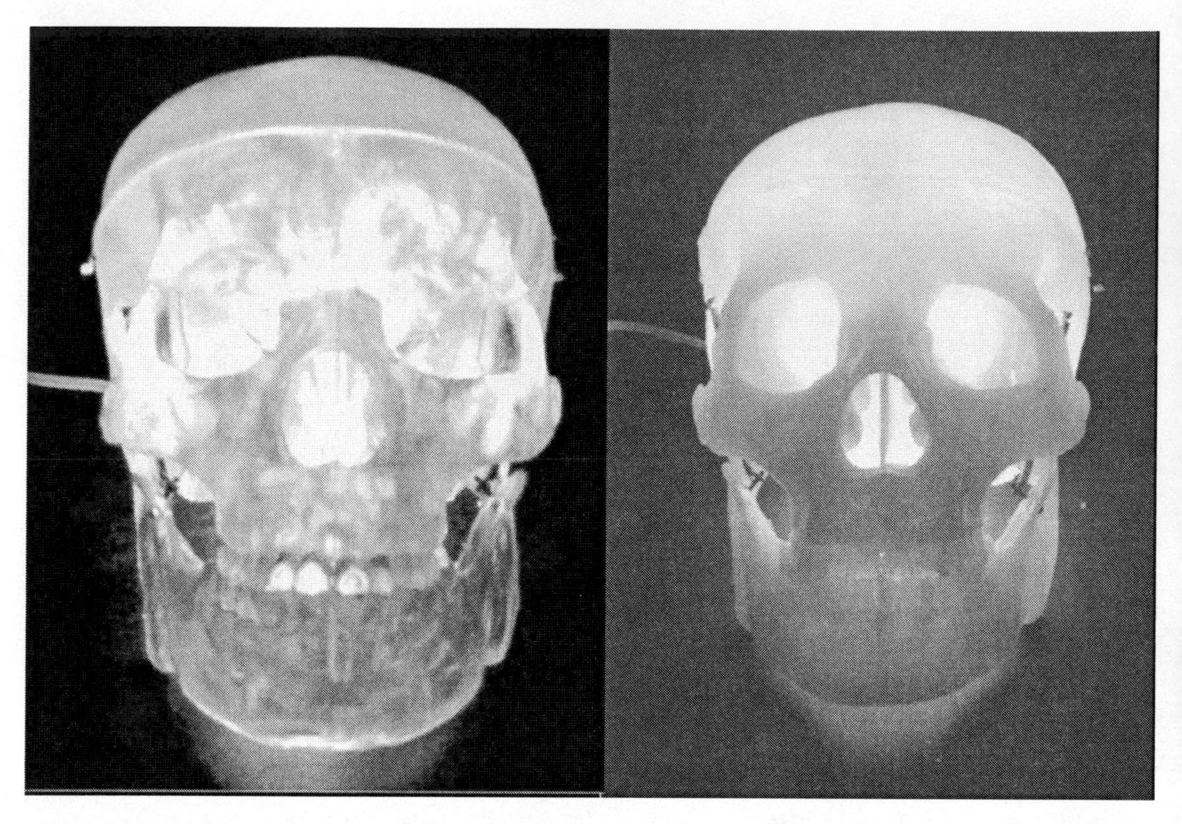

To show how different types of skulls work as skull lights, this picture shows a transparent skull (left) with a glow-in-the-dark skull next to it (right). To see how the two types work with different colors of bulbs, take a look at this book's front cover.

Chart Company and C7 bulbs with no problems whatsoever. I have had these lights continuously on for eight hours and more with no overheating. However, as there are a variety of skulls and lights out there, I cannot guarantee that all combinations will be safe, so you must test to ensure safety. When in doubt, turn it out!

DEVIL EYES

For this project you will need:

- ✓ One pair of hollow, clear eyeballs
- ✓ One package glow-in-the-dark polymer clay
- ✓ Silicone adhesive (optional)
- ✓ A sharp knife

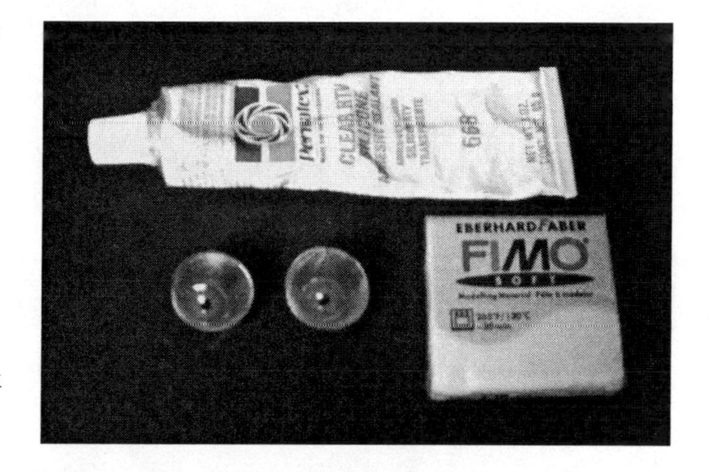

These are the materials you will need to create a set of devil eyes.

Step One: With a sharp knife and great care, cut the back of the eyeball to expose the hollow interior (please be careful so as not to cut yourself). The eyeballs I used were a soft, rubber-like plastic and came from The Anatomical Chart Company (see the Where Can I Find...? section in the back of this book). Again, I am sure there are many eyeballs that will work. I mention where I purchased mine only for those who simply must know.

Step Two: Take a small piece of the polymer clay, work it with your hands until it is soft and then roll it between the palms of your hands into a stick narrow enough to fit into the hole you cut. Polymer clay is available at many craft and hobby stores (see the Where Can I Find...? section in the back of this book). I have tried a couple of varieties of this clay and to me the brand that seems to glow the brightest is the FIMO brand.

Step Three: Gently stuff the polymer clay into the eyeball through the hole you cut earlier. Make sure not to use too much pressure or you may push the iris out of the front of the eye.

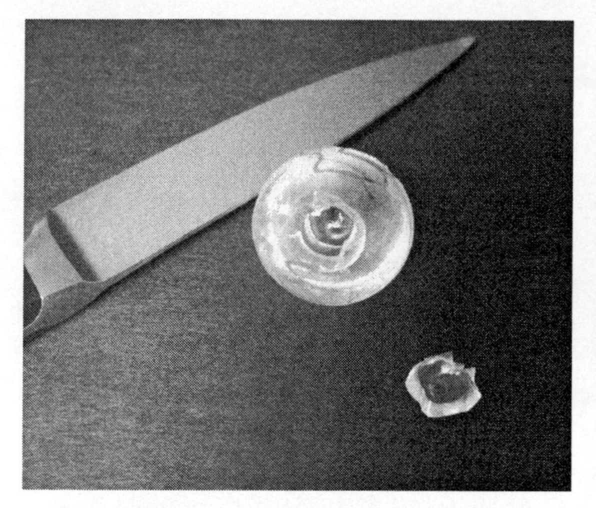

Left: **With a sharp knife and great care, carefully cut the back of the eyeball to expose the hollow interior.** ***Right:*** **Take a small piece of the polymer clay, work it with your hands until soft and then roll it between the palms of your hands into a stick narrow enough to fit into the hole you cut.**

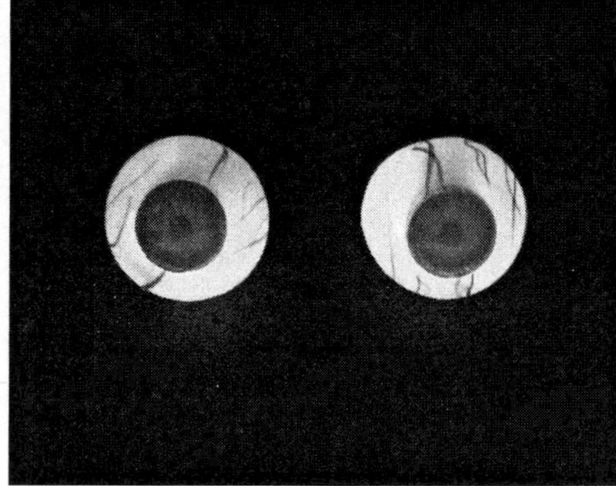

Left: **Gently stuff the polymer clay into the eyeball through the hole you cut earlier.** ***Right:*** **Completed Devil Eyes shown under black light.**

Step Four: Replace the piece of plastic you cut out in step one, or seal the opening with silicone adhesive and you are done.

Your completed Devil Eyes can now be used by charging them in bright light and then placing them in the dark, or just keeping them under black light. These eyes look great when placed in a skull or just use your imagination and see what you can come up with.

DEMON EYES

For this project you will need:

✓ Two hollow prop eyes
✓ Two LEDs

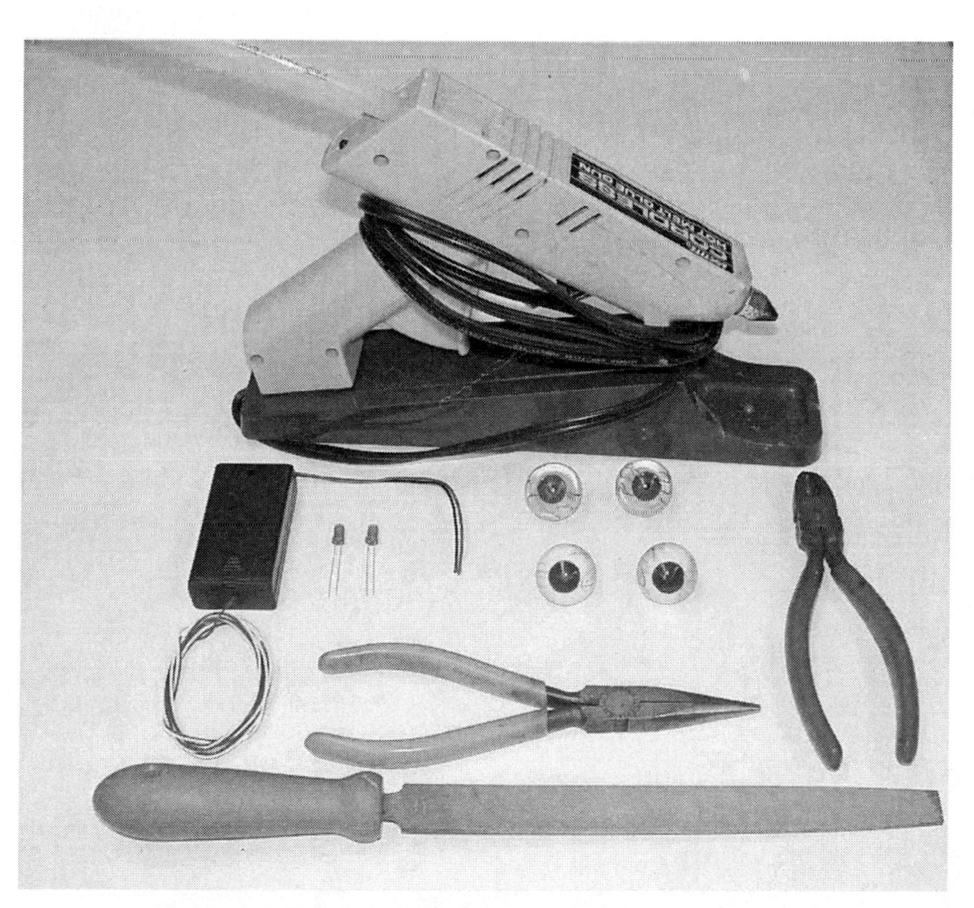

These are the materials you will need to create a set of Demon Eyes.

- ✓ About four feet of wire (about 22 gauge)
- ✓ Hot melt glue gun with glue or silicone adhesive
- ✓ Wire wrap tool or long-nose pliers
- ✓ A drill with drill bit, or a file, or a sharp knife
- ✓ Wire cutters
- ✓ One battery pack with batteries

You will need a pair of prop eyes, which are hollow inside and are transparent or at least translucent, or have a transparent or translucent iris.

Step One: Select your eyes. You will need a pair of prop eyes, which are hollow inside and are transparent or at least translucent, or have a transparent or translucent iris. In order for your eyes to work correctly, they must allow some light to shine through them when a light is put inside. The eyes I used were from The Anatomical Chart Company. I have used both the hard plastic and clear eyes.

Step Two: Make a hole in the back of each eye. You will need to make this hole just large enough for your LED to fit into. How you make your hole will depend on the type of eye you are using. If you are using a soft rubber eye, such as the transparent eyes from The

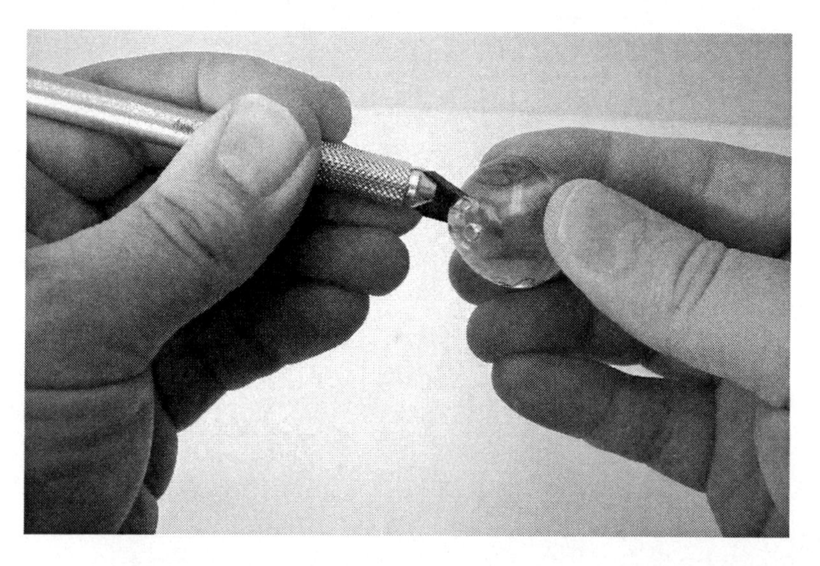

Left: **If you are using a soft rubber eye, such as the transparent eyes from the Anatomical Chart Company, you can carefully cut the hole with a sharp knife.** ***Right:*** **Soft eyes with the backs cut out.**

Anatomical Chart Company, you can carefully cut the hole with a sharp knife.

If you are using a hard plastic eye, you will need to drill or file the hole. As a round object can be difficult to drill, I suggest you use a file to make your hole. If you have a drill press and can make a jig to hold your eye, and you also have the skill to safely use them, you can consider drilling. If you are not expert at drilling holes in round objects, I strongly suggest you use a file to make your holes. This may take a little longer, but at least you get to keep all of your fingers. To make a hole with a file, simply file off the back of the eye until you have a hole large enough for the LED.

Step Three: Connect a piece of wire about one foot long to each lead of the LEDs. At this point, you may want to choose two different color wires, one for the positive lead of the LED, and a different color for the negative lead. This will make it easier to get your polarity correct later on. If you must use the same color wire for both leads there is no need to worry; we will check for correct polarity later. You can solder the wire to these leads, but take care not to damage the LED by overheating it. Another way is to wrap wire around the lead. This is easy if you have a wire wrap tool; just use the right gauge wire for your tool and wrap away.

If you are like most people and do not know what a wire wrap tool is, let alone own one, you can still wrap your connection. Start by stripping off about one and one half inches of insulation from one end of your wire. Place the stripped wire next to one of the leads of the LED so that the end of the insulation just touches the lead.

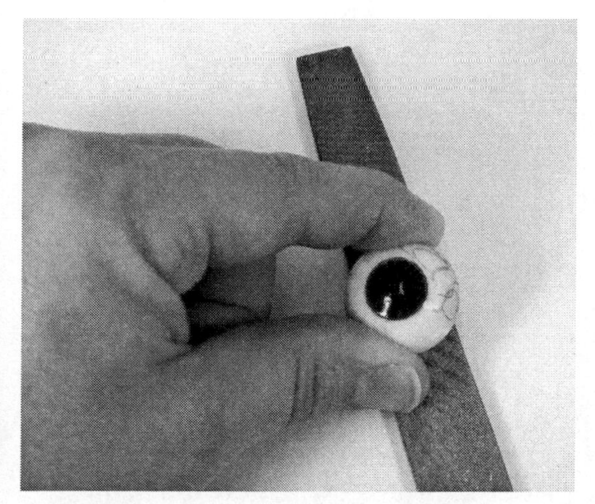

Left: To make a hole with a file, simply file off the back of the eye until you have a hole large enough for the LED. _Right:_ Hard plastic eyes with the back filed off.

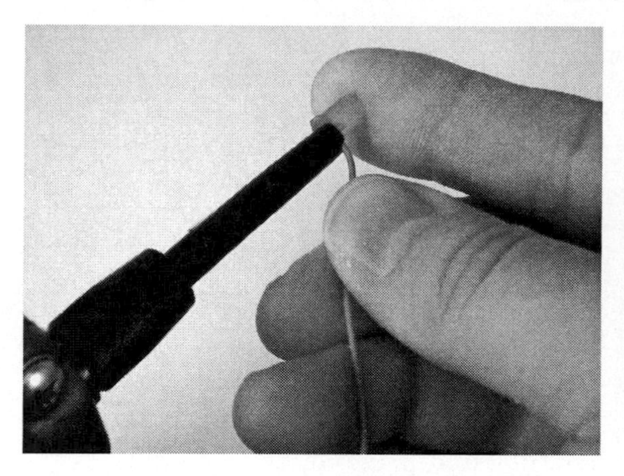

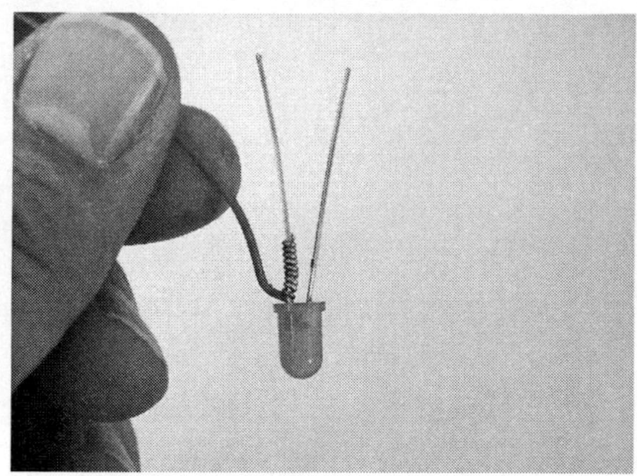

Left: **Connect a piece of wire about one foot long to each lead of the LEDs.** ***Right:*** **If you have a wire wrap tool, just use the right gauge wire for your tool and wrap away.**

Holding the LED and insulated section of the wire firmly, take a pair of long-nose pliers and carefully wrap the wire around the lead. You will want to use solid wire for this because stranded wire will not hold.

Make sure you pull the wire tightly against the lead to make good contact. Once you have the first loop around the lead, use your pliers to push the wire around the lead. To do this, place one side of the pliers against the loop, and the other against the unwrapped wire. Now squeeze on the handles of the pliers to force the wire against the lead. You will have to work in very small sections; and

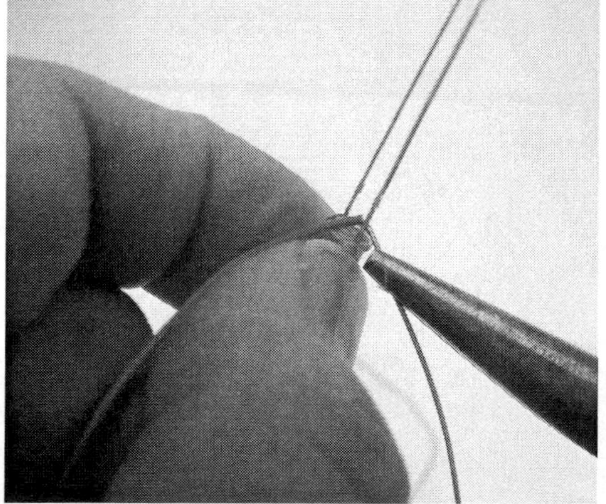

Left: **If you don't have a wire wrap tool, place the stripped wire next to one of the leads of the LED so that the end of the insulation just touches the lead.** ***Right:*** **Holding the LED and insulated section of the wire firmly, take a pair of long nose pliers and carefully wrap the wire around the lead.**

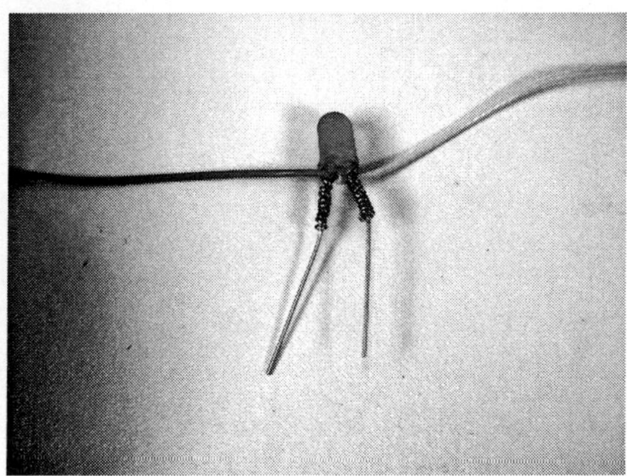

Left: **Once you have the first loop around the lead, use your pliers to push the wire around the lead.** ***Right:*** **An LED wrapped by hand may not look as neat as one done using a wire wrap tool, but done right it will work just as well.**

it will take a long time to get all the way around the lead. Just keep working your way slowly around the lead until all of the stripped section of the wire is used. If you like, you can add a small drop of solder to hold the wrap in place (if you get a nice tight wrap this is not needed).

Once you have completed the first lead, take another piece of wire and wrap it to the other lead the same way.

Now that your wires are connected, you must insulate the bare copper from touching anything else. Start by trimming off any excess lead.

It is very difficult to wrap in-between the leads with electrical tape, though it can be done. Another option is to use liquid electrical tape. This is paint-on tape, but it can be hard to find. I myself like to use the coffee stirrer method. To use this method, take a one-holed coffee stirrer and cut off a piece a little longer than your trimmed lead.

Trim off any excess lead from your LED.

Next, take the wire and fold it back against the lead, then slide the cut section of the coffee stirrer over the free end of the wire. Slide the stirrer down the wire and cover the wire-wrapped lead.

Repeat the process for the other lead and your connections are insulated.

Step Four: Place your

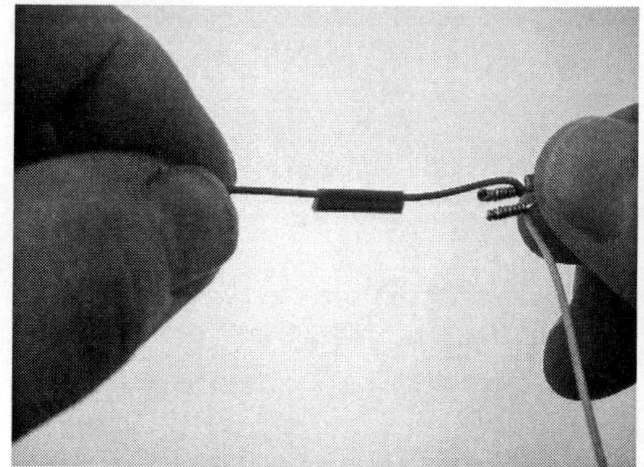

Left: **Take a one-holed coffee stirrer and cut off a piece a little longer than your trimmed lead. *Right:* Slide the stirrer down the wire and cover the wire-wrapped lead.**

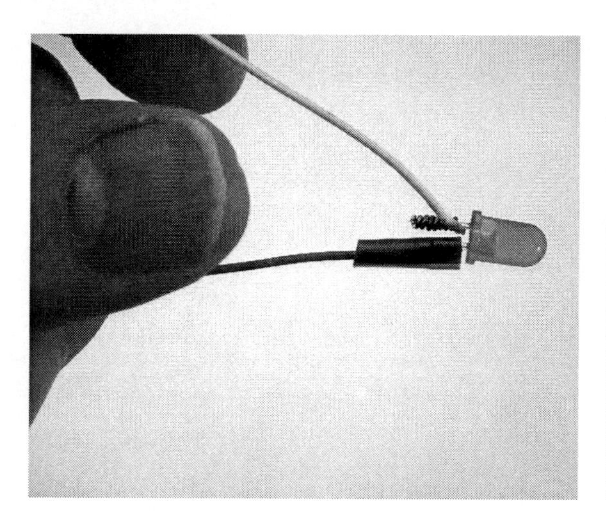

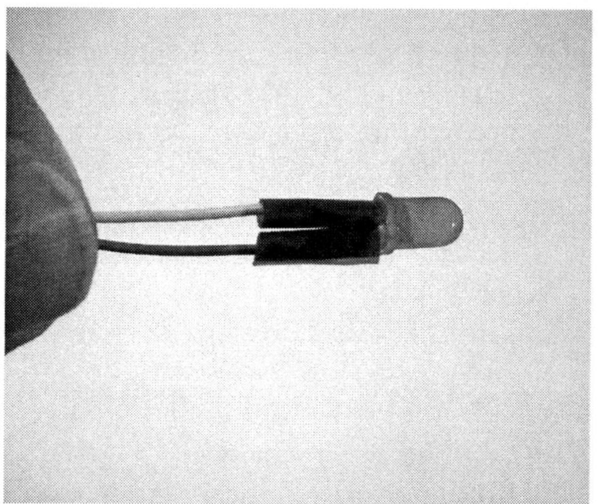

Left: **You can use a small piece of coffee stirrer to keep your leads from shorting out. *Right:* Use two pieces of coffee stirrer, one on each lead.**

LED with the leads insulated inside of the eye. Try to place your LED so that it is positioned in center of the eye with the very ends of the coffee stirrer insulators sticking out of the back of the eye.

Step Five: Now use either hot melt glue or silicone adhesive to seal the LED into the eye. I prefer the hot melt glue on a hard plastic eye because it sets up much faster and makes it easier to keep the LED from shifting while the glue sets up. On softer plastics or rubber, I use the silicone adhesive because the hot melt glue can actually melt the eye. You may have to experiment a little to get the right adhesive for your eye.

Step Six: Complete a second eye or as many eyes as you need for your project.

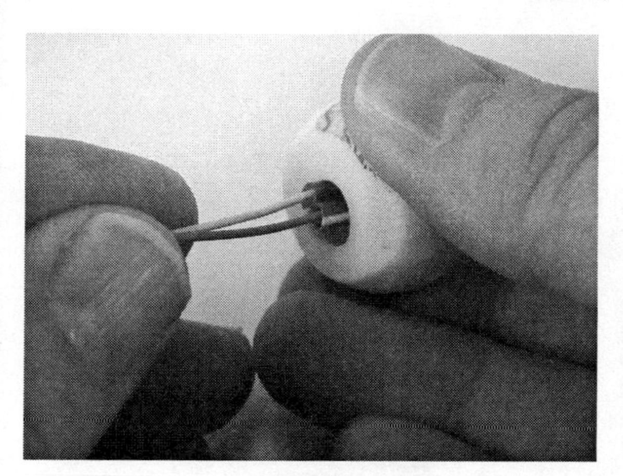

Left: **Try to place your LED so that it is positioned in the center of the eye with the very ends of the coffee stirrer insulators sticking out of the back of the eye.** ***Right:*** **Hot melt glue is a quick and easy way to seal your Demon Eye.**

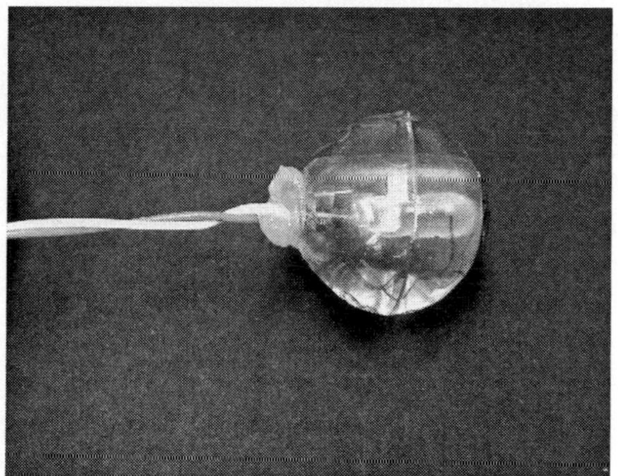

Left: **A rear view of a completed, hard plastic Demon Eye using hot melt glue.** ***Right:*** **A rear view of a completed, soft rubbery plastic Demon Eye using silicone adhesive.**

Step Seven: It is now time to test your eyes and connect them to the power supply. Check the operating voltage for your LEDs and use a battery pack which produces that number of volts. If you do not know the operating voltage of your LEDs, try three volts; this usually works well. You will find that most battery packs that hold two batteries (AAA, AA, C or D) put out three volts. Strip off about one inch of insulation from both wires going to your eyes and both wires going to your battery pack. Keep the stripped ends of the wires from the battery pack from touching each other or anything metal. Put your batteries in the battery pack. Now take one lead from your eye, and touch it to one lead from the battery pack. Then take the other lead from your eye and touch it to the other

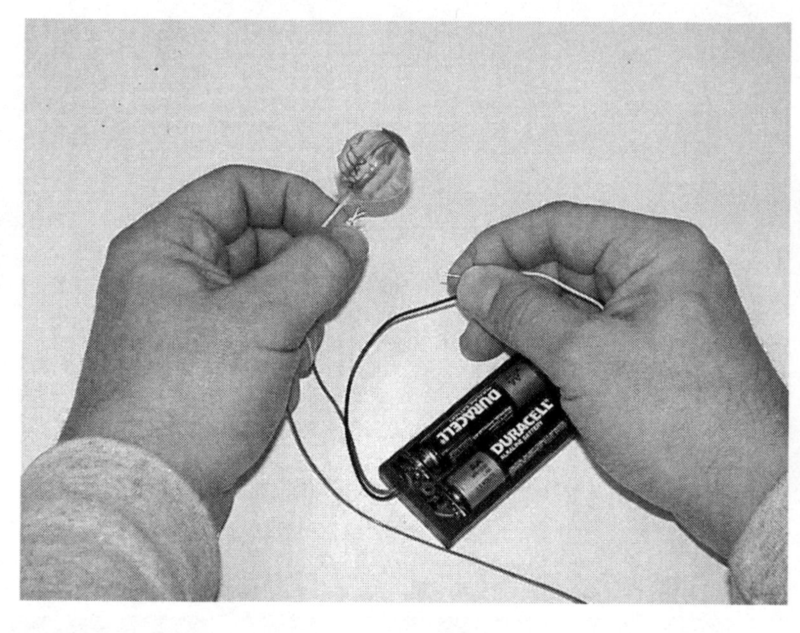

After you complete your Demon Eye, it is a good idea to test it before placing it in a prop.

lead from the battery pack. If your eye lights, you have the correct polarity to your eye. If necessary, mark all your wires so that you can reconnect them in the same way. If your eyes do not light, switch the wires from the eye to the opposite wires from the battery pack. Your eyes should now light. Mark your wires so that you can connect them correctly later. Repeat this process for each eye you made.

Step Eight: You can now put your eyes into whatever prop you want to use them in. In many cases, you will want to put your eyes into the prop before connecting them to the battery pack. This will allow you to run the wires through a small opening, like the eye of a skull.

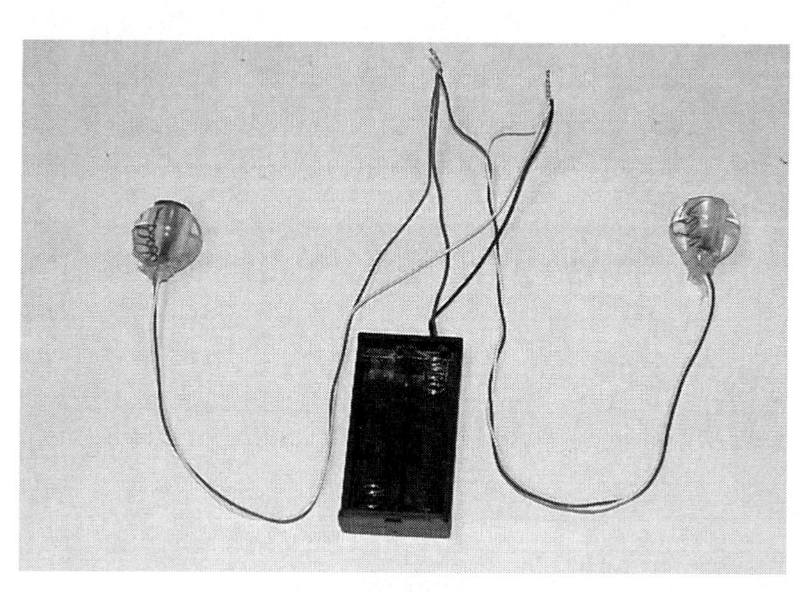

Connect your eyes to your battery pack (if you need more detail on wiring, see the section in this book entitled Put a Light in It).

Step Nine: Connect your eyes to your battery pack (if you need more detail on wiring, see the section in this book entitled Put a Light In It). For most LEDs, this will require a three-volt battery pack. To connect the pack to your eyes, strip off about one inch of insulation

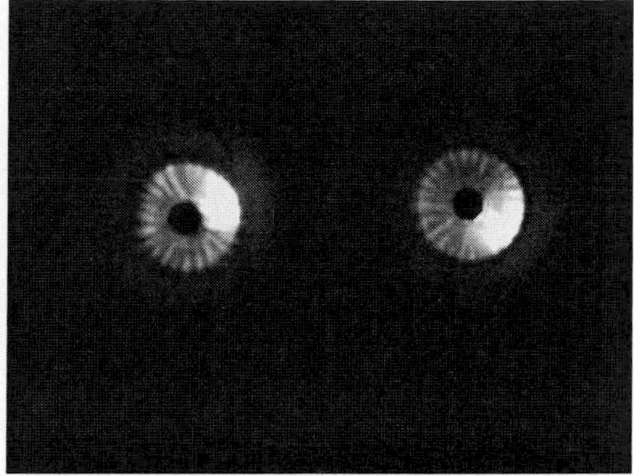

Left: **A completed set of Demon Eyes connected to a battery pack.** ***Right:*** **Red Demon Eyes in use in a dark room.**

from each of the wires from each eye, and each wire from your battery pack. Now just twist the bare wires together. You will want to connect your wires the same way they were when the eyes lighted in step seven.

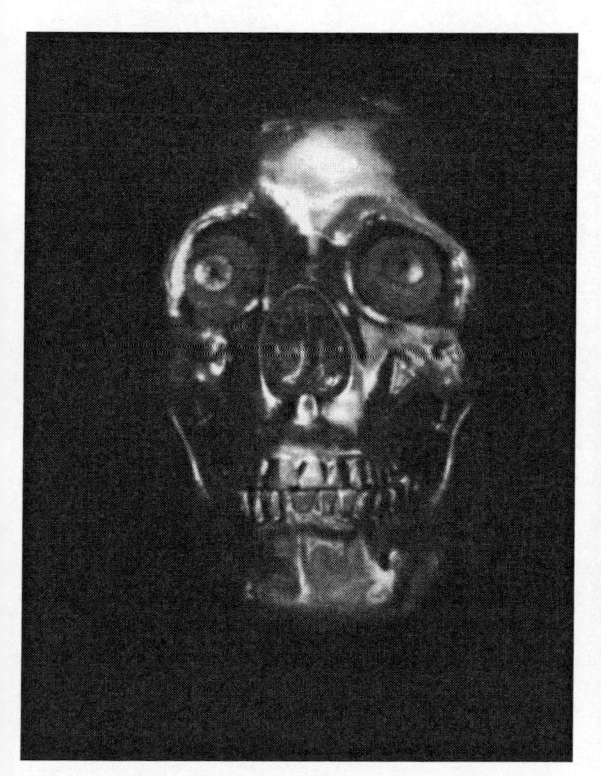

Left: **I call this one my "major motion picture starring a former Mr. Universe who later went on to become governor of California" skull.** ***Right:*** **A picture of hard plastic Demon Eyes built using blue LEDs placed in a wolf mask.**

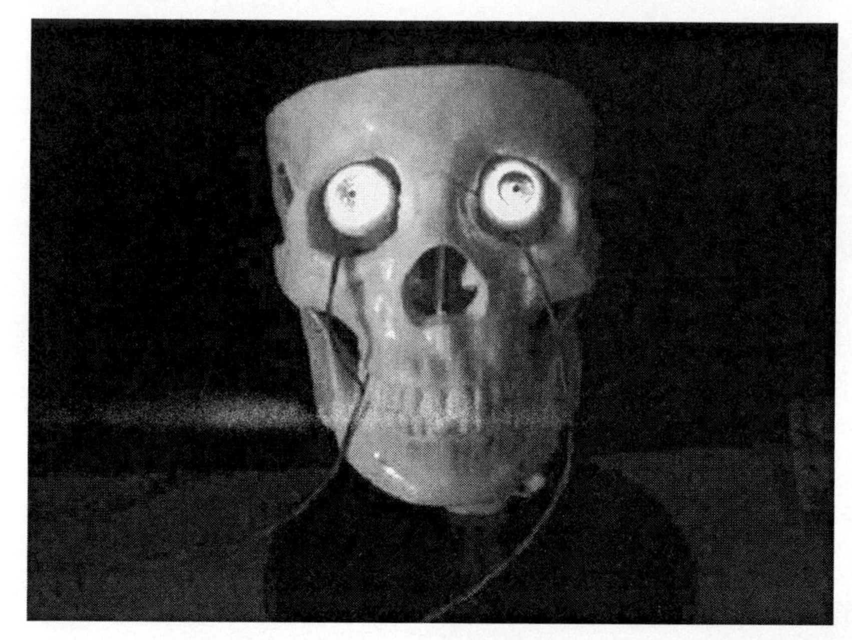

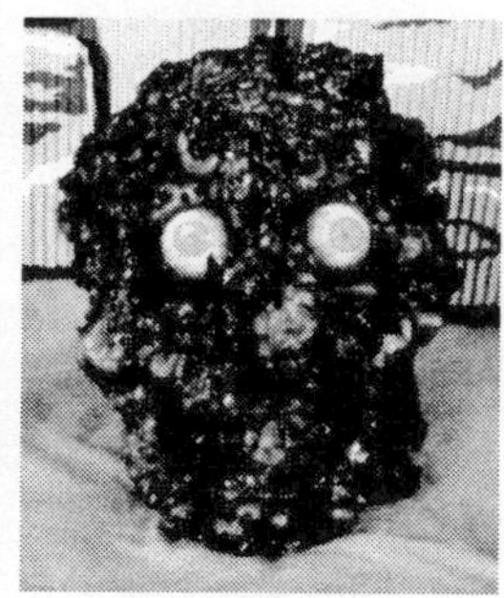

Left: Blue hard plastic Demon Eyes in a skull. ***Above:*** Hard plastic red Demon Eyes in a barbecued skull.

Step Ten: Put the batteries in your battery pack and your eyes are all set.

Here are a few pictures of props I built using Demon Eyes. I call the first one my "major motion picture starring a former Mr. Universe who later went on to become governor of California" skull.

Note: Demon Eyes are very difficult to photograph. They look much better in person than they do in pictures.

Yellow hard plastic Demon Eyes in a mask.

MAGIC BOTTLE

For this project you will need:

- ✓ One bottle with stopper, your choice
- ✓ A small amount of pearlizing agent
- ✓ Food coloring (optional)

Step One: Select your bottle. You will find it best to select a bottle that is clear or only very lightly colored. If you go too dark on the color, you will not be able to see through the bottle to the magic effect.

Step Two: Pour a very small amount of pearlizing agent into your bottle. For the bottle shown here, I used less than one teaspoon. You can always add more later if you need to increase the effect. In fact, if you look closely at the first picture, you can see how much of the pearlizing agent is missing. That amount made several magic bottles. In case you are wondering what

These are the materials you will need to create a magic bottle.

pearlizing agent is, it is a common additive in many soaps and shampoos. It is what gives them that shimmering look. The pearlizing agent I used is called Q-pearl and came from the Chemistry Store.

Step Three: Add enough water to fill your bottle to just below where the stopper will end when pushed tightly into the bottle. Add the water slowly. If you add it very quickly you may cause foaming, which will make it harder to fill the bottle. Do not worry that the pearlizing agent does not mix with the water. We will take care of that later.

Pour a very small amount of pearlizing agent into your bottle.

Step Four: Place your stopper into the neck of the bottle and seal tightly.

Step Five: Repeatedly turn the bottle upside-down and then right side up again, until the pearlizing agent is mixed into the water. You will begin to see the magic effect as you mix. When the mixing is done, you have a magic bottle.

When left undisturbed the bottle will have a cloudy look, but when shaken and then set down, you will see a swirling pattern within the bottle that will last for as long as a full minute. If you would like to experiment to get the maximum effect, you can try adding a little more pearlizing agent to add more swirls (too much and you will actually decrease the effect). If you add too much pearlizing agent, just pour off some of the mixture and add more water. Experiment until you get just the look you want.

Add enough water to fill your bottle, to just below where the stopper will end when pushed tightly into the bottle.

Step Six: This step is optional. You can remove the stopper from your bottle and add a few drops of food coloring to change the color of the water (the pearlizing agent color will not change).

There are other little tricks you can use to change the look of your bottle.

Left: **A completed magic bottle.** ***Right:*** **The author's first magic bottle, made by adding a few drops of red food coloring to the water.**

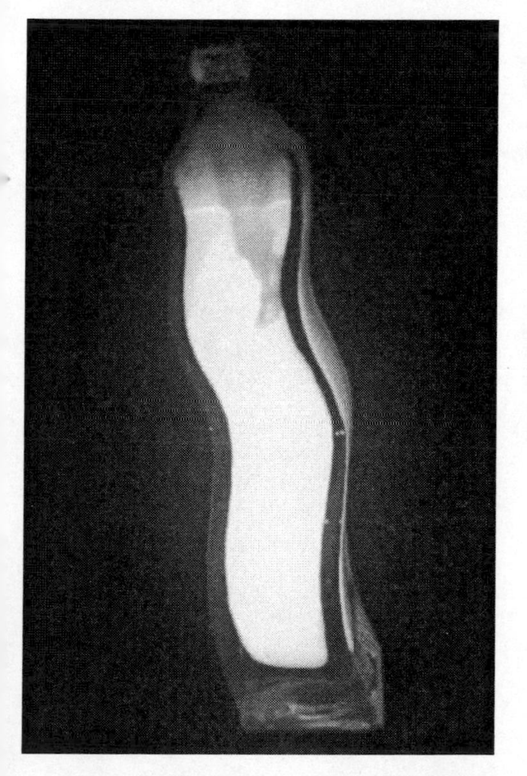

Left: **A magic bottle made with tonic water and photographed under black light. The magic swirls do not photograph well under black light.** ***Right:*** **A magic bottle using tap water dyed with highlighter fluid and photographed under black light. The magic swirls do not photograph well under black light.**

For one, you can use differently shaped bottles for a different look and different patterns of swirls. Or you can try tonic water instead of plain water to make your bottle glow a whitish blue color in black light, or add a UV dye to the water for a different color black light glow (see the section called Working with Black Light). It's your bottle; experiment, and who knows what you may come up with!

***Left:* A magic bottle made with tonic water and photographed under normal light. *Right:* A magic bottle using tap water dyed with highlighter fluid and photographed under normal light.**

I have included pictures of magic bottles using tonic water and a UV dye to give you some ideas. Unfortunately, the magic effect is a little harder to see in black light and much harder still to photograph. In case you were wondering, the UV dye I used was fluid from a highlighter.

BONEHEAD FLATWARE

For this project you will need:

- ✓ Some plain flatware
- ✓ One small plastic skull (with removable top) for each piece of flatware
- ✓ A rotary grinding tool with bit or small round file
- ✓ Hot melt glue gun with glue

Step One: Remove the top of your skull. The skulls I used were Tiny Tim skulls from The Anatomical Chart Company.

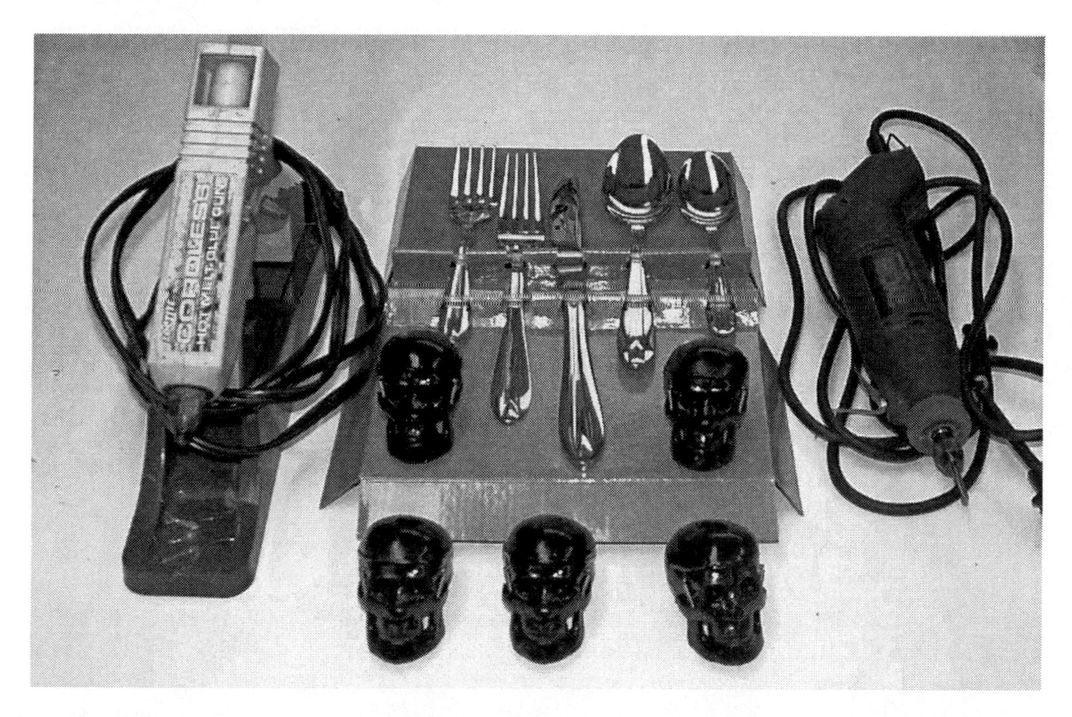

These are the materials you will need to create a set of bonehead flatware.

Step Two: Grind or file a slot in the bottom of the skull just large enough for the end of your flatware to fit into. You will want to make this slot from side to side, rather than front to back. You will also want to make sure it is positioned so that the flatware will lie properly when set down.

Step Three: Place the end of your flatware into the slot you just made. Now lay your flatware and skull on a flat surface and make sure it will lie flat. It does not matter if the skull and flatware will not stay in the exact position you want

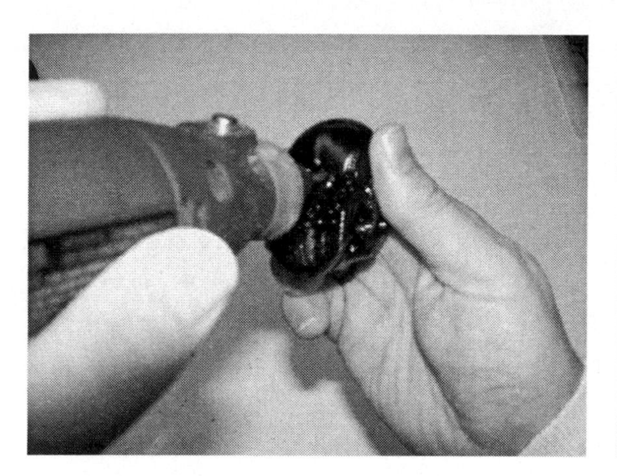

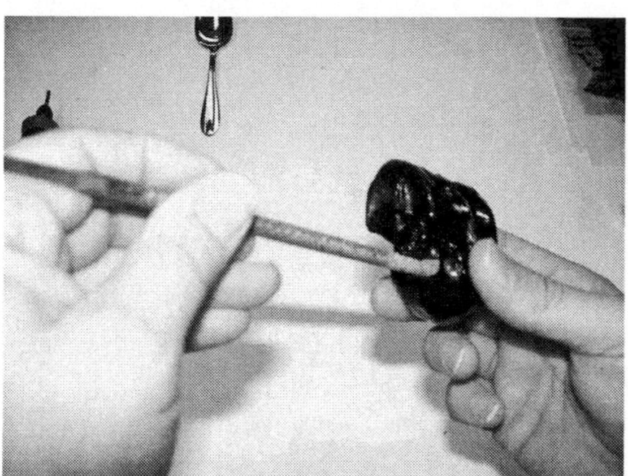

Left: **If you have the right tools, it is easy to grind a hole in your skull.** ***Right:*** **If you do not have a handheld power grinder you can use a small round file to file a hole in your skull.**

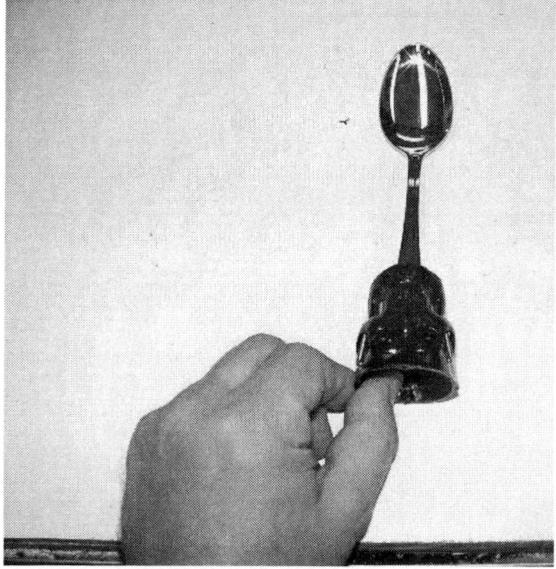

Left: **Your finished slit should run side to side, rather than front to back.** ***Right:*** **Lay your flatware and skull on a flat surface and make sure it will lie flat.**

Left: **Apply a generous amount of hot melt glue around the end of the flatware and onto the inside of the skull.** ***Right:*** **While the hot melt glue is still hot, lay your flatware on a flat surface and adjust it so that the flatware and skull lie as desired.**

on their own, as long as you can position them where you want. Once you glue them, you will make a final adjustment and the glue will hold everything in place.

Step Four: Lift your skull with the flatware in place and hold it so that the skull is upright. Now apply a generous amount of hot melt glue around the end of the flatware and onto the inside of the skull.

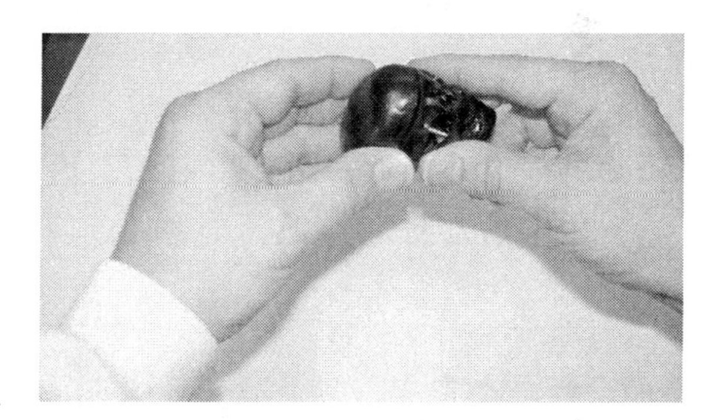

Replace the lid on your skull and you are done.

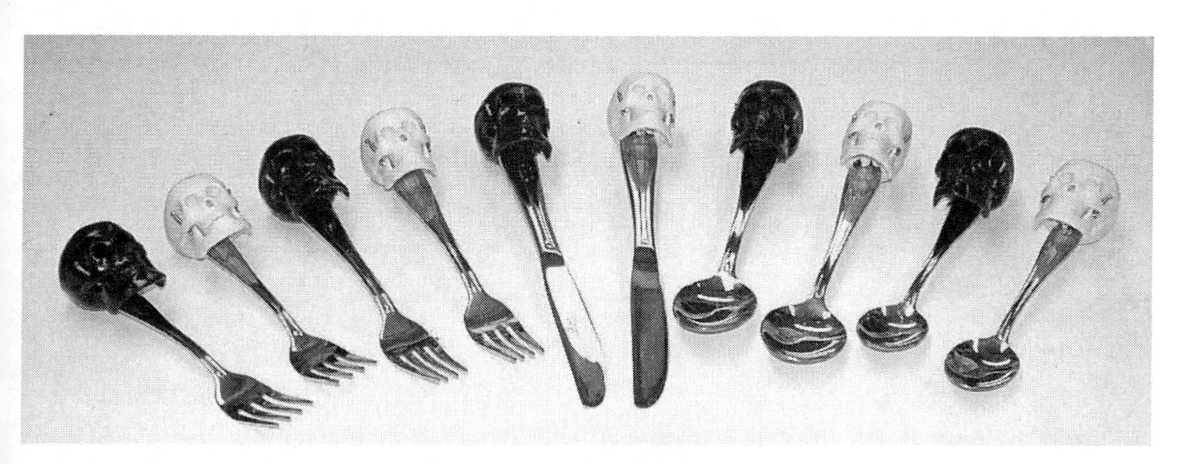

A finished set of bonehead flatware.

Step Five: While the hot melt glue is still hot, lay your flatware on a flat surface and adjust it so that the flatware and skull lie the way you want them to. Hold them in this position until the glue sets up (about one minute). **Caution: Hot melt glue and the glue gun are hot! Be very careful not to burn yourself!**

Step Six: Replace the lid on your skull and you are done with this piece. Now you can continue to follow the above steps until you have finished as many pieces as you like.

BONEHEAD NAPKIN RING

For this project you will need:

- ✓ One vertebra (plastic)
- ✓ A drill with a large spade bit (about ⅞")
- ✓ A piece of scrap wood at least ¾" thick
- ✓ A piece of medium grit sandpaper

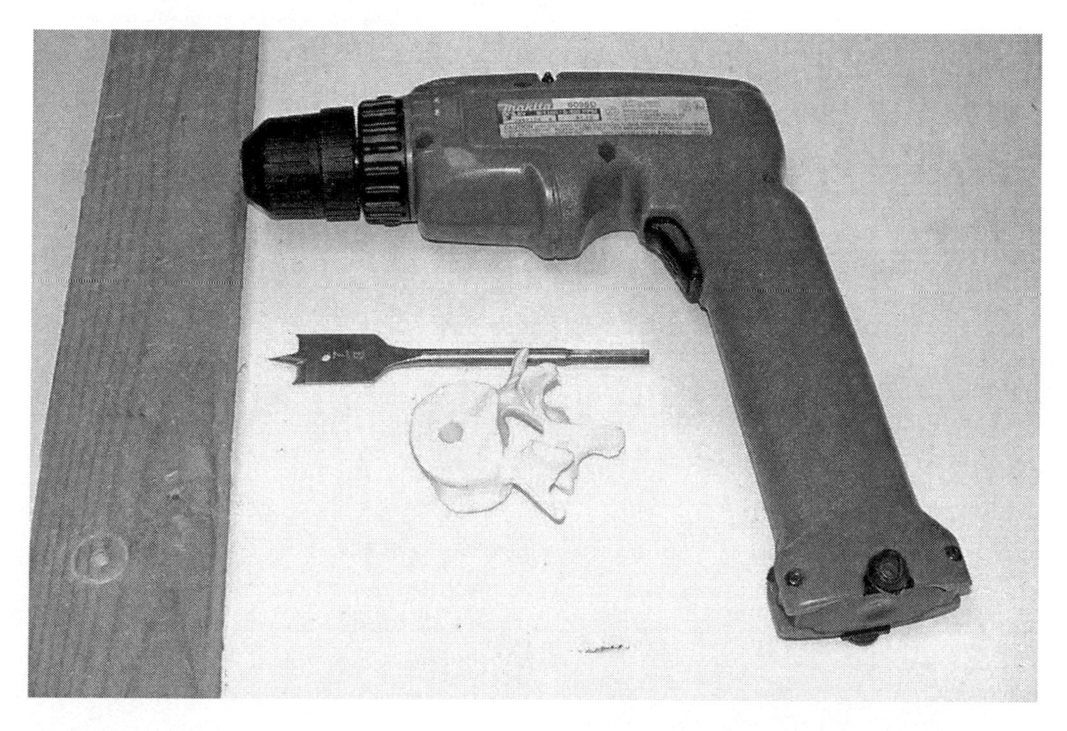

These are the materials you will need to create a bonehead napkin ring.

Step One: Place your vertebra on the piece of scrap wood. You will want to select a larger vertebra from the lower back; this will give you a larger hole to place the napkin through.

There are several ways in which to purchase the vertebra for this project. You can purchase a complete spine and take it apart for the individual vertebra, you can buy loose bones by the pound and hope to get a few vertebrae or you can purchase vertebra-shaped pencil holders.

Now you would think that placing a vertebra on a piece of wood would be easy, but just like anything else there is a right way and a wrong way to do it. If you look closely at your vertebra, you will notice it has a slight curve to it. You want to place the vertebra so that the ends of the curve go up (concave); this will make drilling much easier.

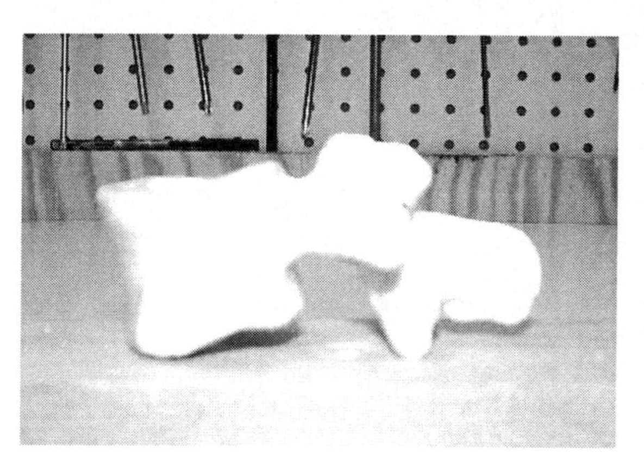

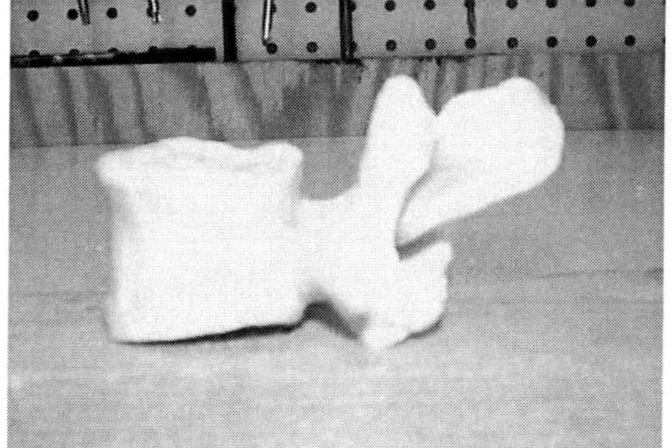

***Left:* A vertebra placed the wrong way for drilling. *Right:* A vertebra placed the right way for drilling.**

Step Two: Use the drill and drill bit to enlarge the hole in the vertebra. The size of the bit you want to use will depend upon the size of the vertebra you are using. You will want to drill as large of a hole as you can while still leaving enough of the sides intact to keep your ring from breaking. I used

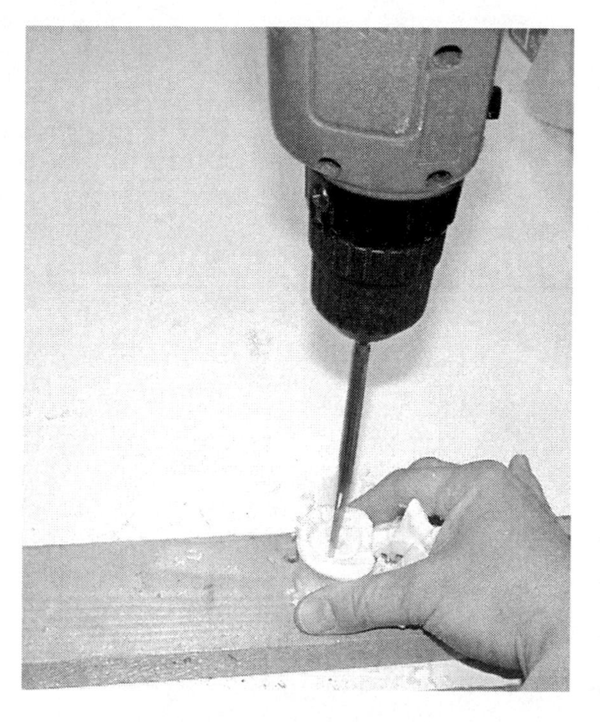

Use the drill and drill bit to enlarge the hole in the vertebra.

one of the largest vertebrae and a ⅞" spade bit. This seems to work well. It allows enough room inside to easily push a napkin through, and yet the sides are still nice and strong.

You will want to drill slowly and carefully; use light pressure and let the drill do the work. This is especially important at the beginning and as you get near the end of the hole as these are the times the bit is most likely to jump off the vertebra or catch and cause the vertebra to spin. If you have a vise, it is best to do this step in the vise; if not, just proceed with extreme caution. As you drill through the vertebra the tip of the drill bit will go through it into the scrap wood; this protects the table or workbench below. Do not keep drilling until you are through the scrap wood.

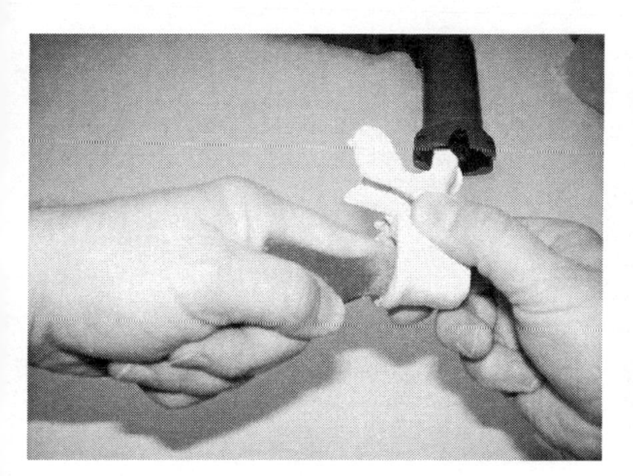

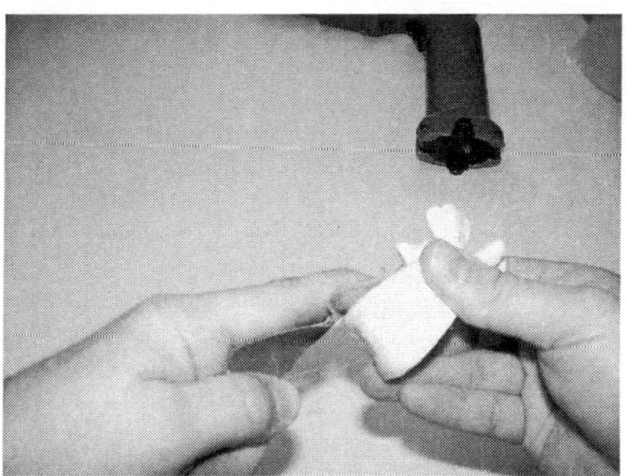

Left: **Take a strip of sandpaper about one inch wide, curl it so that it will fit into the hole you have drilled, place one finger over the sandpaper and work it up and down around the vertebra until the inside of the hole is smooth.** ***Right:*** **Take your strip of sandpaper and curve the first joint of your finger around it, inside the hole. Work your finger and the sandpaper around both ends of the hole.**

Step Three: This and the following step are optional. You will find the drilling process left the new hole in your vertebra somewhat rough. This can be corrected easily with a little sandpaper and some work. Take a strip of sandpaper about one inch wide, curl it so that it will fit into the hole you have drilled, place one finger over the sandpaper and work it up and down around the vertebra until the inside of the hole is smooth.

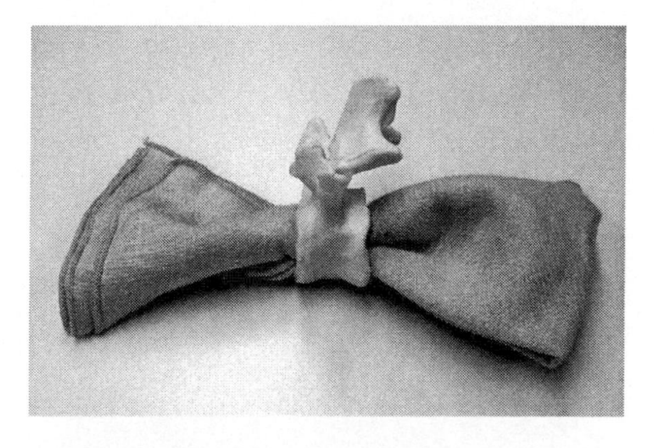

A completed bonehead napkin ring.

Step Four: This step is optional. Take your strip of sandpaper and curve the first joint of your finger around it, inside the hole. Work your finger and the sandpaper around both ends of the hole. This will help remove any burrs or rough spots which may catch and tear your napkins.

Now you can add a napkin and your project is complete. Of course, you may want to do a few more, so as to have a complete set.

BONEHEAD SALT AND PEPPER SHAKERS

For this project you will need:

- ✓ One pair of salt and pepper shakers with removable tops
- ✓ One small white plastic skull (with removable top)
- ✓ One small black plastic skull (with removable top)
- ✓ A rotary grinding tool with bit or a small round file

These are the materials you will need to create a set of bonehead salt and pepper shakers.

✓ Hot melt glue gun with glue (optional)
✓ A drill with a small drill bit

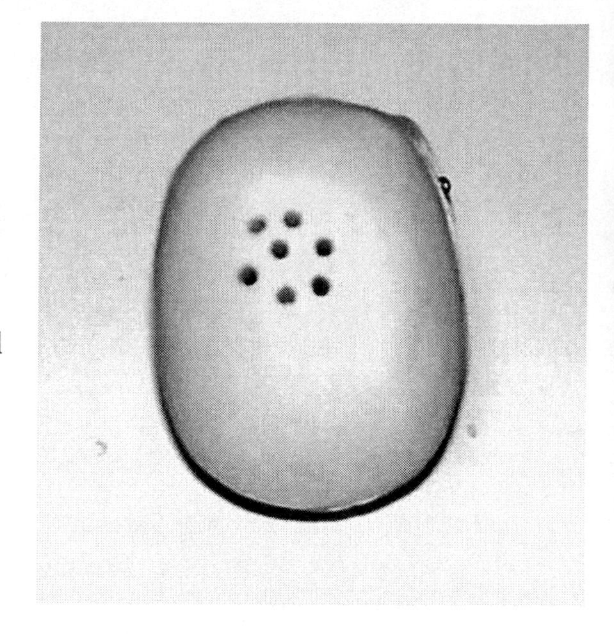

Drill several small holes in the top center of each skull.

Step One: Drill several small holes in the top center of each skull.

Step Two: Remove the tops of your skulls. The skulls I used were Tiny Tim skulls from The Anatomical Chart Company.

Step Three: Remove the tops of your shakers and discard them, or better yet save them until you figure out how to turn them into another prop.

Step Four: Grind or file a hole in the bottom of the skull just large enough for the top of your shakers to fit tightly into. I do not suggest trying to drill this hole. The small skulls are much too difficult to hold, and they tend to catch the bit and spin. This can result in some cut and torn fingers.

Step Five: Firmly and carefully screw your skulls onto your shakers.

Step Six: This step is optional. You may find it a good idea to glue your skull to the shaker; this is particularly helpful if you did not get a

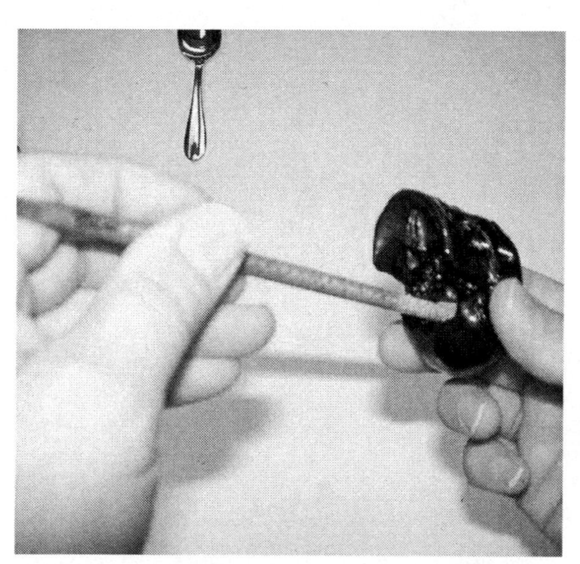

Left: **If you have the right tools, it is easy to grind a hole in your skull.** ***Right:*** **If you do not have a handheld power grinder you can use a small round file to file a hole in your skull.**

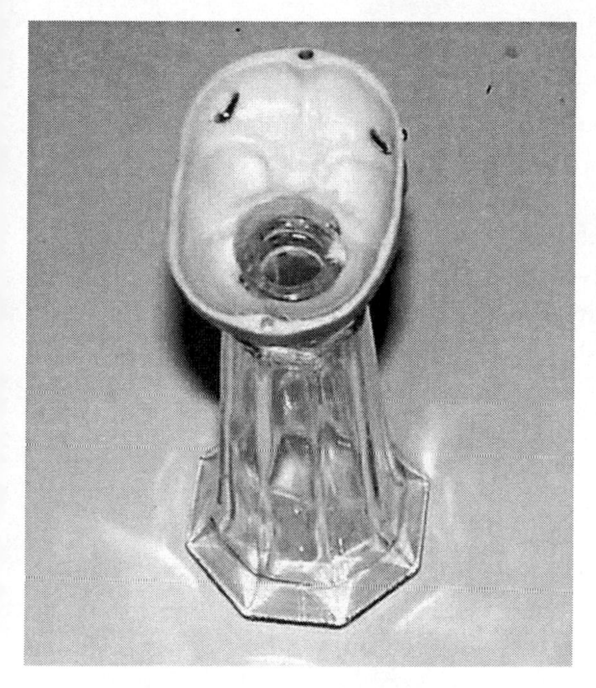

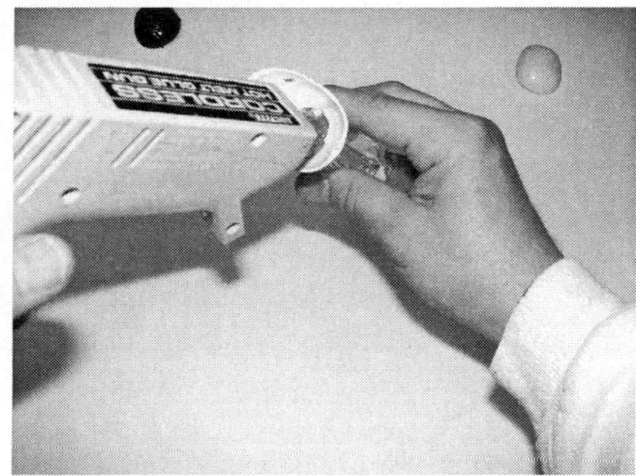

Left: **Firmly and carefully screw your skulls onto your shakers.** ***Above:*** **You may find it a good idea to glue your skull to the shaker.**

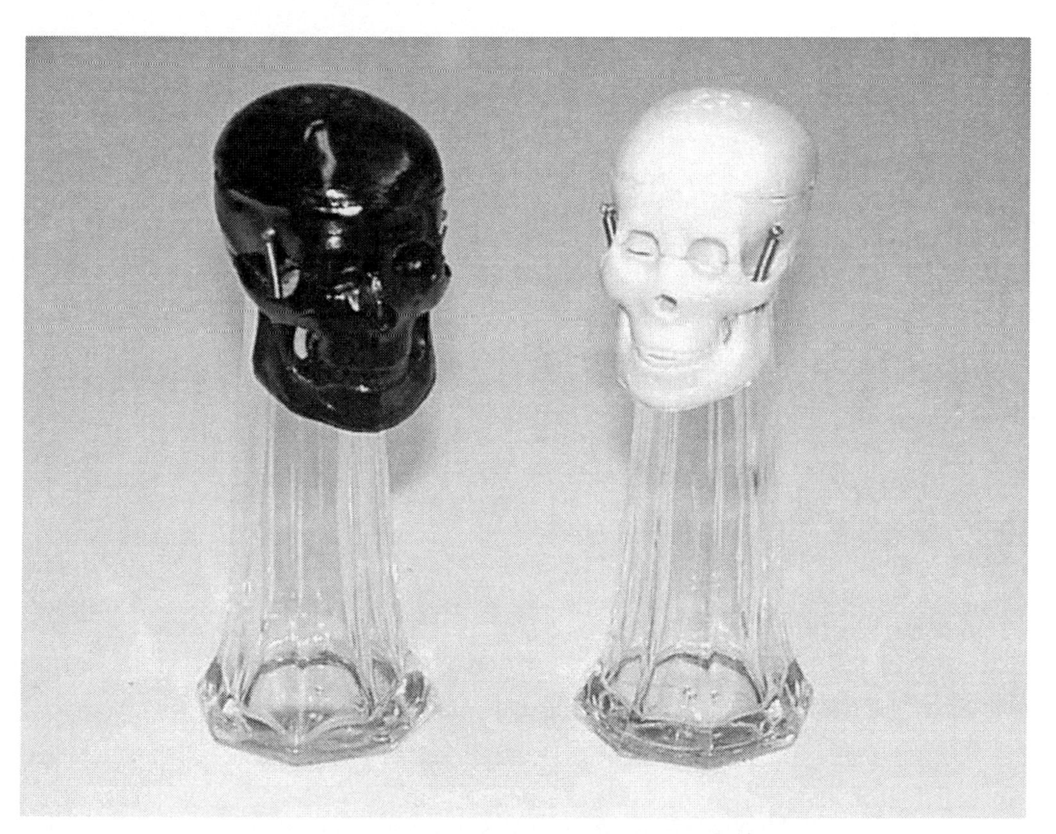

A completed set of salt and pepper shakers.

good fit when grinding the holes in your skulls. I like to use hot melt glue for this because it sets up very quickly. You can use a silicone adhesive or any glue which will bond plastic to glass. **Caution: Hot melt glue and the glue gun are hot! Be very careful not to burn yourself!**

Step Seven: Once your glue has set, fill your bonehead shakers with salt and pepper, replace the tops of the skulls and you are all set.

Warning: **The plastics and adhesives used for this project may not be food grade, and should not be used for food! These are intended as props only. The salt and pepper from these shakers should never be used on food!**

SKULL FLOWERS

For this project you will need:

- ✓ A small bunch of artificial flowers
- ✓ One flower pot
- ✓ One piece of floral foam
- ✓ Several small skulls
- ✓ A handful of floral moss
- ✓ Spray paint (optional)
- ✓ Hot melt glue gun, with glue

These are the materials you will need to create a set of skull flowers.

Step One: Select the artificial flowers you wish to use. This really should not be difficult, as most any flowers will do (of course, it still took me over an hour). There are a few things, however, you should look for that will make your finished project just a little nicer. Make sure the flowers are about the same size as the skulls you plan to use. This will give you a more realistic look when you are done. You will also need to be certain the stems will be strong enough to support your skulls, which tend to be much heavier than flowers. In addition, it will help if you select flowers with green leaves at the very bottom of the flower. Ideally, these should be large enough to extend past the ends of your skulls. Finally, if you choose flowers which allow the leaves to be repositioned along the stems, it will give you more flexibility to control the overall look of your finished plant.

Step Two: If the flowers you have selected are one tight bunch, as the ones I selected were, you will find it best to cut the several small stems loose. This will make them easier to work with and give you much more flexibility in the final arrangement. Of course, the final choice is yours. Experiment with designs until you get the perfect plant for you.

If the flowers you have selected are one tight bunch as the ones I selected were, you will find it best to cut the several small stems loose.

Step Three: Now for the fun part: rip those pretty colored flowers off their stems. On some flowers, this will still leave the green leaves just below the flower firmly in place, and on others they will come off with the flowers and will need to be separated from them.

Step Four: If the green leaves from just below the flowers came off the stem while removing the flowers, slide them back over the stem.

Step Five: Prepare the

skull for placement. There are a number of skulls you can use; the ones I selected were the Tiny Tim skulls from The Anatomical Chart Company. If you have chosen a skull with a removable top, remove the top at this time.

Step Six: Again what you do at this point will depend on the type of flower and skull you have selected.

If you have chosen a flower where the green leaves below the flower remained firmly attached to the stem, simply apply a generous amount of hot melt glue to these leaves and position the skull on the stem as you like it. **Note: When working with hot melt glue, it is very hot, and can cause a nasty burn. It will remain hot for some time, so be careful!** Hold the skull in place and allow the glue to cool a minute or two before going on to the next step.

If the leaves below the flower came off with the flower, you will need to make sure your skull has a small hole in the bottom. If the skulls you selected do not have holes already in them, you will need to grind or file a small hole in the center of the bottom of your skull just large enough for your stem to pass through. Make sure you have placed the green leaves from beneath the flowers back on the stem. Place a generous amount of hot melt glue in and around the hole and position the skull on the stem, as you would like it. Be sure the

Rip those pretty colored flowers off their stems.

If you have chosen a skull with a removable top, remove the top.

stem extends well into the skull, but not so far as to prevent the top from being replaced. **Note: When working with hot melt glue, it is very hot, and can cause a nasty burn. It will remain hot for some time, so be careful!** Hold the skull in place and allow the glue to cool a minute or two before going on to the next step.

Step Seven: If your flowers were the type where the green leaves below the flowers remained firmly attached to the stem, skip to step nine. If you inserted the stem through a hole in the bottom of the skull, you will need to glue it from the inside. After your first gluing has set, turn the flower so that the skull is right side up. You can now apply additional glue to the inside of the skull to hold it securely in place. **Note: When working with hot melt glue, it is very hot, and can cause a nasty burn. It will remain hot for some time, so be careful!** Hold the skull in place and allow the glue to cool a minute or two before going on to the next step.

Step Eight: Place the top back on your skull. Slide the leaves you removed from the bottom of your flowers and position them on the bottom of the skull. You may want to take a few seconds to try different positions of the leaves to get the best look. Once you have decided where you want your leaves, add a small dab of glue and secure the leaves to the skull. **Note: When working with hot melt glue, it is very hot, and can cause a nasty burn. It will remain hot for some time, so be careful!** Hold the leaves in place and allow the glue to cool a minute or two before going on to the next step.

Step Nine: This step is optional, but I feel it adds a lot to the finished prop.

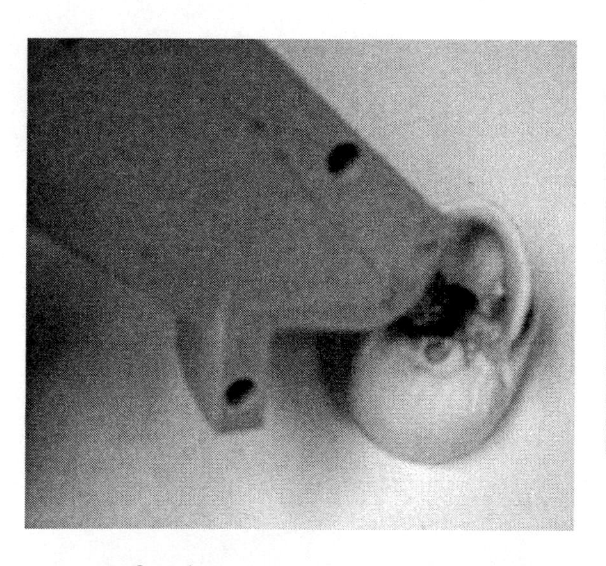

Left: **Place a generous amount of hot melt glue in and around the hole.** ***Right:*** **If you inserted the stem through a hole in the bottom of the skull, you will need to glue it from the inside.**

Above: **Slide the leaves you removed from the bottom of your flowers and position them on the bottom of the skull.** ***Right:*** **With a sharp knife, cut a piece of floral foam to the rough size and shape of your pot; you will want to leave the foam just a little oversized so that it will be a tight fit in the pot.**

Above: **Add some moss on top of the floral foam.** ***Right:*** **Here is a picture of my first skull flower plant; I hope yours looks better!**

You may want to spray paint your flowerpot black for a more haunted look. Or, if you prefer, use some other color. After all, it is your prop.

Step Ten: With a sharp knife, cut a piece of floral foam to the rough size and shape of your pot. You will want to leave the foam just a little oversized so that it will be a tight fit in the pot. It is also a good idea to cut the foam so that it is about one inch below the rim of the pot. Place the foam in your pot and press firmly to the bottom.

Step Eleven: Add some moss on top of the floral foam.

Step Twelve: Insert your skull flowers in the foam. Simply push the stem into the foam; they should slide in easily and stay firmly in place.

By now, I hope, you are thinking of all the modifications you can make on the basic skull flower design. To name a few: You can change the types of stems you use, change the skull type, change the arrangement, mix different types of flowers, change the moss type, change the flowerpot (use a large skull perhaps) or

Left: **Skull flowers using different stems.** ***Right:*** **Skull flowers using glow-in-the-dark skulls (photographed under black light).**

try painting the small skulls you use. On the previous page are pictures of a few combinations I have tried.

One last little tip: skull flowers are a great way to deaden up an otherwise lively flower arrangement. Just add a few skull flowers into a pot with a live plant or a vase with cut flowers.

BONEHEAD VASE AND CANDY DISH

For this project you will need:

- ✓ One three-piece skull
- ✓ A small Phillips screwdriver
- ✓ Wire cutters
- ✓ Hot melt glue gun, with glue
- ✓ Your choice of paints (optional)

Step One: Select the skull you will use. I selected a fourth-quality, three-piece skull from The Anatomical Chart Company. In fact, I selected the absolute worse skull I had, as I planned to paint my finished product and the color mismatch would not matter. **Note: It is extremely rare to receive a skull in such poor condition. I was just lucky I guess.**

Step Two: Remove the top of your skull; this will become your candy dish. Using your small Phillips screwdriver, remove the hooks from the lid and the pins from the top of your skull.

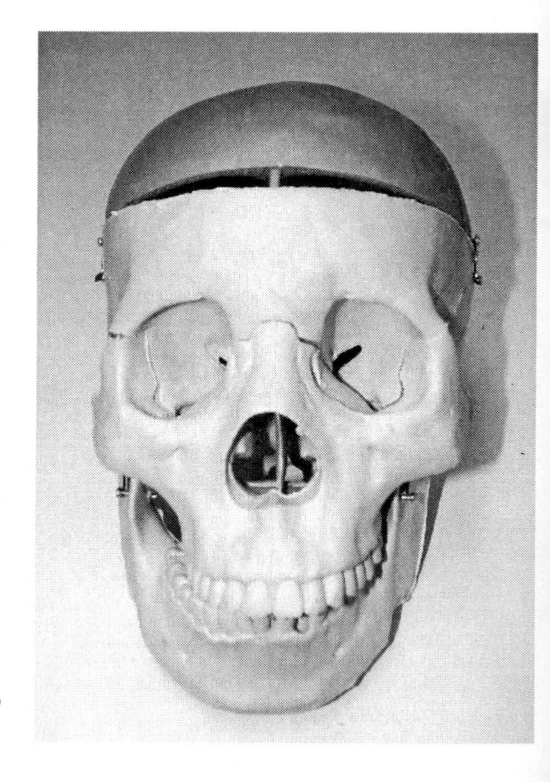

These are the materials you will need to create a bonehead vase and candy dish.

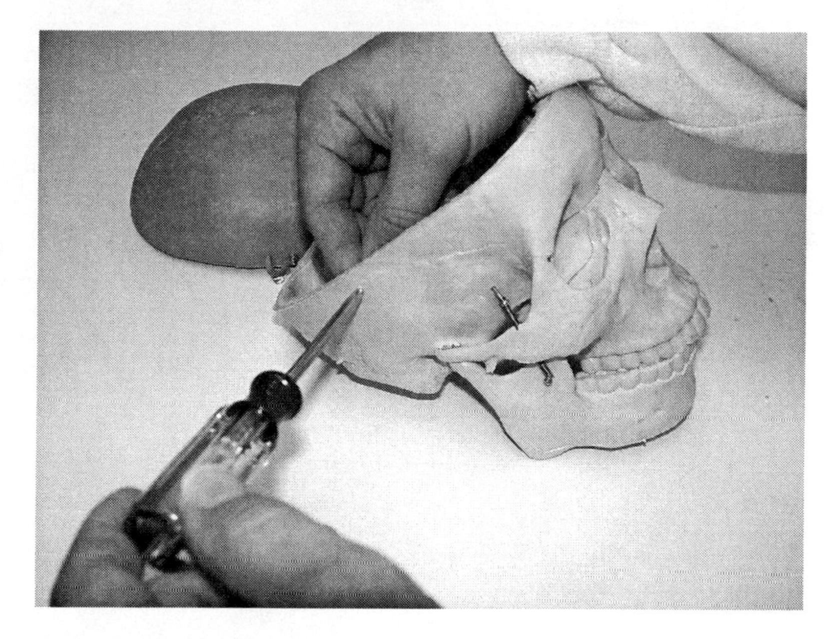

Remove the hooks from the lid and the pins from the top of your skull.

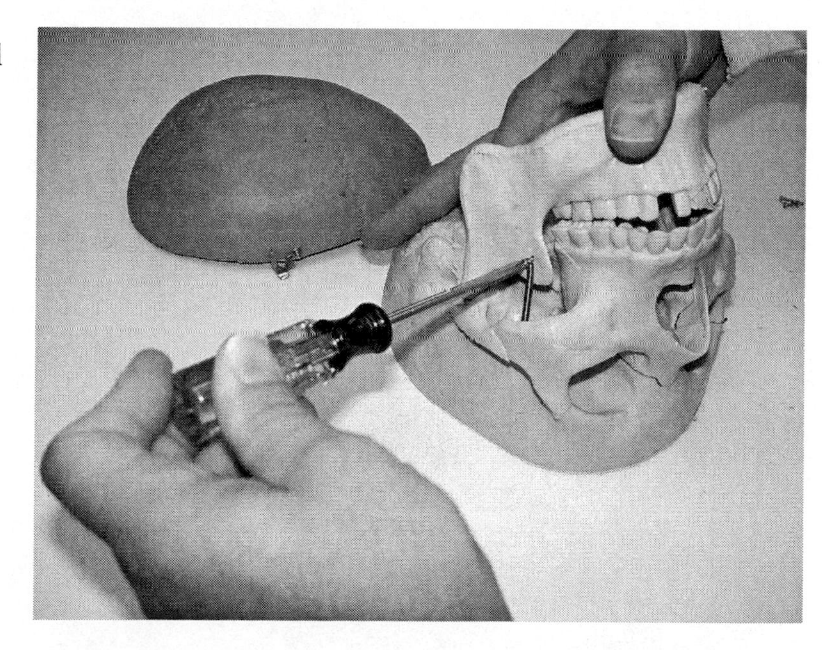

Remove the screws and springs which hold the jaw to the skull.

Step Three: Remove the screws and springs which hold the jaw to the skull. I like to save all the hardware I remove in case I ever need it to repair another skull.

Step Four: Remove the jaw from your skull. You will later use this as a support for your vase.

Step Five: Use the jaw you just removed as a support for your vase by placing it under your skull with the teeth facing rearward. This will constitute your vase. If you like you may use hot melt glue to attach the jaw to the bottom of the skull. If you prefer not to glue the jaw in place, you can just set the skull on the jaw. It will remain quite stable unless you decide to move the vase.

Your vase is now ready to be painted, if you wish, or you can now fill it with whatever you like. I chose to paint mine as described in the section Aged Skull and filled it with skull flowers. You may, of course, also use the vase as a second candy dish.

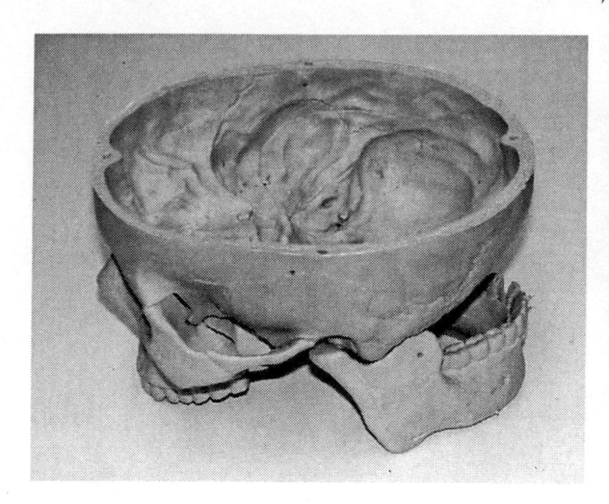

Left: **Use the jaw you just removed as a support for your vase, by placing it under your skull with the teeth facing rearward.** ***Right:*** **Use your wire cutters to trim the pegs off the top of the skull.**

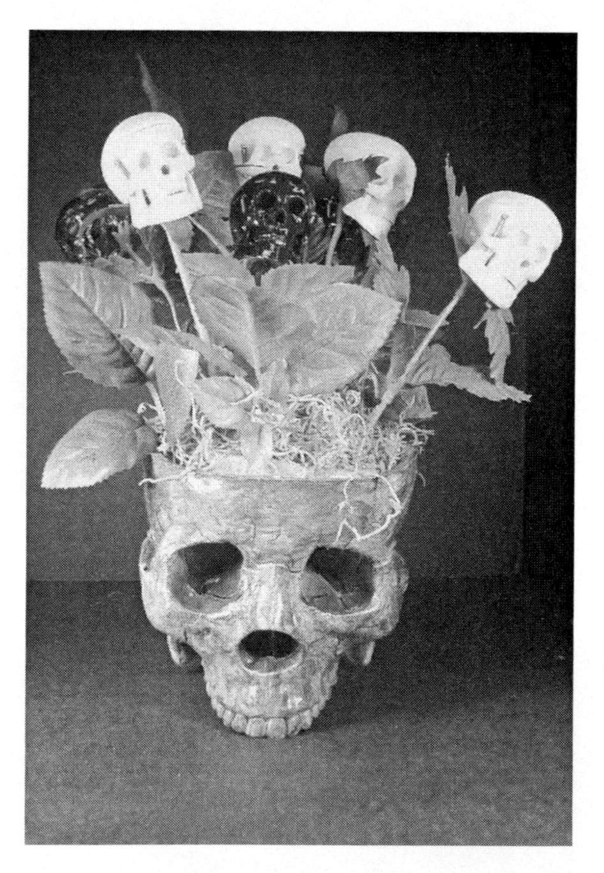

Left: **A front view of the finished project used as a vase for skull flowers.** ***Right:*** **A side view of the finished project used as a vase for skull flowers.**

Step Six: Use your wire cutters to trim the pegs off the top of the skull.

You now have a candy dish, ready to paint if you like or to use as is. I chose to paint mine as described in the section Aged Skull.

***Warning*: The plastic in the skulls is not food grade, so you should use only wrapped candy in your candy dish.**

GLOWING BRAIN

For this project you will need:

- ✓ One brain-shaped gelatin mold
- ✓ One small paintbrush
- ✓ Some polyester or cotton batting
- ✓ Liquid latex
- ✓ Fabric whitener
- ✓ Rubber gloves
- ✓ Some tap water

These are the materials you will need to create a glowing brain.

Note: This project will take several days to complete, due to the long drying time for the many layers of latex.

Step One: Working outside, or in a well-ventilated area, stir the fabric whitener into the liquid latex; use about one-half envelope (one-half ounce) to one quart of latex. Mix thoroughly, to evenly distribute the whitener throughout the latex. This will make your brain black light reactive; you may of course skip this step if you do not wish your brain to glow under black light. The whitener I used was Rit Whitener & Brightener. There may be others that will work; however, this is the only one I have tried and therefore the only one I know will work. The liquid latex I used was Professional Grade Mold Latex from Polyproducts Corporation. I prefer the mold latex, as it is much thicker than other liquid latexes, meaning you get more of the solid latex (which is, after all, what you are paying for).

Step Two: Using the brush, apply a layer of liquid latex to the inside of the gelatin mold. While applying you will find it better to dab the latex on rather than brush it; this will give you better coverage. Do not worry if your first coat is very uneven or even leaves a few small bare spots. You will be adding several additional layers to cover these. Set your coated mold aside to dry. How long this will take will depend on the thickness of your layer. It could vary from a few hours to a few days.

When you have finished your first layer, you must now do something to protect your brush so that you can use it again for additional layers. You have three options: The first is to thoroughly wash the brush in running water to remove all the leftover latex (this is the best option if you plan to wait several days before your next layer). The next is to wrap the brush tightly in plastic wrap to keep it from drying out (this is good if you plan to leave the brush no longer than 24 hours before using it again). The last option is to place the brush in a container of water deep enough to cover any area which was exposed to the latex (this method is good for many days, as long as you make sure to keep the container filled with water). If you choose to keep your brush in water, remember to wipe it dry before using it again. You do not want water thinning the latex, making it harder to apply.

Using the brush, apply a layer of liquid latex to the inside of the gelatin mold.

Step Three: Repeat step two until you have a latex thickness of about 1⁄16".

Step Four: Once you have your mold coated with latex, it is time to add the batting. Start by dabbing a small amount of liquid latex into the mold; this will help hold the

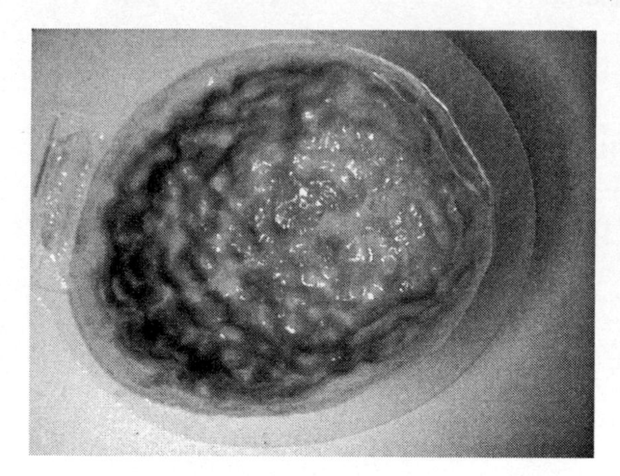

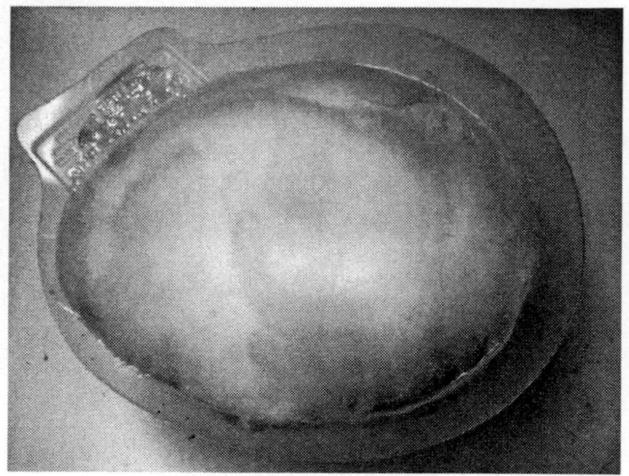

***Left:* Repeat step two until you have a latex thickness of about 1⁄16". *Right:* Then take a generous amount of batting and place it into the mold.**

batting in place. Then take a generous amount of batting and place it into the mold. Press the batting down firmly, and keep adding tightly packed batting until the inside of the mold is slightly overfilled.

Step Five: Now, it is time to seal your brain. If you are using a thin, watery latex, proceed to step six. If you are using a thicker latex, such as mold latex, you will need to thin it in order to apply it over the batting. If you use a very thick latex for this, the batting will just stick to the brush and pull out of the mold. You will want to make your mixture thin and watery. For the mold latex, I used a mixture of about one part latex to one part of tap water. Combine the latex and water in a small container and mix well. You will need about one cup of mixture.

Step Six: Apply the latex mixture over the batting. Load the brush heavily

***Left:* Combine the latex and water in a small container, and mix well. *Right:* Apply the latex mixture over the batting.**

with the mixture and dab to the top of the batting. Continue to add mixture until the batting is saturated and begins to pack down.

Step Seven: Again saturate the brush with your latex and water mixture and pass it between the batting and the set latex in the bottom of the mold. This will make sure you have a good seal between the top and bottom of your brain. Keep adding the mixture to the brush and make as many passes as needed to completely seal the edge.

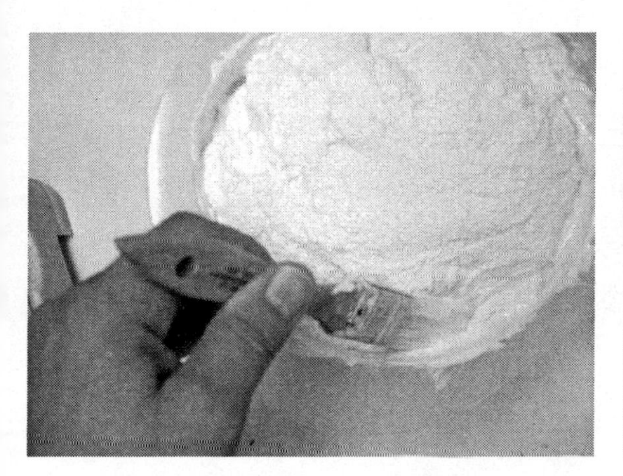

Left: **Saturate the brush with your latex-water mixture and pass it between the batting and the set latex in the bottom of the mold.** ***Right:*** **Working with a brush wet with the latex and water solution, work the coated batting from the center toward the edges until it is as flat as possible.**

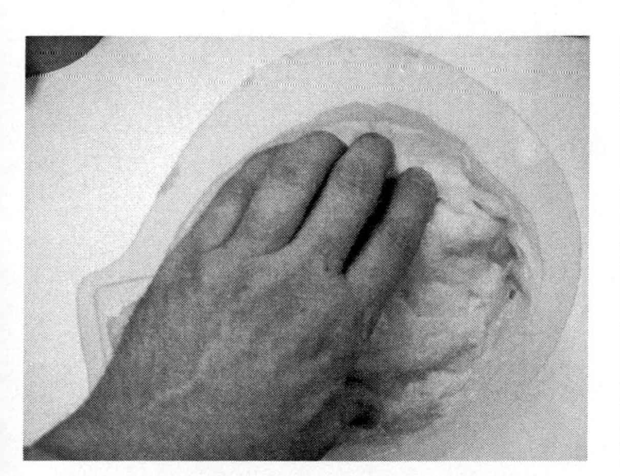

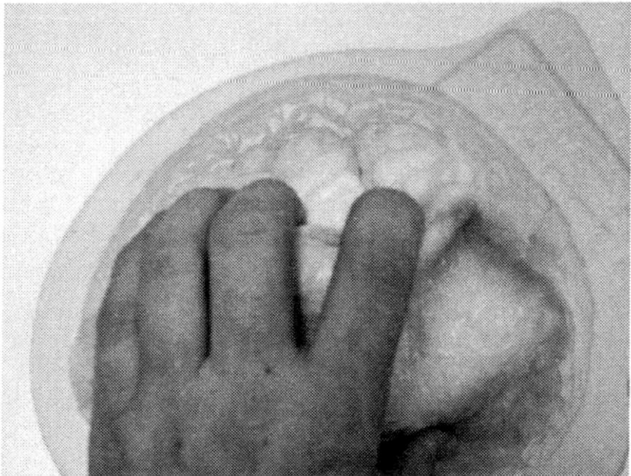

Left: **Start by grasping the latex at the edge where it meets the mold and pull toward the center of the mold until the brain pulls away from the mold about one inch down.** ***Right:*** **Grab the brain and pull toward the center until it pulls away from the mold to a depth of about three inches, almost to the bottom.**

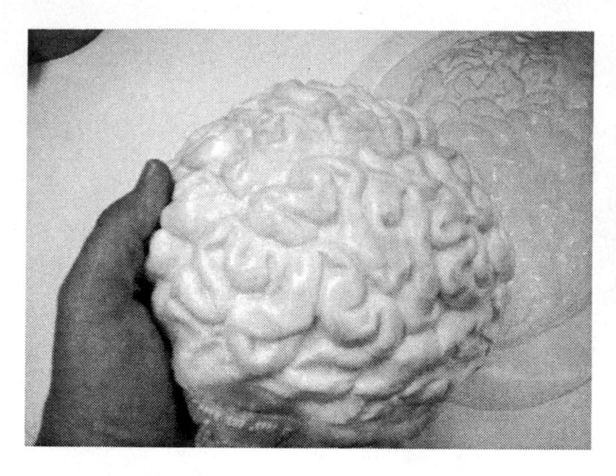

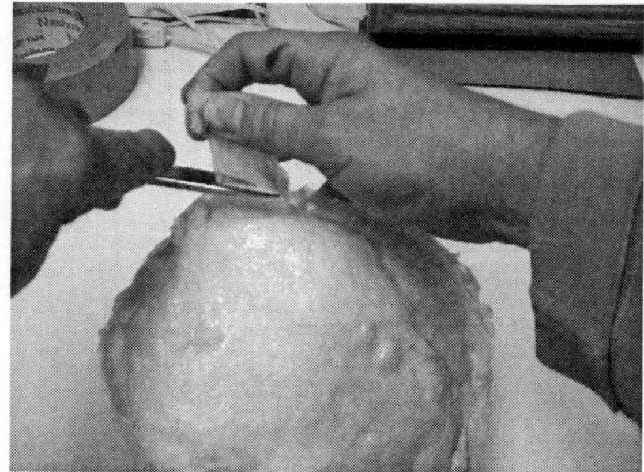

Left: **Pull your brain completely from the mold.** ***Right:*** **Trim away any extra latex.**

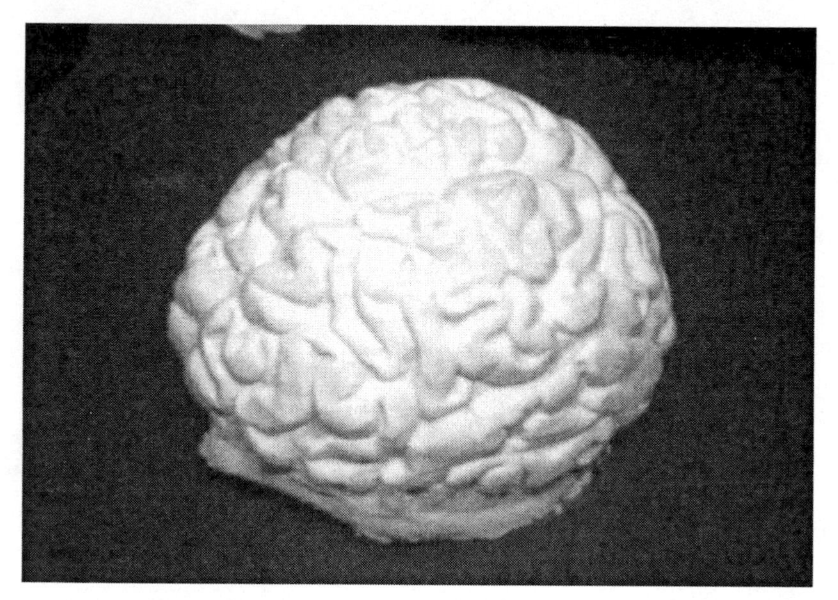

A finished glowing brain shown under black light.

Step Eight: Working with a brush wet with the latex and water solution, work the coated batting from the center toward the edges until it is as flat as possible. Once done, set the mold aside overnight to dry.

Step Nine: Add additional layers of undiluted latex until you have a layer about 1⁄16" thick. Again, apply it in thin layers and allow one layer to dry before adding the next.

Step Ten: Once your brain is thoroughly dried, it is time to unmold it. Start by grasping the latex at the edge where it meets the mold and pull toward the center of the mold until the brain pulls away from the mold about one inch down. Move over a few inches and repeat until you have worked your way all the way around the brain.

Next, start over. Grab the brain and pull toward the center until it pulls away from the mold to a depth of about three inches, almost to the bottom. Again, work your way around the brain.

Now you are ready to pull your brain completely from the mold.

Step Eleven: Take a pair of scissors and trim away any extra latex.

And your brain is finished. On the previous page is what it will look like under black light.

PARTIALLY EATEN HAND

These are the materials you will need to create a partially eaten hand.

For this project you will need:

- ✓ One hand-shaped gelatin mold
- ✓ Two or three small paintbrushes
- ✓ Some polyester or cotton batting
- ✓ Liquid latex
- ✓ One skeleton hand (left or right depending on whether your mold is left or right handed)
- ✓ One set of fake fingernails
- ✓ Silicone adhesive
- ✓ Flesh tone acrylic paint

- ✓ Blood red acrylic paint
- ✓ Crackle paint (optional)
- ✓ Rubber gloves
- ✓ Some tap water
- ✓ A pair of wire cutters
- ✓ A pair of long-nose pliers
- ✓ A pair of sharp scissors
- ✓ Safety glasses
- ✓ A very small sharp knife

Note: This project will take several weeks to complete, due to the long drying time for the many layers of latex.

Step One: Using the brush, apply a layer of liquid latex to the inside of the gelatin mold. While applying, you will find it better to dab the latex on rather than brushing it on. This will give you better coverage. Remember, you are making a partially eaten hand, so this is the point at which you must decide what part of your hand you would like to have eaten. On my hand, I decided to do the little finger and the ring finger, next to it. To achieve the effect just leave some of the mold uncoated with latex; when you add the bones, it will appear as if the hand has been eaten down to the bone. Do not worry if your first coat is very uneven, or even has a few small bare spots; you will be adding several additional layers to cover these. Set your coated mold aside to dry. How long this will take will depend on the thickness of your layer. It could vary from a few hours to a few days.

When you have finished your first layer, you must now do something to protect your brush so that you can use it again for additional layers. You have three options. The first is to thoroughly wash the brush in running water to remove all the leftover latex (this is best if you plan to wait several days before your next layer). The next is to wrap the brush tightly in plastic wrap to keep it from drying out (this is good if you plan to leave the brush no longer than 24 hours before using it again). The last option is to place the brush in a container of water deep enough to cover any area which was exposed to the latex (this method is good for many days, as long as you make sure to keep the container filled with water). If you choose to keep your brush in water, remember to wipe it dry before using it again. You do not want water thinning the latex, making it harder to apply.

You should try to find the most detailed mold you can, as these details will be transferred to your finished hand. The mold I used came from The Anatomical Chart Company. It is a very detailed, high quality mold, with such fine details as fingerprints. After all, the more detail, the more realistic the finished hand will look. The liquid latex used was mold latex from the Polyproducts Corporation. It is a very thick, heavy latex and gives excellent coverage, compared to some very thin and watery liquid latex solutions.

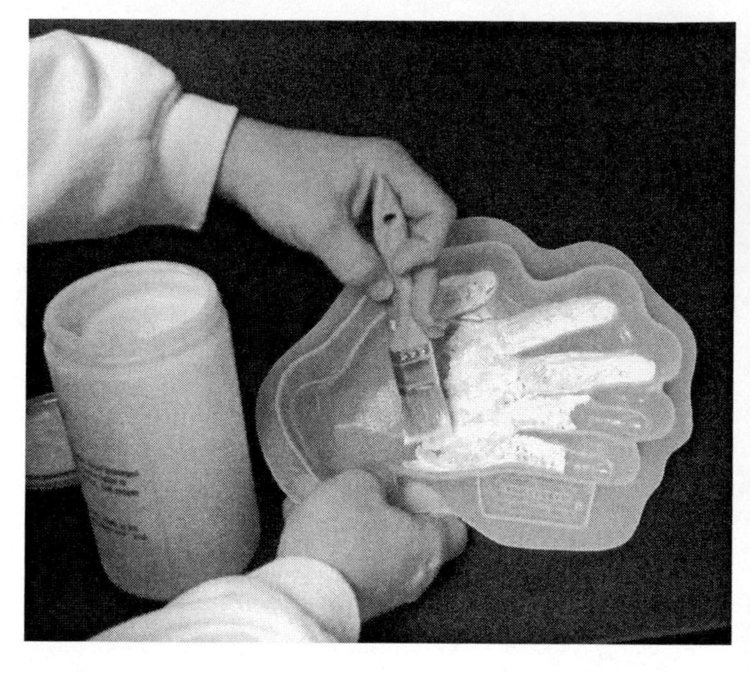

Apply a layer of liquid latex to the inside of the gelatin mold.

Step Two: Repeat step one until you have a latex thickness of about 1/16".

Step Three: Take your long-nose pliers and partially unroll the wire loops at the ends of the fingers of the skeleton hand. You need to straighten the loops at the ends of the fingers only enough to add about a tenth of an inch to the length of the wire. This will make it easier to move the individual bones around when you add the hand to the mold. Do not completely straighten the loops.

Step Four: Cut the loop off one end of the wire which runs through the knuckle area of the fingers, joining them together. It is a good idea to cover this

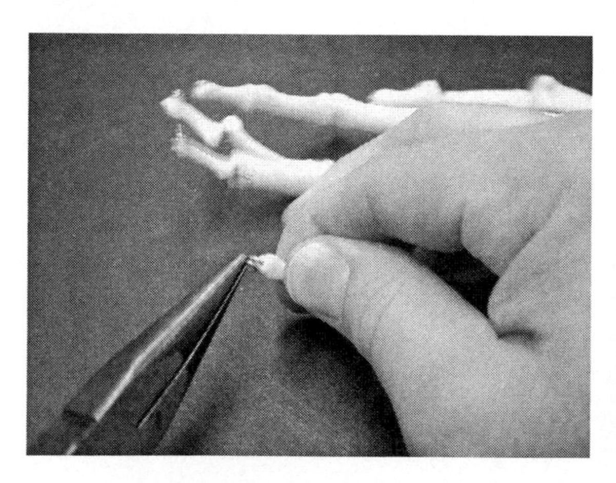

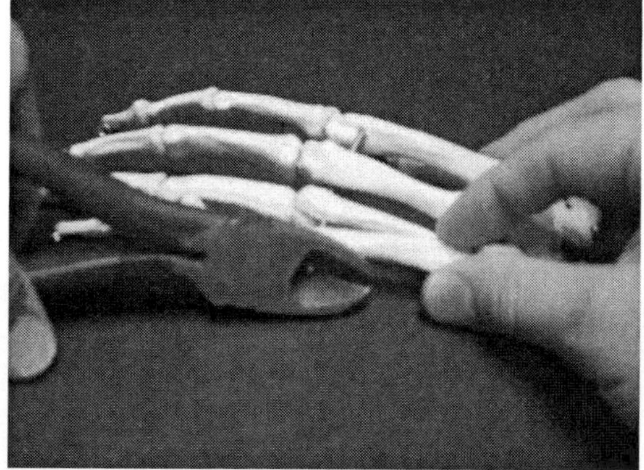

Left: **Partially unroll the wire loops at the ends of the fingers of the skeleton hand.** ***Right:*** **Cut the loop off one end of the wire, which runs through the knuckle area of the fingers, joining them together.**

operation with a towel before cutting, so that the clipping does not fly off and hit you or someone else. Of course, everyone in the room should be wearing safety goggles.

Step Five: Remove the wire between the fingers. This will allow you to spread the fingers to fit the mold.

Step Six: Apply a thin layer of liquid latex to the dry latex in the mold, and on both sides of the skeleton hand. Put a thin layer of batting into the mold and add the skeleton hand to the mold, spreading the skeletal fingers out so that they are positioned in the center of the fingers of the mold.

Step Seven: Add a layer of batting on top of the hand. You will want to have the batting a little higher than the fingers of the mold, as it will compact when you add latex over it.

Step Eight: Now, it is time to seal your hand. If you are using a thin, watery latex, proceed to step nine. If you are using a thicker latex, such as mold latex, you will need to thin it in order to apply it over the batting. If you use a very thick latex for this, the batting will just stick to the brush and pull out of the mold. You will want to make your mixture thin and watery. For the mold latex, I used a mixture of about one part latex to one part of tap water. Combine the latex and water in a small container, and mix well. You will need about one cup of mixture.

Step Nine: Apply the latex mixture over the batting, load the brush heavily with the mixture and dab onto the top of the batting. Continue to add the mixture until the batting is saturated and begins to pack down.

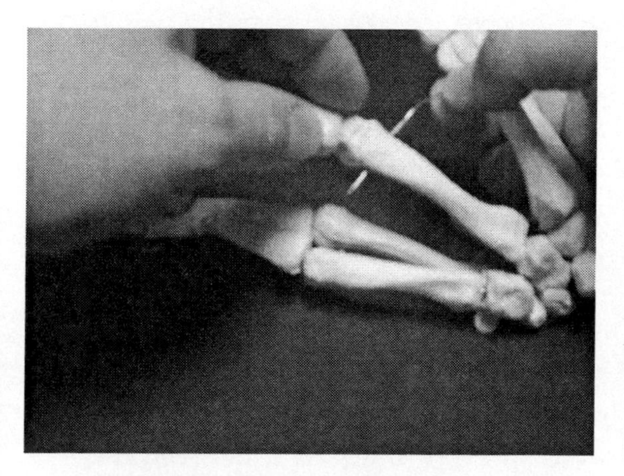

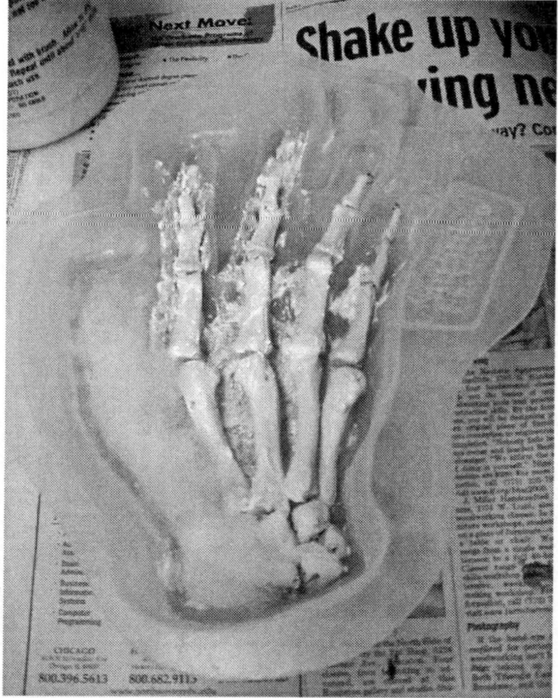

Left: **Remove the wire between the fingers.** ***Right:*** **Add the skeleton hand to the mold.**

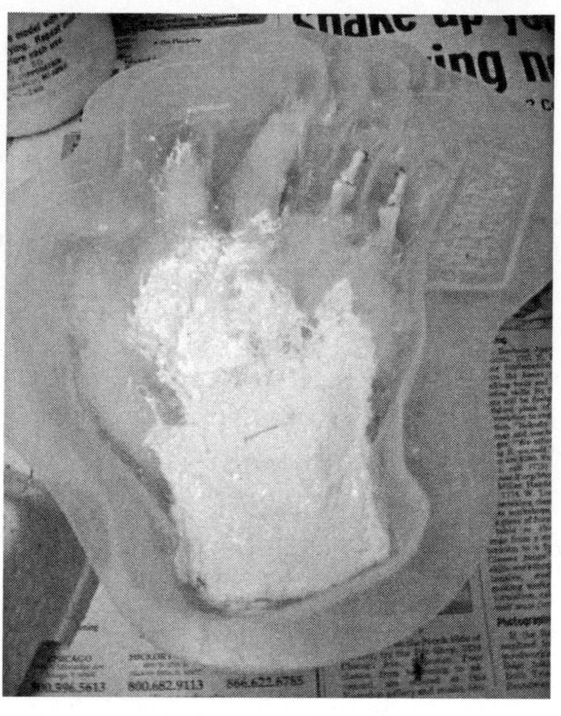

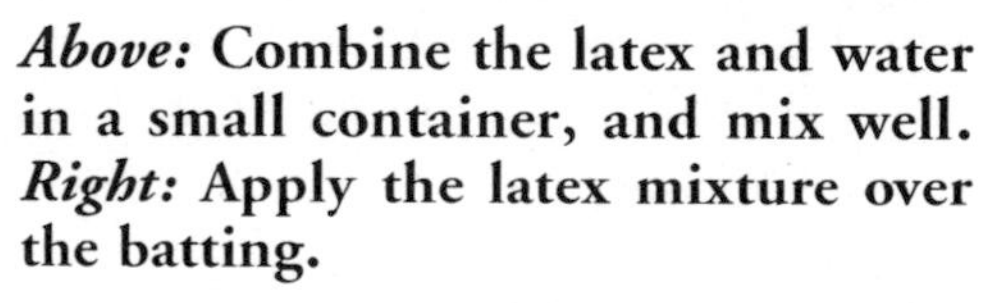

Above: **Combine the latex and water in a small container, and mix well.** ***Right:*** **Apply the latex mixture over the batting.**

Step Ten: Again, saturate the brush with your latex and water mixture and pass it between the batting and the set latex in the bottom of the mold. This will make sure you have a good seal between the top and bottom of the hand. Keep

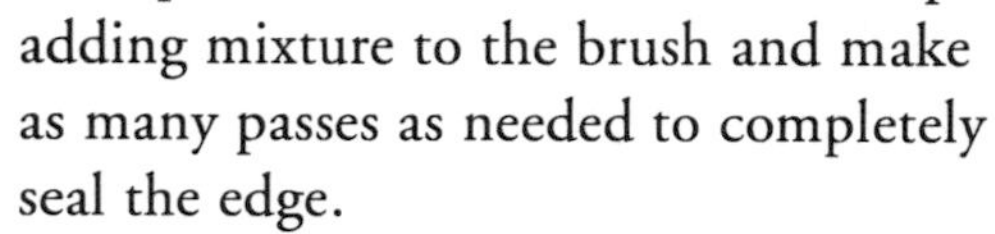

adding mixture to the brush and make as many passes as needed to completely seal the edge.

Step Eleven: Working with a brush wet with the latex and water solution, work the coated batting from the center toward the edges until it is as flat as possible. Once done, set the mold aside overnight to dry.

Step Twelve: Add additional layers of undiluted liquid latex until you have a layer about 1/16" thick. Again, apply in thin layers and allow one layer to dry before adding the next.

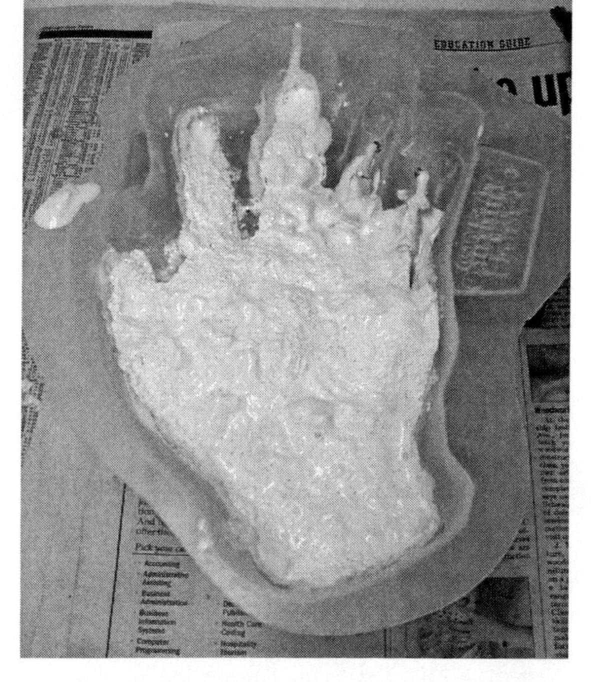

Saturate the brush with your latex and water mixture and pass it between the batting and the set latex in the bottom of the mold.

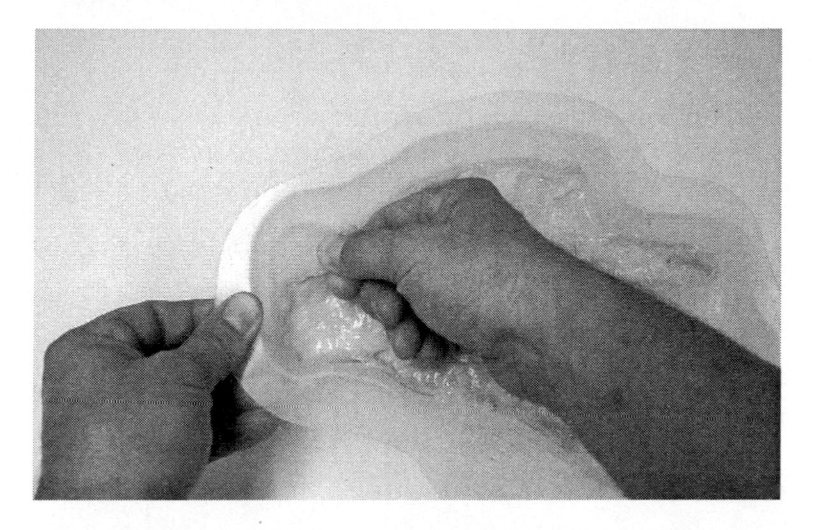

Grasp the hand at the wrist area and pull towards the center of the mold.

Step Thirteen: Once your last layer of latex has completely dried, grasp the hand at the wrist area and pull toward the center of the mold. Once the cured latex begins to separate from the side of the mold, carefully pull the hand up and out.

Once your hand is free of the mold, you will probably notice that the latex that was in contact with the mold is quite white compared to the other dried latex. This is because it has not been in contact with air, and has therefore not set completely. Allow your hand to set overnight and it should all be a uniform color and ready for you to continue.

Step Fourteen: Once your hand has fully cured, take a pair of sharp scissors and trim away any extra latex that does not belong on the finished hand.

Step Fifteen: At this point, you must decide what you would like your finished hand to look like. You can simply paint the ends of the cut-off and eaten sections of your hand (wrist and fingers) blood red. If you want a more battered look, you can use the optional crackle paint.

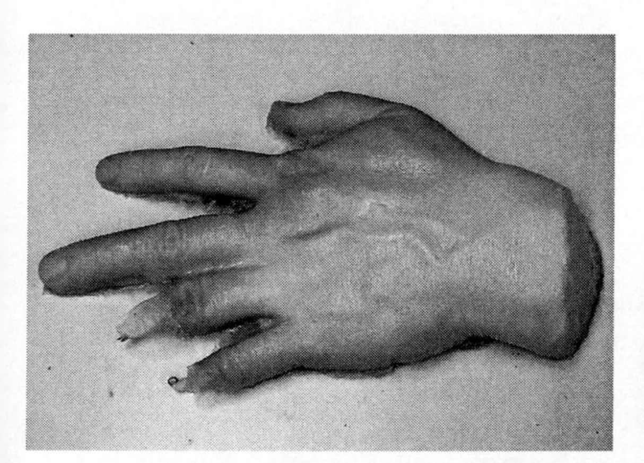

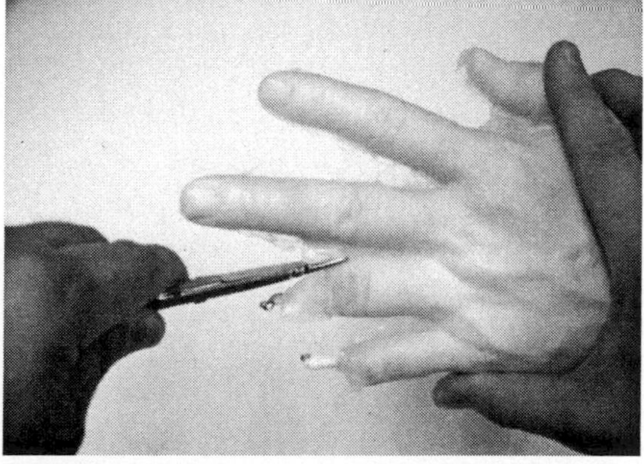

Left: The unmolded hand may look very white where it was in contact with the mold. This means it is not yet fully cured. _Right:_ Once the hand is fully cured, trim away any extra latex that does not belong on the finished hand.

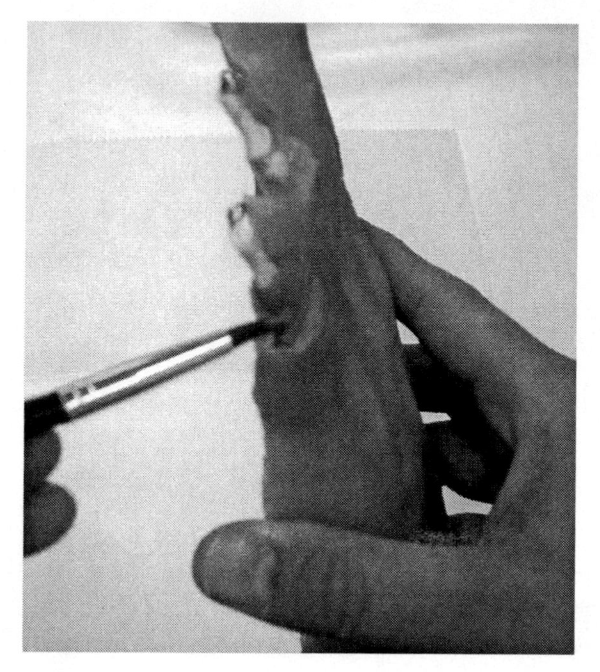

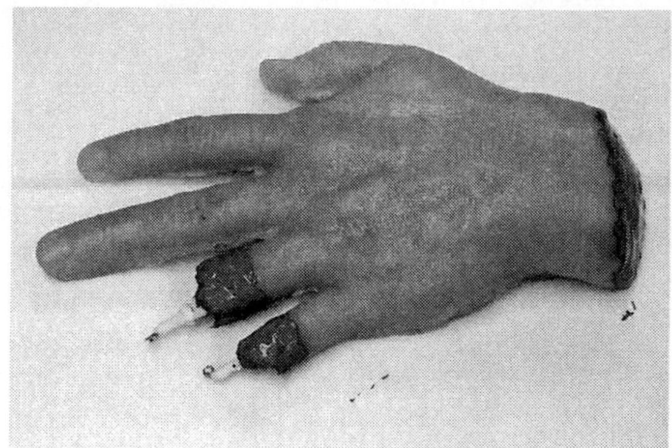

***Left:* You can simply paint the ends of the cut-off and eaten sections of your hand (wrist and fingers) blood red. If you want a more battered look, you can use the optional crackle paint. *Above:* If you plan to use crackle paint, extend the red further down the hand.**

The crackle paint that I used is available in most craft stores, in the same section where you would find the acrylic paints. It is used by first painting a base coat of one color, applying the crackle paint and then placing another color on top of that. After a few minutes, the topcoat of paint will split and crack in a random pattern, showing the color below. I like this look because it makes the hand look more mangled and abused.

If you decide to try the crackle effect, you will want to apply the blood red paint down an inch or so onto the hand. When you have finished painting, set your hand aside to dry. How long this takes will depend upon the paint you used, and how thick of a coat you applied. I suggest that you let the paint dry as long as the manufacturer suggests, and a little extra to be sure.

Step Sixteen: If you are not using the crackle paint, skip to step seventeen.

Apply the crackle paint over the sections of red paint where you would like the mangled look. Stop just short of the end of the red to avoid covering bare latex. Again, follow the manufacturer's directions for proper drying time. This paint usually requires that the flesh color be applied while it is still tacky. Check the directions on the paint you buy.

At this point, you may find it a good idea to hang your hand. This will allow you to paint all sections of the hand without smearing the paint. Simply tie a string or piece of wire through one of the finger loops, and tie off to any convenient overhead location.

Step Seventeen: Apply the flesh colored paint to the non-severed parts of the hand and over any crackle paint.

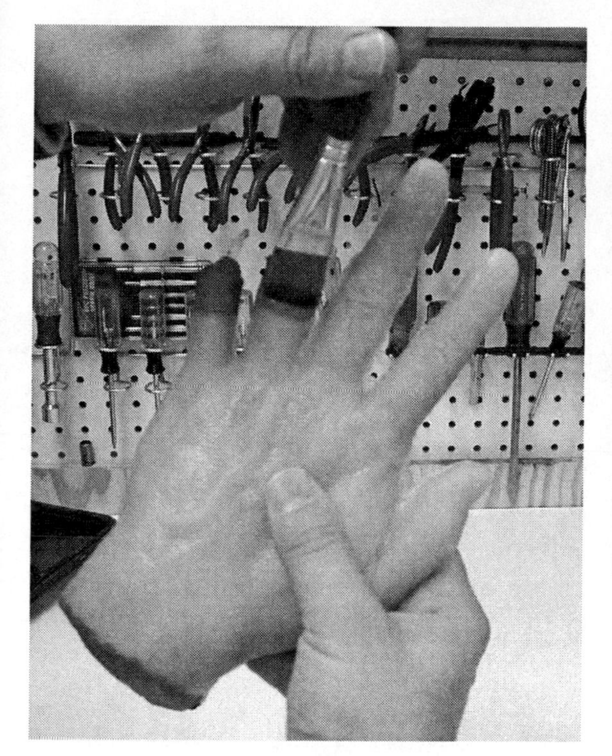

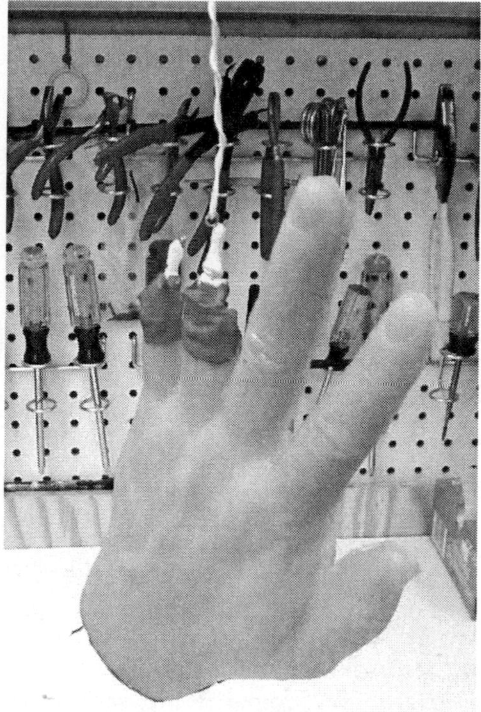

***Left:* Apply the crackle paint over the sections of red paint where you would like the mangled look; stop just short of the end of the red to avoid covering bare latex. *Right:* You may find it a good idea to hang your hand.**

You will find it best to brush in the direction of deeply grooved areas, like the knuckles, rather than against them. This will help avoid filling these low spots in and losing definition in the details.

When finished, set your hand aside to dry. If needed, apply a second coat. You will want to avoid adding too many additional layers as they will cause you to lose detail. When you have a finish that you are happy with, let it dry overnight. If your finish is a little uneven, remember this is a severed hand and you would expect some discoloration.

Step Eighteen: Separate your fake fingernails according to which finger they go onto.

Step Nineteen: One at a time place the nails over the appropriate fingernail section of the hand, then take your knife and carefully mark the back of nail by scoring the latex hand with your knife. You may skip this, and the next step, if you like. However, I do feel that making a cut for the nail to slide into adds to the realism. You will find that the latex is very hard to cut.

Step Twenty: Again, you may skip this step if you like and still have a very realistic hand. However, the perfectionist will find it worth the effort. With the blade parallel to the finger, **very** carefully cut back into the hand about $1/32$" along

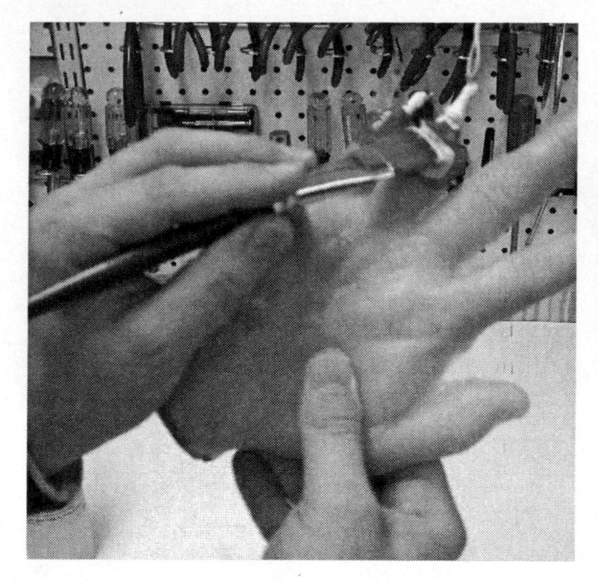

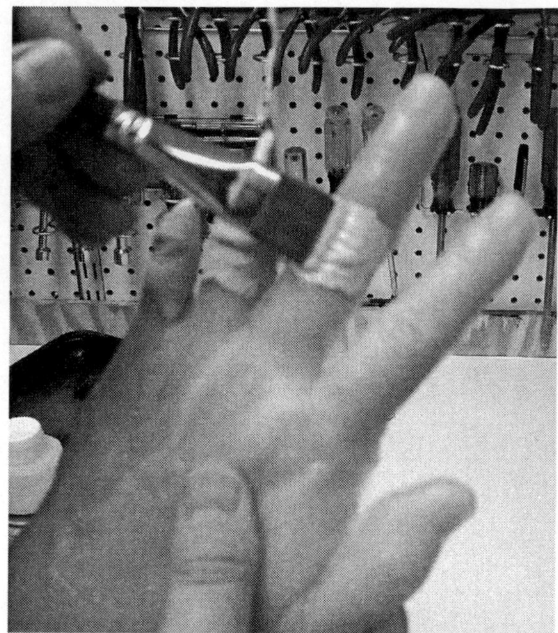

Left: **Apply the flesh colored paint to the non-severed parts of the hand and over any crackle paint.** ***Right:*** **You will find it best to brush in the direction of deeply grooved areas, like the knuckles, rather than against them.**

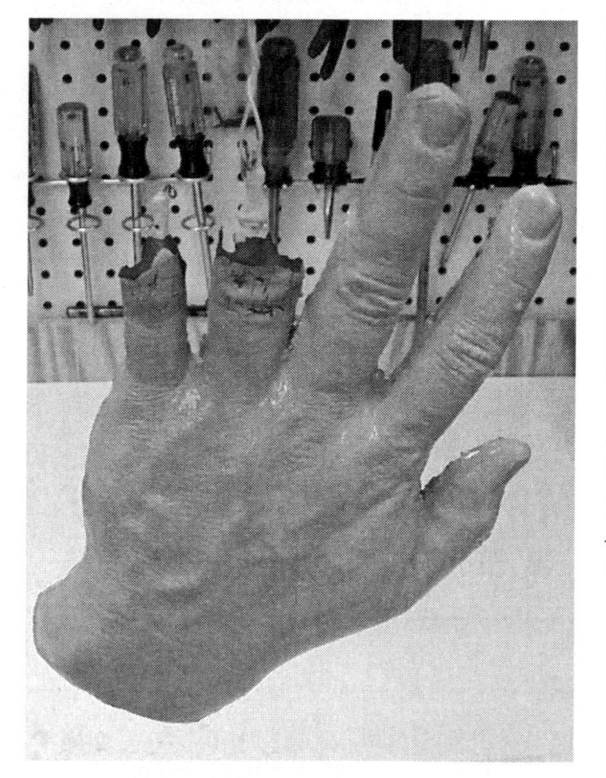

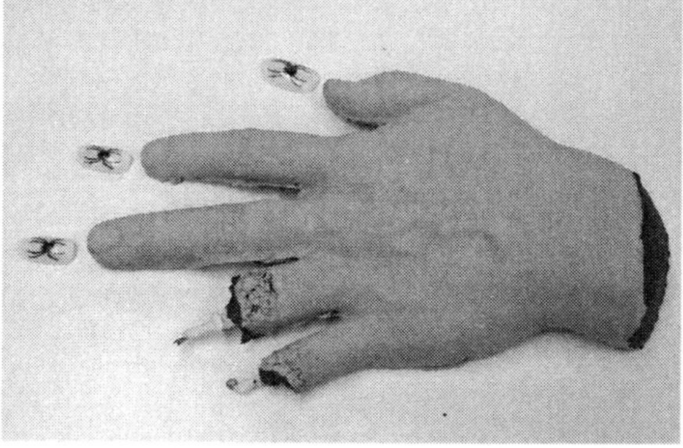

Left: **If your finish is a little uneven, remember this is a severed hand and you should expect some discoloration.** ***Above:*** **Separate your fake fingernails according to which finger they go onto.**

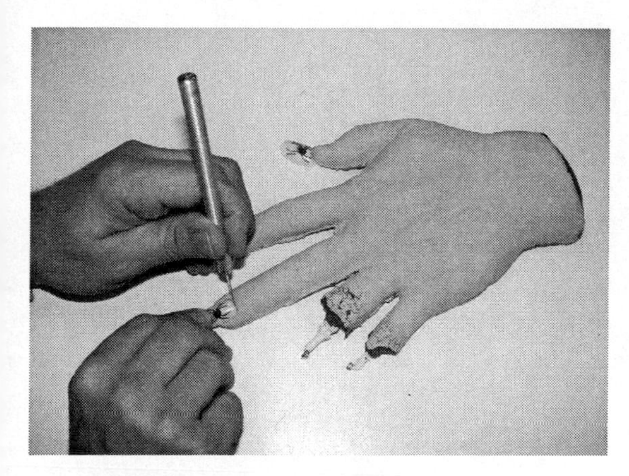

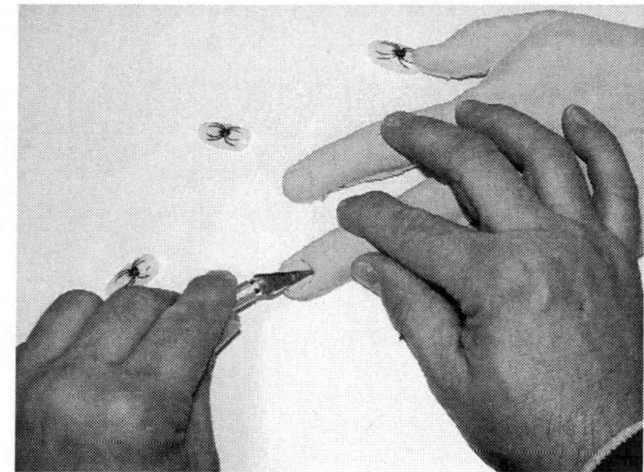

Left: **Carefully mark the back of the nail by scoring the latex hand with your knife. *Right:* Very carefully cut back into the hand about 1/32".**

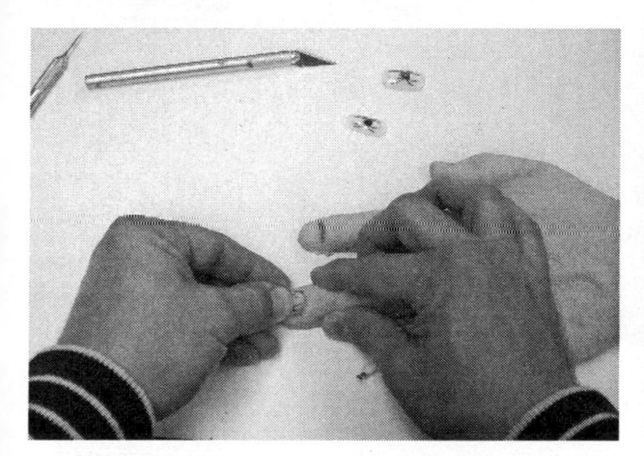

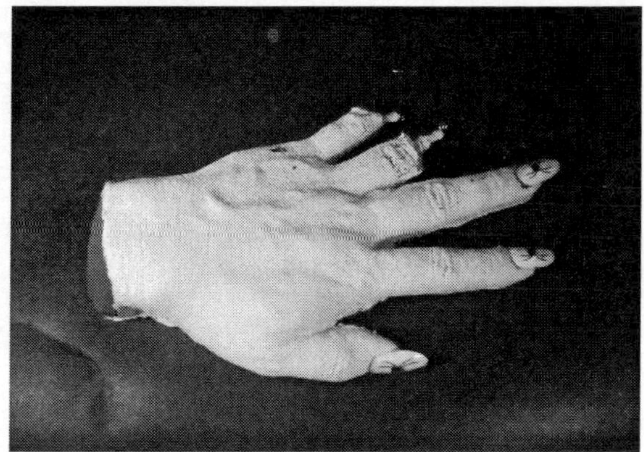

Left: **Take the nails one at a time and insert them into the slit you previously cut into the nail bed, then press down to set the adhesive. *Right:* A completed partially eaten hand.**

the line you marked in the previous step. You will find you need to stab at the latex rather than cutting by dragging the knife across the finger. Be very careful not to cut yourself. This can be a little tricky. If you find this step is not worth the effort, just retouch any paint you chipped off and skip to the next step.

Step Twenty-one: Place a small

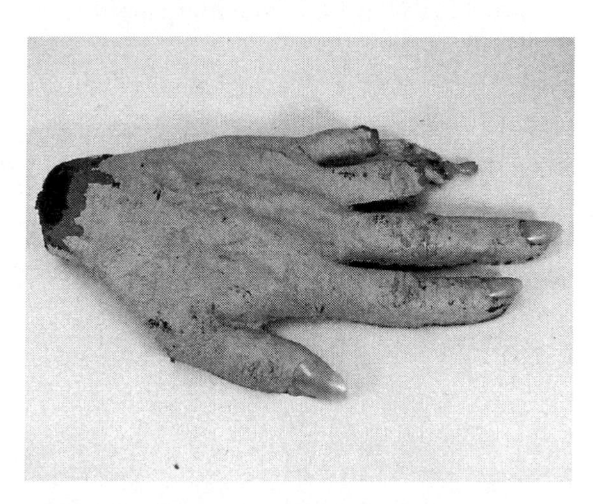

The author's first partially eaten hand.

A partially eaten hand used in a Halloween display.

amount of the silicone adhesive on the back of each nail. Take the nails one at a time and insert them into the slit you previously cut into the nail bed, then press down to set the adhesive.

Set your hand aside overnight to allow the adhesive to cure, and your hand is finished.

For the hand I made here, I chose some different nails that I found in the Halloween aisle rather than the cosmetics section. I had already built my first hand with realistic nails and thought I would try something different, so I picked glow-in-the-dark nails with spiders.

Above is a picture of how I use a partially eaten hand in a Halloween display.

X-RAY HAND

For this project you will need:

- ✓ One hand-shaped gelatin mold
- ✓ One skeleton hand
- ✓ One box unflavored gelatin
- ✓ One bottle tonic water (you may use plain tap water if you do not want the hand to be black light reactive)
- ✓ Long-nose pliers
- ✓ Wire cutters
- ✓ Safety goggles

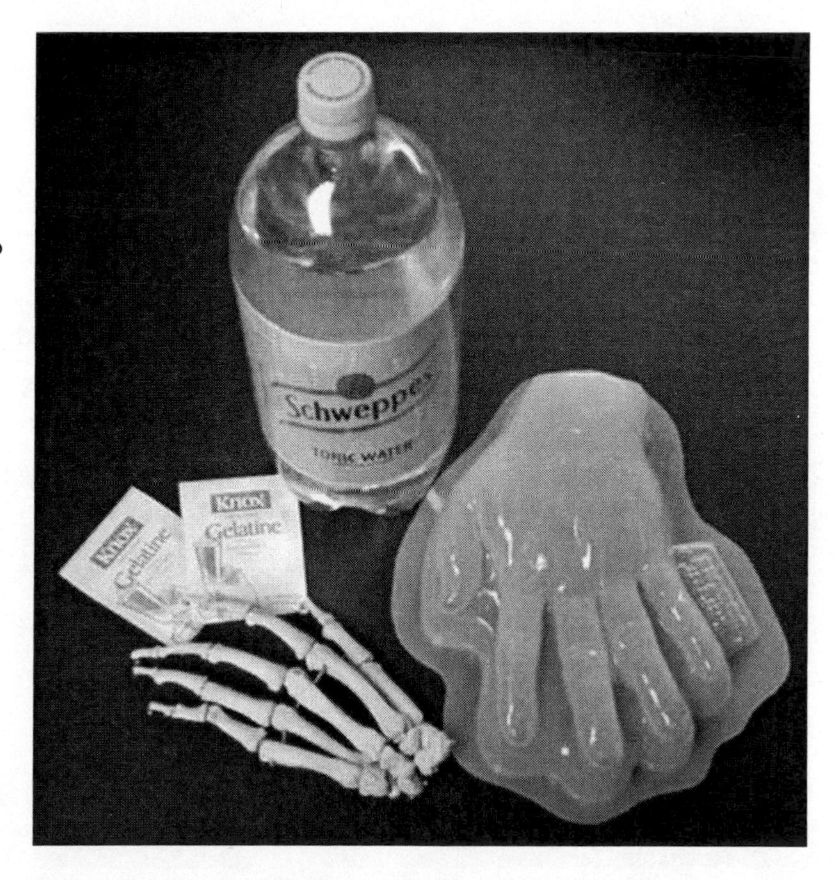

These are the materials you will need to create an X-ray hand.

Step One: If you would like your hand to be black light reactive, prepare one-half of the gelatin using tonic water instead of tap water (to avoid bubbles in the hand, it is best to let the tonic water go flat before using). If you do not wish your hand to be black light reactive, prepare the gelatin with tap water. For a more durable hand, you may want to use about 25 percent less water or tonic water than called for on the package.

Step Two: Pour enough gelatin mixture into the hand mold to fill it so that the fingers are filled for their full length, and to about one-half of their depth, then place in a refrigerator to cool. You will need to carefully adjust the mold in the refrigerator so that all the fingers are filled equally, about halfway. The fill level in the rest of the mold is less important than in the fingers. Leave the mold in the refrigerator until the gelatin is firm, about two hours.

Step Three: While the gelatin cools, take your long-nose pliers and partially straighten to loops at the ends of the fingers of the skeleton hand. You need add only about a tenth of an inch to the length of the wire. This will make it easier to move the individual bones around later on when you add the hand to the mold.

Step Four: Cut the loop off one end of the wire which runs through the knuckle area of the fingers, joining them together. It is a good idea to cover this operation with a towel before cutting, so that the clipping does not fly off and hit you or someone else. Of course, everyone in the room should be wearing safety goggles.

Step Five: Remove the wire between the fingers. This will allow you to spread the fingers to fit the mold.

Step Six: Add the skeleton hand to the cooled mold (note: you can tie string or wire to the hand as shown here, so that your finished prop can be tied

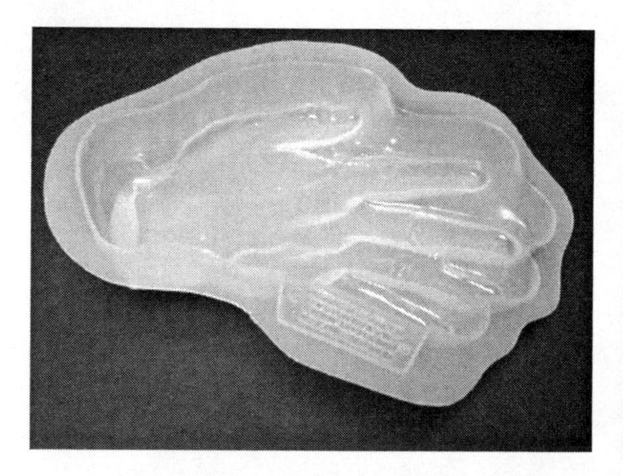

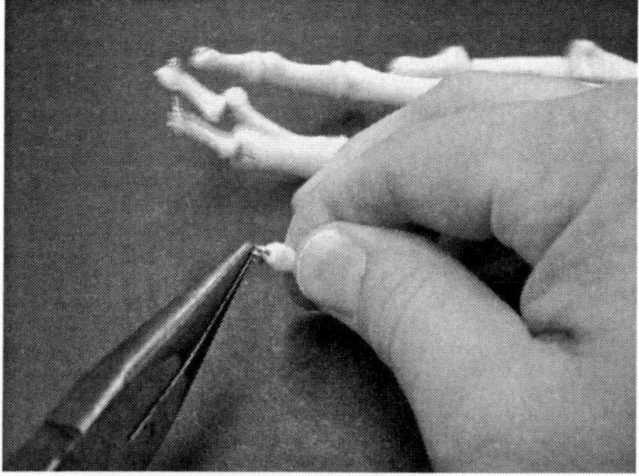

Left: **Pour enough gelatin mixture into the hand mold to fill it so that the fingers are filled for their full length, and to about one half of their depth.** ***Right:*** **Take your long nose pliers and partially straighten the loops at the ends of the fingers of the skeleton hand.**

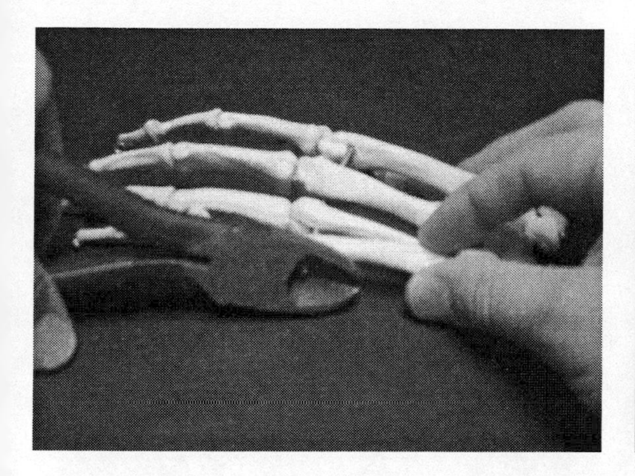

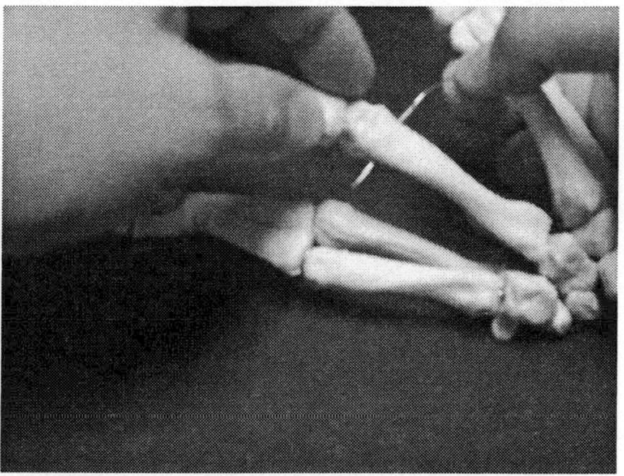

***Left:* Cut the loop off one end of the wire, which runs through the knuckle area of the fingers, joining them together. *Right:* Remove the wire between the fingers.**

in place). Spread the skeletal fingers out so that they are positioned in the center of the fingers of the mold.

Step Seven: Prepare the second half of the gelatin as before.

Step Eight: Add enough of the gelatin mixture to completely cover the bones. At this point, it may be necessary to add gelatin to the point that the spaces between the fingers are partially filled. This is not a problem, as it can be cut out after your hand is unmolded. Place the mold back in the refrigerator, being careful to angle it so that all the fingers are properly filled, and leave overnight to set up.

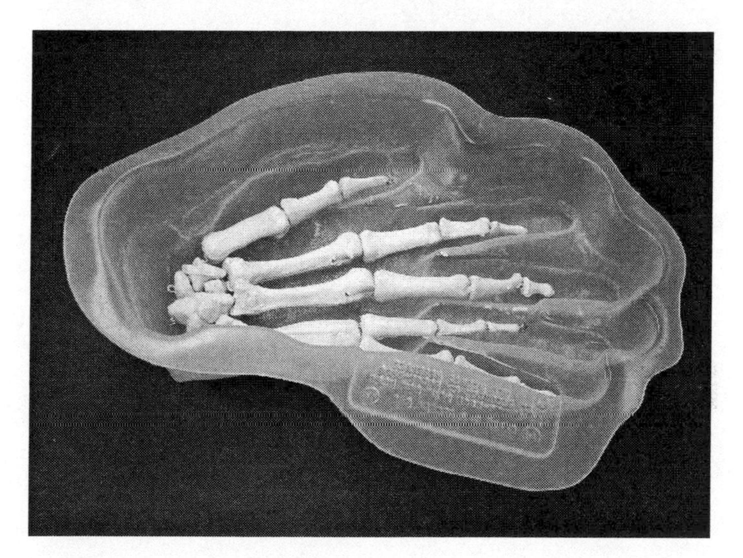

Add the skeleton hand to the cooled mold (note: you can tie string or wire to the hand as shown here, so that your finished prop can be tied in place).

Step Nine: After your mold has chilled overnight, unmold it as you would a regular gelatin dessert. That is to say, fill a sink or pan large enough to hold your entire mold with hot water. Place the mold, with the open side up, in the hot water (being careful not to put your hands into the hot water and burn yourself). The mold should float on top of the water. Let it do so for about thirty seconds to a full minute. This will melt the gelatin just enough to let it fall out of the mold with ease. Place a plate upside-down over the opening of the mold, turn them over quickly, and the hand should fall right out. Once again, place the mold back into the refrigerator for about one hour. After that you may trim any excess gelatin from between the fingers and elsewhere, and your new x-ray hand is finished. The picture here shows what my very first x-ray hand looked like. Does yours look better?

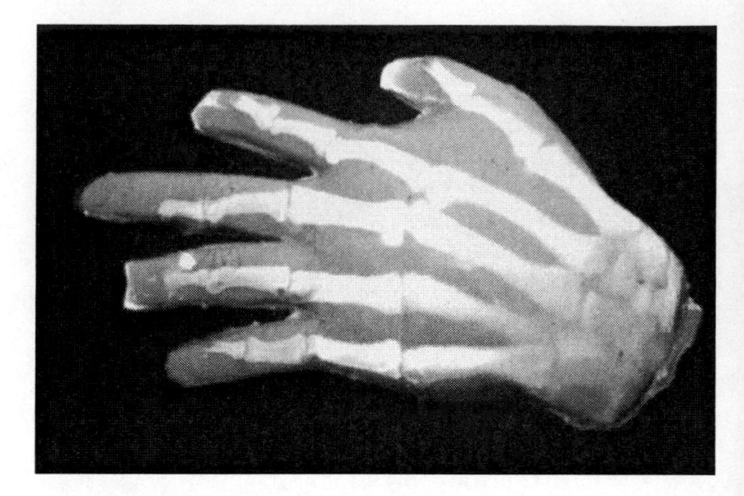

The X-ray hand made with tonic water shown under black light.

SPIDER DROP

For this project you will need:

- ✓ One large inflatable spider or similar large, soft, lightweight prop
- ✓ Some string
- ✓ A conveniently located tree, or other high object from which you can hang your prop

If you have the layout for it, this is without a doubt one of the easiest scares you will find. It is also one of the most effective. It is so simple, in fact, that I do not need to give you step-by-step directions. Once you have the basics, you will easily be able to adapt it to your own haunt. The concept is simple; the proper execution can be more difficult. What you are trying to do is to drop a large prop in front of, or on, an unsuspecting victim. After reading this section, I hope you will find this easy to do and well worth the effort.

The first thing we must discuss is safety. In this effect, you will be dropping your prop right on your victim's head. Therefore, you must select it very carefully. **You must make sure your prop is very lightweight.** You will find that a large prop is more effective than a small one. An inflatable or foam rubber prop is ideal.

You must also make certain your prop has no sharp edges or small protrusions. Your prop may be falling very rapidly, not to mention the fact that a victim will be reacting to your prop and may be moving quickly to get away. You do not want any sharp edges which may cut someone, or protrusions which may poke them in the eye. Select your prop carefully and you can have some very startled, uninjured victims.

After safety, the second most important consideration is placement. You will be trying to drop your prop directly in front of your victim, or perhaps even right on his head. You will find most victims do not want to cooperate with you. They will tend to want to walk their own path and will stop everywhere except where you would like them to. It is up to you to make them want to stop right where you want them to. A second placement consideration is that you will need something overhead from which to suspend your prop. When suspended, your prop should be pulled up high enough to be out of the line of sight of your victim. It also helps if there will be something around the prop to hide it. I have found a tree to be perfect for this.

Let me first discuss how to perform the effect, and then we will discuss how to get your victims where you want them. First, you will need to get your string over the branch or other high object you will drop you spider from. For me, this was done by throwing a roll of string over a tree branch. Once your string is over the support, tie one end to your spider or other prop. Now run the other end of the string to a convenient hiding place or some spot where you will not look out of place. You can now pull on the string to lift your prop up out of sight. Once you have lifted your prop up, let go of the string, and your prop should drop to the ground. Try this several times to get the correct timing; you will need to have a good feel for how long it takes your prop to drop.

The spider hanging in a tree hidden by branches, waiting to pounce.

If the prop seems to fall at a good rate, fast enough so that it will appear quickly, but not so fast as to pose a risk of injury, you may proceed to finish setting up your scare. If the prop falls too slowly, there are two things you can do to try to speed it up. The first is to add some weight to your prop. If you choose to do this remember you must be certain the total weight will not be enough to cause injury if it falls on someone's head. The second is to reduce the friction between your string and the tree branch, or whatever supports your string. You can do this by using a small pulley or running the string over a smooth surface rather than a rough one.

If you think your prop falls too quickly, you can try to slow it down. Again, the first way to do this is to adjust the weight of the prop. Often, it will not be practical to remove weight, so you will need to increase the friction between the string and its support. Try adding a rough surface to the support or run the string between two blocks, which apply a slight squeeze on the string. Another option is to add a counterweight to the string. To do this, select a weight that is lighter than your prop. Then with your prop lifted up to its high position, take your string and bring it straight down to the ground and mark this point on the string. Once you have this point marked, attach your counterweight at this point. The counterweight should be securely attached to the string so that it will not come loose and fall on someone. You also should use a counterweight which is soft enough that if it were to come loose and fall it would not injure anyone.

Once you have the prop dropping at a rate you like, it is time to determine where you would like your prop to stop so that it can have the maximum impact. A prop falling to the ground from above may give someone a little bit of a start, but if you want maximum impact you will want your prop to stop at right about eye level. To do this, simply raise your prop by pulling the string, and then lower it to the height where you feel it will have maximum impact. Once you have the prop at the right height, simply tie off the free end of your string. Now you can raise your prop and every time you drop it, it will fall and stop right where you want it to. I usually have the low portion of my prop stop about four feet above the ground. This is a good height for shorter people and children. With a prop that is about two and a half feet long, it is still high enough to be in the face of a six-footer.

Now that you know how to set up the spider drop, how do you get people to stop where you can drop your prop on them? If you become expert in timing the drop of your prop, you can simply force people along a narrow path and drop your prop, so it will reach the right height just as they arrive. The problem with that is I have found people to be most uncooperative. If I release my prop at the perfect moment, that is when people tend to stop and turn away. By the time they look back, the spider is there and is not much of a surprise.

The way I like to work it is to give people something to look at and one

The spider in the dropped position.

good spot to see it from. That one good spot just happens to be under my spider! For my home haunt, I channel everybody up a narrow walkway; at one point along the walkway is the one spot to get a really good look into the mad scientist lab I have set up. While my victims are standing there looking into the lab, my spider drops right on them. I have things positioned so that if they are a few feet behind my target zone, the spider drops right in front of them. The effect is just as good as if the spider lands directly on them. If they are a few feet in front of my target spot, the spider drops in silently behind them. This is sometimes even better, because when they turn to leave, they have a spider starring at them from six inches away. This is usually good for about a three-foot jump and a 120-decibel scream.

That is about all there is to the spider drop; it is very easy and yet one of the most remembered parts of my haunt. The only problem is that after I used it for a few years in a row, too many people came to expect just where the spider would attack. Now I have had to retire my spider for a couple of years, awaiting his return when he is least expected, and in a different spot. I can hardly wait to drop my spider again; I can almost hear the screams now!

BUCKY'S HOME REMODELING

You can turn an ugly room into a beautiful, modern mad scientist lab with Bucky's remodeling service.

A room before remodeling.

The same room after remodeling.

However, what do you do if you can not afford to have Bucky and his crack crew of professionals redo your home for Halloween? Do it yourself! That's right, now you can have professional results right at home. Just follow the simple procedures outlined here, and you too can create your very own wonderful modern mad scientist lab.

Just what do you need to accomplish this totally amazing metamorphosis? You may be surprised how little it really takes. For the lab here I used simply:

- ✓ 1" × 2"s
- ✓ A few pieces of scrap pegboard
- ✓ Some faux stone corrugated paper
- ✓ A few screws
- ✓ A drill with bits
- ✓ A screwdriver
- ✓ A staple gun with staples
- ✓ A table

✓ An old board I had lying around the house
✓ Some white plastic sheeting (a plastic tablecloth)
✓ Some black plastic sheeting
✓ Some tape
✓ An assortment of my Halloween props, both homemade and store-bought

I began by cleaning out all the furniture; it just did not look right for a lab. Next came the walls. There are many ways to do walls; here I was lucky in that most of the new walls would be able to lean up against existing walls. If you need your lab to be freestanding, you will need to do some heavier construction. This section will deal solely with rooms where most of the lab walls will be supported by existing walls. If you have any real carpentry skills, you can easily adapt the ideas here to build freestanding structures.

When building your new lab, the first thing you need to do is measure the space in which you will be building your walls. I was lucky in that the area I was building in had eight foot ceilings, allowing me to use 1" × 2" × 8's for the uprights (floor to ceiling), without having to cut them. If you have a ceiling height of less than eight feet you will need to trim your 1" × 2"s. Measure your height floor to ceiling and cut two 1" × 2"s per wall, to this height, or if you want to make things a little easier to install, cut them about a half an inch shorter.

Next, measure the length of the first wall you plan to do. Cut three 1" × 2"s to this length minus the width of two 1" × 2"s. This works out to the measured length of the wall minus 2⅝." Do not let the numbers scare you; the way we will be building our walls is very forgiving of an error or two. If the section of wall you are building is over 8' 2⅝", you will have to build two or more sections of wall to cover it.

Now take some pegboard or other thin wood and cut or break it into pieces about 2" × 4". You will need six of these pieces per section of wall you are building.

Now it is time to start assembling the frame for your first wall. For this you will need to have handy: two upright 1" × 2"s, three 1" × 2"s you cut to the length of your wall, 6 pieces of pegboard, 12 wood screws (or if you are like me a few more because you will lose a few), a drill with a small bit and a screwdriver or driver bit for the drill. You need not be too fussy about the screws you choose except that they should be no longer than ¾" so that they do not protrude through the back of the 1" × 2"s when screwed in place. Sheet metal screws can be used instead of wood screws. The screws I used were 8 × ¾", that is a number eight screw ¾" long. If the whole screw thing is a little confusing to you, just go into your local hardware store, and ask for "eight by three quarters wood screws"; your helpful hardware person will know what you need.

Before we actually begin to assemble the frame for our first wall, let me explain, how we will be connecting the 1" × 2"s together. First, we will be connecting the top and bottom boards to the uprights. For this operation, it is highly advisable to have a second person help you. Take one of your upright 1" × 2"s and place it at a right angle to one of the 1" × 2"s you cut for the length of your wall.

You will now attach the two 1" × 2"s. Place one of the pieces of pegboard, you made earlier, over the corner where the two 1" × 2"s come together. Now drill a small hole (a pilot hole for your screw) through the pegboard, into one of the 1" × 2"s. Without moving anything, or letting your assembly shift, drill another hole into the other 1" × 2". This hole should be small enough so that your screw must be screwed into it, not so large that it just slides in. For a number eight screw, this hole should be $\frac{5}{64}$". If you like you can go through one of the factory holes in the pegboard and it will hold just fine.

Now take two of your screws and screw them into the holes you just made.

Next, go to the other end of the bottom 1" × 2" and repeat this joining process, then do the same for the top 1" × 2". When you are done you should have a nice square frame. Do not worry if your frame is a little wobbly; we will soon fix that. Placement of the center 1" × 2" is a little more tricky, but still very easy.

Now add the center 1" × 2" into the frame you have made. This 1" × 2" will serve two purposes: it will add strength to the frame, and give you a place to attach your faux stone cardboard. The positioning of the center board is very

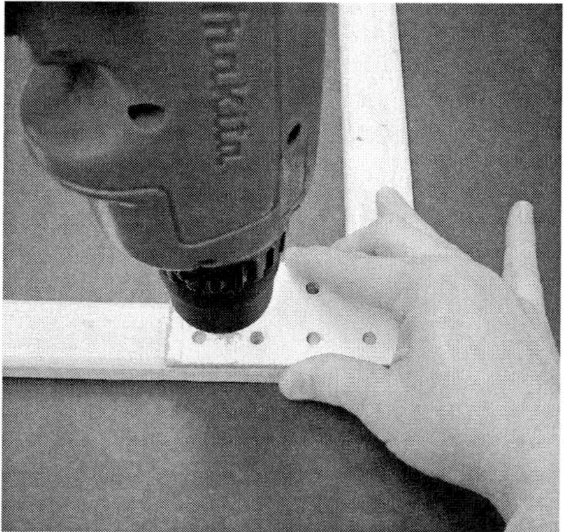

Left: **Take one of your upright 1" × 2"s and place it at a right angle to one of the 1" × 2"s you cut for the length of your wall.** ***Right:*** **Predrill holes for your screws.**

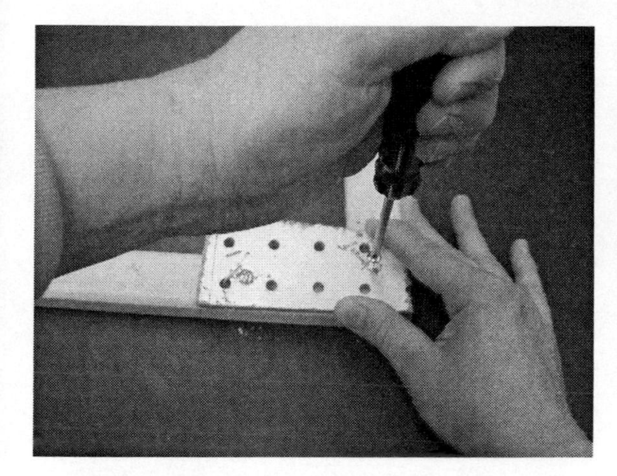

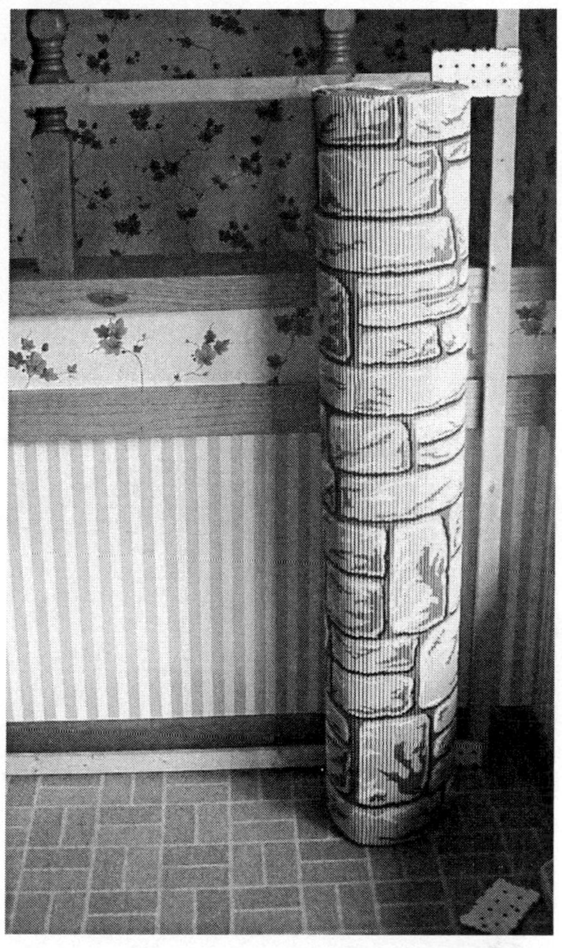

Above: **Take two of your screws and screw them into the holes.** ***Right:*** **The easiest way to position the center board is to stand the frame where it will be used, and stand your cardboard roll next to it.**

important. It must be placed at the right height and be level, or else you will have problems later.

The easiest way to position the center board is to stand the frame where it will be used, and stand your cardboard roll next to it. You can then position your center board so that the center of the board is even with the top of the roll. Attach your board at this point and repeat at the opposite end.

You have now finished your first frame!

So far, our wall does not look very impressive, does it? It is time to change that! First, let me take a moment to tell you about the wall covering I used on my wall. It is called Flagstone Corobuff, and it is sold as a background for store displays. Corobuff can be hard to find. My wife first found it at a party store, which later discontinued it. After a long search, I have finally found where it can be ordered through the mail, and have included that information in the Where Can I Find...? section of this book.

On the roll, Corobuff looks rather unimpressive. However, once up on a wall it looks very much like a real stone wall. While this product looks like flimsy corrugated cardboard, it is really very durable. I have used the same Corobuff in my lab for five years now and see no reason why I cannot get another five years or more out of it.

Now that you know more than you ever wanted to know about Corobuff, let me tell you how to put it on your frame. Start by taking one end and wrapping it around one of the upright 1" × 2"s.

Continue to stretch the Corobuff along the frame. Cut it about an inch or two longer than the wall and wrap it around the other upright. Starting at one end, staple the Corobuff tightly to the frame. You can use any kind of staples and staple gun you like, as long as you can drive the staple far enough into the wood to hold the Corobuff tightly in place. Remember to staple the top, bottom and both sides, spacing your staples about twelve inches apart.

A close-up view of the proper location for the center board.

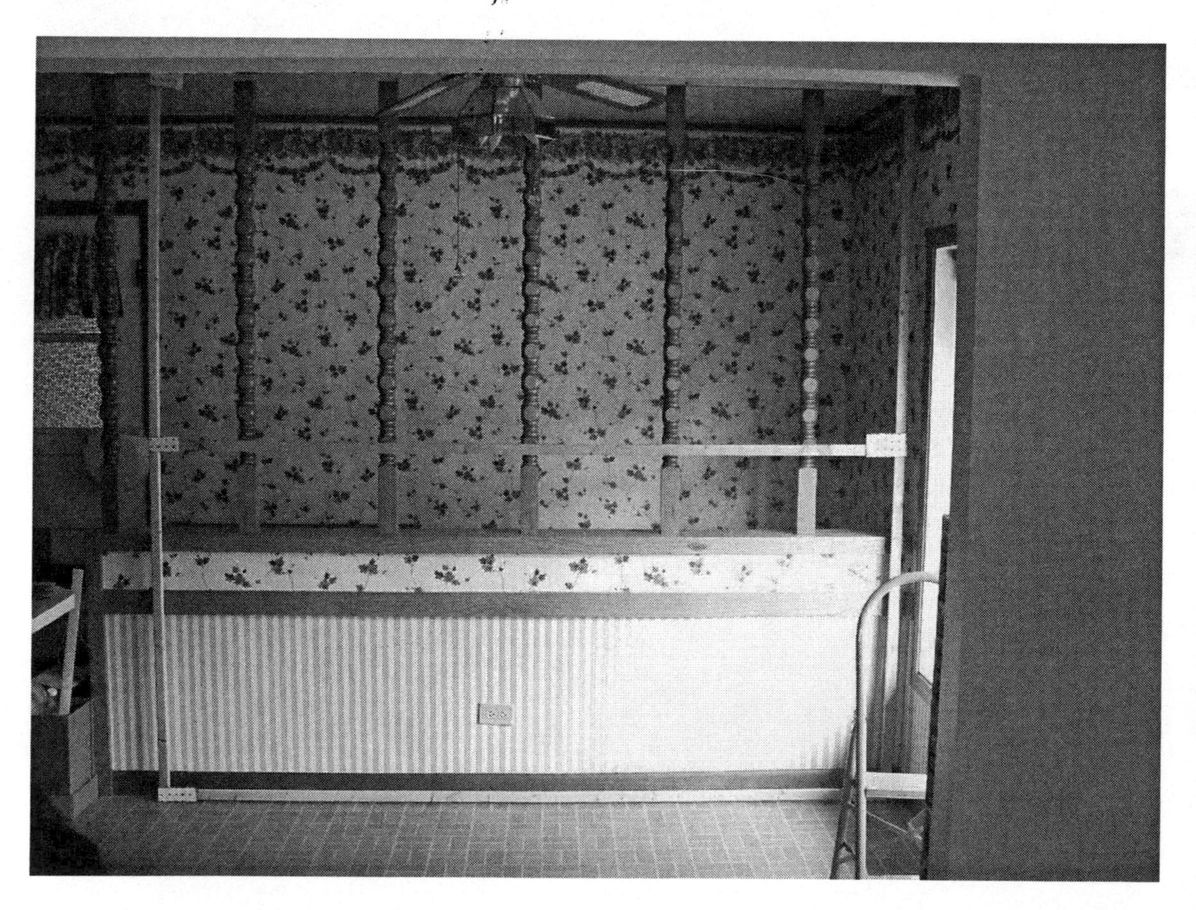

A finished frame.

Left: **Start by taking one end and wrapping it around one of the upright 1" × 2"s.** ***Right:*** **Use a staple gun to attach the wall sheeting to the frame.**

Once you have finished the bottom section of the wall, take your roll of Corobuff and line up the bottom of the roll with the top of the section you have just applied. Wrap the upright, stretch out the roll, wrap it around the other upright, and cut and staple it in place just as you did with the first section. You

The first wall frame half covered.

The first wall completed.

An ordinary table can be transformed to look like a lab bench.

now have one finished wall. If your wall is less than eight feet high, you will need to trim the second row of Corobuff.

I think our room is looking better already! You can now continue to build the remaining walls for your room in the same way you built the first. My lab is visible to visitors only from the outside, looking in through a bay window, so I do only three walls.

Now that you have your lab built, it is time to furnish it. Of course, no lab is complete

Left: **A one-inch-thick board on top helps to transform a table into a lab bench.**
Right: **Cover the board with a sheet of white plastic.**

without a lab bench. These are usually heavy-duty benches with stone tops. Such a bench would be a little expensive for most budgets, not to mention heavy, so we will make our own out of much cheaper and lighter materials. I use a simple craft table. If you do not have a craft table you can use just about any table. I have even used several boxes stacked up.

Finish off your bench by wrapping black plastic around the bottom to cover the legs of the table.

I like to put a one-inch-thick board on top of the table. I use this board to simulate a one-inch-thick slab of stone.

I then cover the board with a sheet of white plastic (in this case a white plastic tablecloth). You can staple or tape the plastic to the board and it will give you not only the look of a stone top, but also a good contrasting background for the props you place on the table.

Finish off your bench by wrapping black plastic around the bottom to cover the legs of the table. You can tape or staple this to the table, leaving the white on the side of the top board showing.

Top off your table with a few props and you have a respectable lab bench. You can probably spot a few of the props from this book on the finished bench pictured on the next page.

After I add a few more props to the lab, the view visitors have from the outside is shown on page 217.

In that picture, let us take a better look at some of the props added to the

Top off your table with a few props and you have a respectable lab bench. You can probably spot a few of the props from this book on the finished bench.

lab to give it that homey feel. The most obvious is the seven-foot-tall Frankenstein's monster. Sorry, but this is a rather expensive store-bought prop. The glow-in-the-dark skeleton is also one I cannot show you how to make; sometimes you just have to go with store bought. So, we will look at ways to add not only the props we build ourselves but also those we buy ready made.

My all-time favorite addition to the lab is what I like to call the bat mobile. I am fortunate enough to have a ceiling fan in my lab, which allows me to have bats flying around the room. To achieve this effect, I start with some glow-in-the-dark bats. I then add a little extra string to allow the bats to hang lower, and tie them off to the blades of the fan.

I then turn the fan on low and the bats fly around in circles. You just have to make sure to use only the lowest speed for the fan or the bats have a tendency to fly off the fan. Always make sure no one is where they could be injured by bats flying off the fan. Also, you must make certain to use only light bats so as not to damage the fan. This effect looks best in a dark room lit with black light.

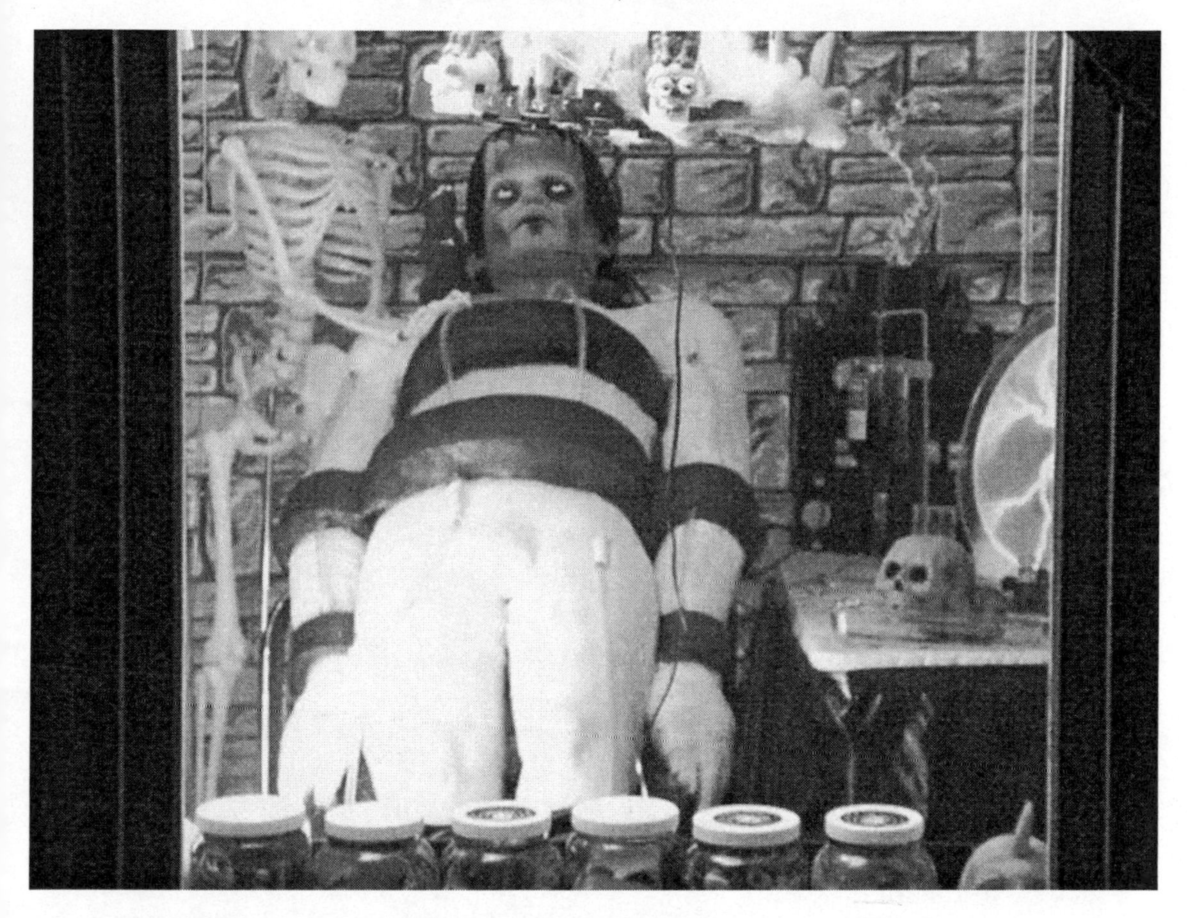

After I add a few more props to the lab, this is the view visitors have from the outside.

Now let us take a close-up look at the interior of the lab, section by section, starting with what I call the monster maker.

The monster maker is what you use to bring a monster back to life; it is the black box to the left in the picture on page 216. My monster maker, in reality, is a collection of garbage on a cardboard box. Starting with the chassis, the monster maker is a cardboard box painted black. I then attached some broken volt-ohm meters, literally rescued from the garbage pile (they can be seen on top, left front). Below the meters is a very large fuse (it takes a lot of electricity to reanimate a monster) rescued from old equipment being updated with circuit breakers. The apparent large metal clips, which hold the fuse, are actually pieces of 1" × 2" left over from the construction of the walls. I just covered the 1" × 2" pieces with metal tape to make them nice and shiny. The tubes on top of the monster maker are old burned-out bulbs from mercury vapor lamps (used in industrial lighting). The white bases they sit in are Styrofoam protectors that came on the tubes of my black lights (I never throw anything away if I can help it). On the next version of the monster maker, I plan to add a lot of knobs and buttons by gluing on a bunch of old toothpaste caps, etc.

To the right of the monster maker, behind the bottles, is the blood recirculation apparatus: a cardboard box painted black with some stickers on it. From this box, I run some red plastic tubing to the monster and back. This gives the impression that the box is taking blood from the monster, processing it in some way and then returning it to the monster. The *Book of the Dead*, above this apparatus, is a store-bought prop. The bottles in front of it are just old bottles filled with water and food coloring. Of course, if you like, you can make these bottles glow under black light for a more dramatic effect (see section in this book Working with Black Light).

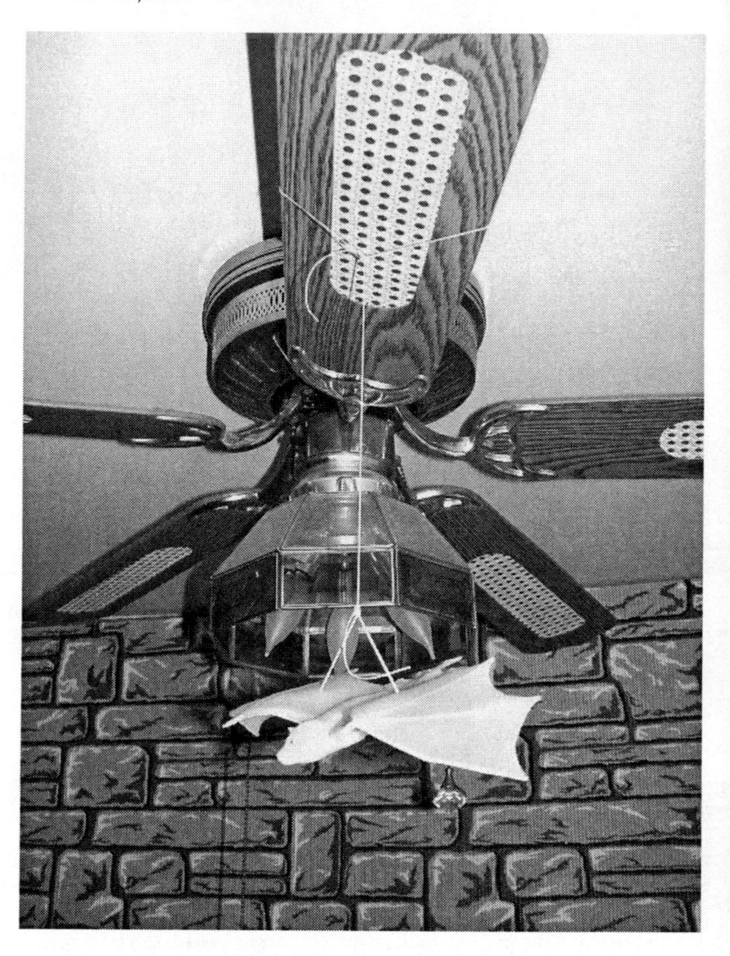

One of my all-time favorite effects is the bat mobile. To achieve this effect, start by hanging glow-in-the-dark bats from a ceiling fan.

To the right in the picture, you can see some store-bought organs and a store-bought plasma disc. I topped off this section of the lab with a few plastic bugs for an extra bit of yuckiness.

Looking farther down the bench, we have a prop hand to which I added a couple of lizards having lunch. This picture was taken before I developed the partially eaten hand, described in this book. In future years, I will be using my homemade prop in this spot. To the left, we have a store-bought glow-in-the-dark skull, flanked by two store-bought skullblets (goblets shaped like skulls). Again, I have a couple of store-bought plasma devices (they look great in a darkened lab). To the right, you can see the tail of a store-bought prop rat.

The pictures on page 221 show what the whole bench looks like and what the bench looks like at night under black light.

A view of the finished lab showing the bat mobile in action.

A view of the lab bench showing the homemade monster maker on the left.

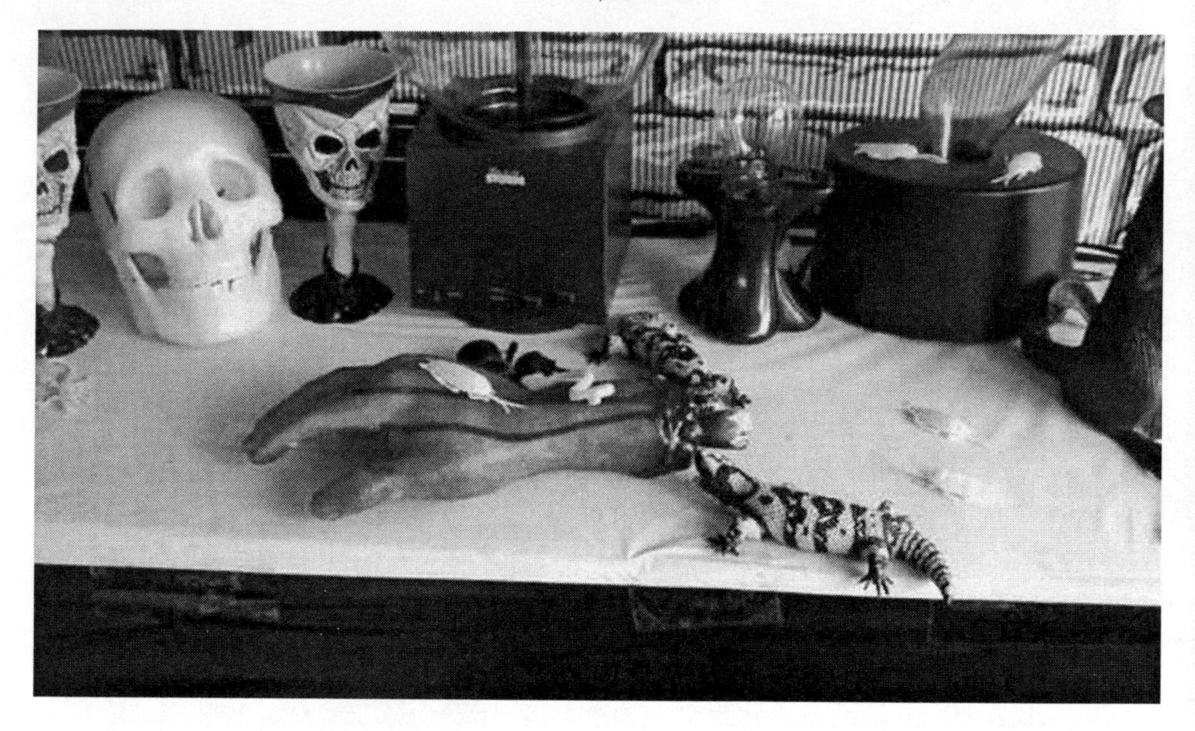

Looking further down the bench, we have a prop hand to which I added a couple of lizards having lunch.

I also added a few wall hangings. These were easy to hang; I just straightened half a paper clip, pushed it through the wall, and hung the wall hanging on the unstraightened part of the paper clip. Not to worry, the bat flies upright when the bat mobile is turned on.

I also like to add a number of what I call "thing in a bottle props." These are the store-bought props you see where you get a prop and a jar to put it in. You then add water to the jar to make it look like a lab specimen (of course you can always get a jar and add your own prop). I add different colors of food coloring or UV dye to the bottles and place them in the front window, where visitors can get a close look.

Once your lab is built and equipped, you must decide how to light it. The problem is usually that some of your props will show up better in the dark, under black light, while others show up only under normal light. This was quite a conundrum for me until I hit upon the idea of using a strobe light. I fill the lab with a number of black lights, placed so as to illuminate my black light reactive props. The black lights are on all the time. I then take one very bright strobe light and place it in a corner of the lab. I try to position the strobe so that when it is lit it casts a number of eerie shadows and yet lights the props which best benefit from bright light. The effect is that the lab alternates from a black light lab to a daylight look. This shows off all of the props reasonably well.

A view of the entire finished bench in daylight.

A view of the entire finished bench at night with the black lights on.

A few wall hangings added to the walls for that homey feel.

A few thing-in-bottle props added to the lab.

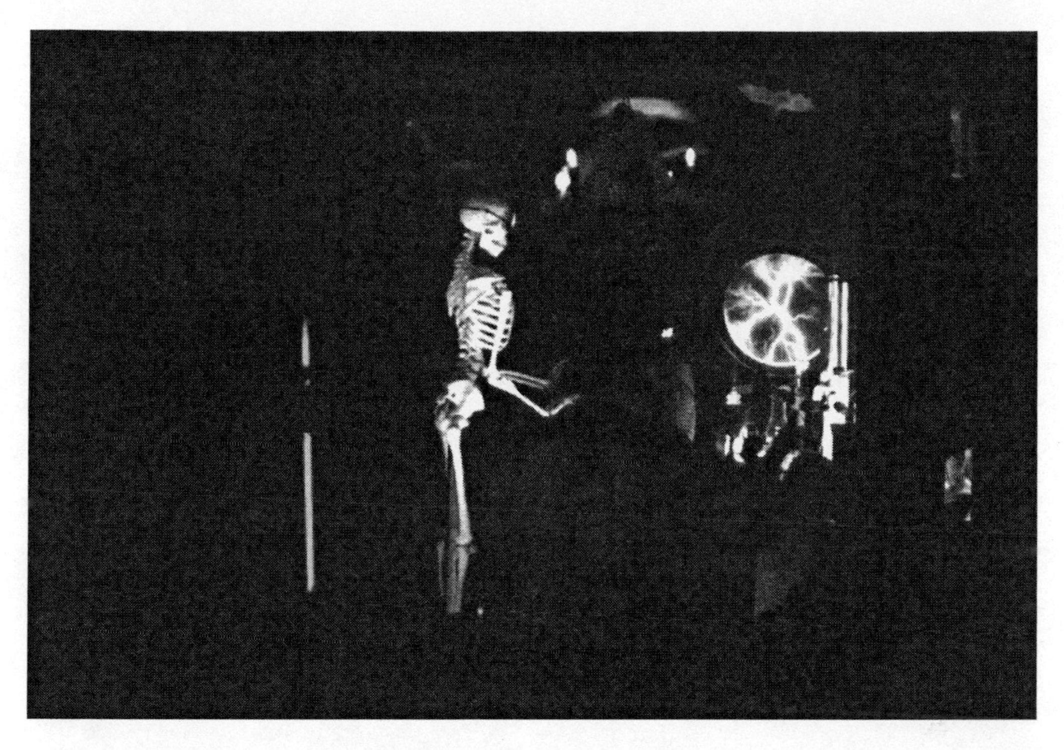

The finished lab shown in black light when the strobe is off.

The finished lab shown when the strobe is lit.

Here is the view visitors get when walking up to the door.

My lab seems to get a little more elaborate every year; it also seems to get easier every year. What I learn one year helps me the next and many of the props I build or modify can be used the next year, with little or no additional work or time spent. It has gotten to the point where I spend less time setting up the lab than the rest of my display, yet it remains the most impressive and popular part of it. With boards and paper already cut and props packed together, the lab can go up in less than a day. Yet, it looks like it takes weeks.

While I do not expect anyone to be able to build an exact replica of my lab, from the information presented here I hope I have set the groundwork for a reader to design and build his own lab. Of course, you can use the same basic ideas to build other rooms, say maybe a dungeon or perhaps a torture chamber. Once again, the possibilities are endless. Just use your imagination and see what you can come up with.

BLOOD, WORMS, AND ALL THE REST: MISCELLANEOUS RAMBLINGS FROM A DISTURBED MIND

In this section you will find ideas and techniques so simple that they do not need detailed instructions. While these are without a doubt some of the simplest ideas to implement, they can still find many a use in your haunt.

BLOOD

What would Halloween be without blood? The problem with real blood is that it spoils quickly and can be hard to come by. Sure you could go out and buy stage blood, but it can be hard to find and the price can make you want to open a vein. The solution to this problem is to simply make your own fake blood. There are a number of recipes for homemade stage blood, but I will limit our discussion to the two I like best. I will not give you exact proportions, as you may wish to vary the color and consistency of your blood to suit your application. I will rather discuss the materials which can be used, and give you a few hints on how to use them.

Most blood recipes call for three things: water, something to thicken the water and coloring. Water, of course, is usually the easiest to come by and ordinary tap water works fine. There are a number of things which can be used to thicken the water; the two I prefer are glycerin and light corn syrup. Glycerin makes for a somewhat less sticky blood; however, it tends to cost more than corn syrup and can be harder to find. I normally use water and corn syrup.

Glycerin can be found in many drug stores or can be purchased from chemical suppliers. Light corn syrup can be found in the baking goods section of most grocery stores. Corn syrup comes in both light and dark; using the light color gives you a little more control over the finished color of your blood.

To make your blood, start by mixing water and corn syrup (or glycerin if you prefer) until you get the consistency you want. Use more water to make the mixture thinner, and more syrup to make it thicker. Just how thick you make your blood will depend upon how you plan to use it. For a blood fountain or waterfall, you may want to use all water so that your blood will flow nicely and not be too thick to pump. If you want to apply your blood to a vertical surface and have it stay or move slowly, you will want to use syrup and little or no water.

Once you have the right thickness, it is time to color your blood. To do this, most people just add a little red food coloring. Red food coloring works OK, but it lacks the true blood color. Getting a dark red requires using a lot of food coloring (which tends to carry a ridiculously high price). You can get a darker, more realistic color by adding a little blue food coloring to the mix. Start by coloring your blood a moderately dark red, and then add a drop or two of blue. You will find it gives you a darker, more blood-like color and you will use less total coloring. Adjust the color of your blood by adding food coloring until you get the shade that is just right for your project. If you go too dark, just add more water and syrup to lighten the mix.

I said earlier that I feel food coloring is overpriced. You do have a bit of an alternative; you can use a powdered drink mix to color your blood. Just pick up a few packs of a red colored drink mix (cherry, fruit punch, etc.) and a blue or purple drink mix (blueberry, grape, etc.). I suggest the unsweetened kind of drink mix; it gives you more color for volume used. Just add the drink mix powder to your blood mixture, a little at a time, until you get the color you want. You can use them just like a powdered food coloring. Aside from being cheaper to use than plain food coloring, they will give your blood a nice fruity smell. If you use water and corn syrup to make your blood, it will taste good and be safe to eat.

I recommend using water, corn syrup and drink mix to make your blood. It gives you a safe, edible product and tastes good. The corn syrup blood is a good one to use if you want to be dripping blood out of the corner of your mouth. If you do this, you will want to make your blood extra thick (your saliva will tend to thin it out a bit). One word of warning: almost all red colorings and dyes stain

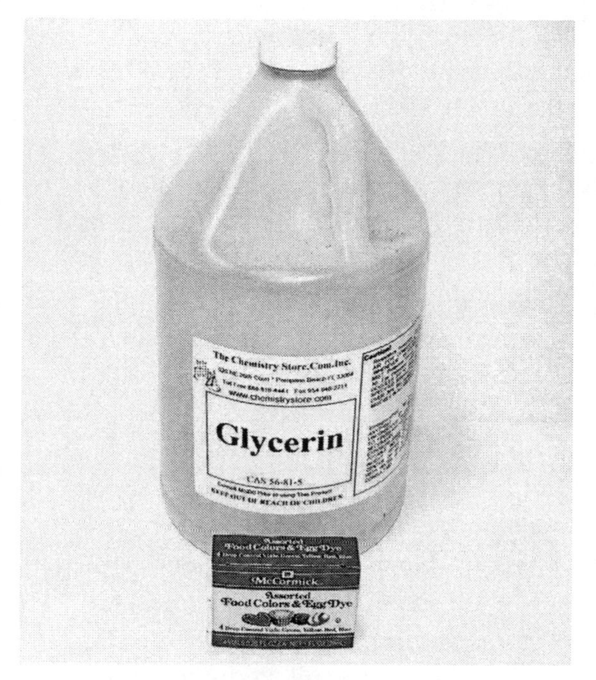

***Left:* One recipe for homemade blood is glycerin and water with food coloring added. *Right:* A cheaper version of blood can be made using corn syrup, water and powdered soft drink mix.**

and are very difficult to remove. Use your blood only on items that you do not mind having stained. This includes your skin. Following is a picture of a prop I set up using homemade blood for added effect. The blood mixture used was corn syrup, water, cherry drink mix and grape drink mix. This mixture stores well in a tightly sealed container. In fact, the blood used with the prop shown was over a year old when I used it.

Homemade blood used to enhance a prop.

Another way to

simulate wet blood is to mix oil-based red paint with polyurethane. Just mix the two until you get the combination of color and shine that you want (I use about equal amounts of each). You can then apply the mixture to a prop or scene and let dry. Once it dries, you will have the look of wet blood, but your blood will not run, smear, or change colors. Needless to say, this mixture should be used only on inanimate objets. Do not use paint and polyurethane blood on people or animals!

Once you have your paint and polyurethane mixed, you will want to apply it. You can simply pour it out to form a large pool of blood, but I prefer a splattered look. To achieve this look simply dip a screwdriver, stick or similar object into the mixture, then dab it onto your prop for the look of large drops. For smaller drops, dip your stick in the mixture and then shake it over the prop.

Set your prop aside overnight to dry and it is ready to use. While it is completely dry, your blood will have that shiny look of freshly spilled blood.

Another little trick you can do with poly-paint blood is to make blood pools and splatters which can be transferred from where you make them onto another object. To do this, start with a piece of melamine shelving or other type of board with a smooth, hard surface. Apply a few drops of household oil to the top of the board, and then rub it over the surface of the board with a small piece of cloth or paper towel.

Now, mix your red paint and polyurethane and apply as before. Let the mixture dry for a few days to make sure it is completely dry and set up. Take a putty knife or similar object and pry up one corner of one of your spatters.

Once you have the corner just started, carefully grab the edge with your finger and work the splatter up.

Left: **Red paint and polyurethane can be used to make fake blood that looks wet even after it dries.** ***Right:*** **Mix paint and polyurethane.**

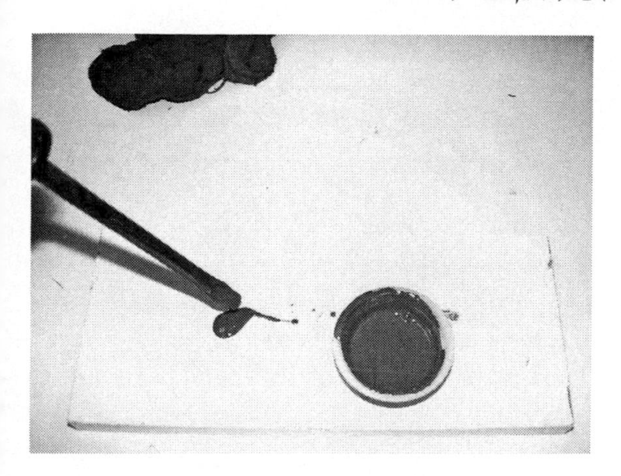

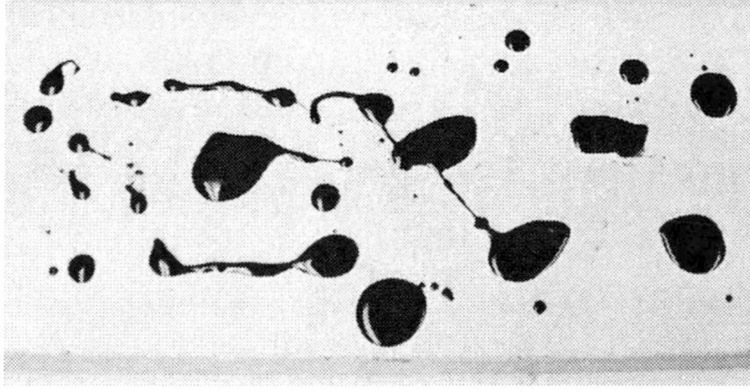

Left: **Dab or splatter your mixture onto your project.** ***Right:*** **A finished test board, showing the dried mixture.**

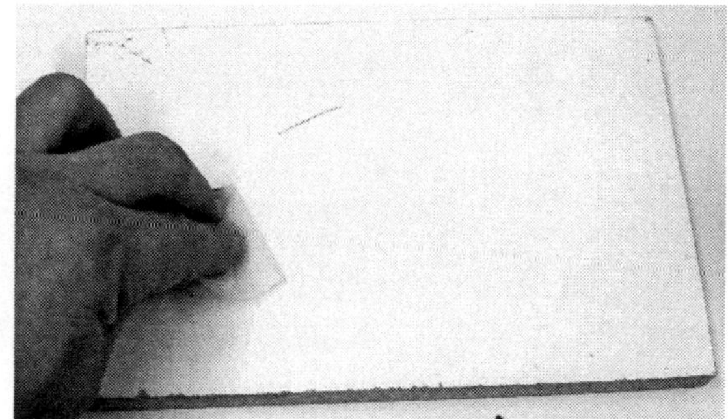

Left: **Put a few drops of oil onto a smooth board.** ***Right:*** **Rub the oil to spread it over the entire board.**

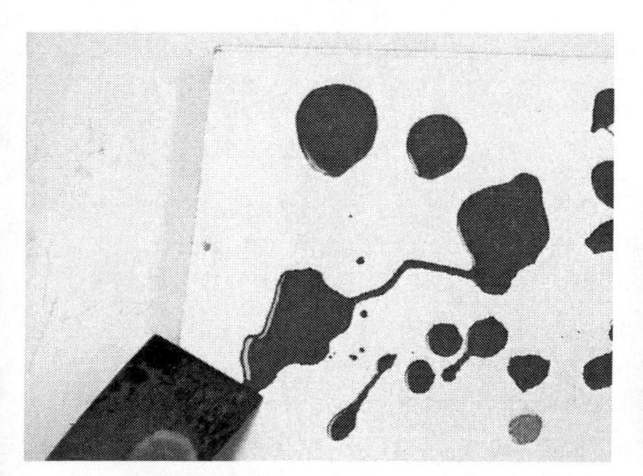

Left: **Take a putty knife or similar object and pry up one corner of one of your spatters.** ***Right:*** **Carefully grab the edge with your finger and work the splatter up.**

***Right:* Continue to lift the splatter off until it is completely free of the board.**

Continue to lift the splatter off until it is completely free of the board.

Your splatters can now be placed on your prop without becoming a permanent part of it.

If you are using your blood splatters on a prop that absolutely cannot be marred in any way, you may want to test your splatter first to make sure it will not damage the prop. The poly-paint splatter should be safe on any painted surface such as a table top, but a little caution is sometimes well advised.

Your splatters can now be placed on your prop without becoming a permanent part of it.

VOMIT

There may be a time you want to add a little vomit to your haunt. I personally feel the real stuff just smells too bad to use; this leaves us no alternative other than to make our own. You could always use the old reliable pea soup, but since a certain movie, that is kind of a cliché. So let us talk about some of the alternatives. There are any number of things which can be used to simulate vomit. Most are everyday food items (after all, isn't that what the real stuff is made of?).

One of the nice things about using food products to make your fake vomit is that if all the materials used are fresh and the vomit is used in a timely manner, an actor can hold the mixture in his mouth until the perfect time for discharge. To make a good quality vomit, you need to start with a liquid or semi-liquid base. Plain water is just too thin and the color is all wrong, so I like to use canned cream of mushroom soup. This soup makes a great base; the color is about right and it is nice and thick. In fact, this soup is often so thick it needs to be thinned with water to get the proper consistency.

Cream of mushroom soup makes an excellent base for vomit.

Of course, what is vomit without chunks? I actually like mine extra chunky. You can add any number of things to your vomit for chunks. After all, it is your vomit and it should reflect your taste. A good start is to add a little canned corn. Corn is one of those things the body has a hard time digesting, so there always seems to be a little left undigested. If you use a whole kernel corn, you may want to squash and mangle the pieces a little, to give them a masticated look.

For chunkier vomit, try adding corn.

Another good item to add for chunks is oatmeal. Oatmeal allows you to make nice big chunks and allows you to control and vary the size of the chunks. To

Oatmeal also makes for nice chunky vomit.

use oatmeal, just cook up as much as you need for the quantity of vomit you wish to make. You will want to make sure your oatmeal is good and thick; if you want runny vomit just use a thinner soup-water mixture.

Add red oil-based paint if you want bloody vomit.

If you want to be a little extra sick you can add a little blood to your vomit. To do this, simply add a little oil-based red paint to your vomit (**if you add paint to your vomit it is no longer safe to eat or put in your mouth!**). As the old saying goes, "Oil and water don't mix." You will find the oil-based paint tends to form small pools and streams in the vomit.

If you wish to have an actor appear to vomit using the bloody vomit, you can fill a plastic bag with your vomit mix. The actor can then hold the bag of vomit up to the side of his face away from the audience and squeeze out the vomit.

At this time, I cannot help but recount a story I heard, which may or may not be just an urban legend. As the story goes, a man attending a wedding quietly pulled a bag of mushroom soup and corn vomit from his pocket, and proceeded to pretend to vomit in the middle of the dance floor. Needless to say, this had many of the guests a little unhappy and somewhat queasy. But they were totally unprepared for what came next. The man's friend immediately went over to the mess and said, "Oh, it looks like there's still some corn left," and proceeded to pick out and eat the pieces of corn. This spectacle then produced substantial quantities of real vomit from the other guests. I do not know if this story is true or not, I just love telling it! Please remember: do not try this at home, or at a wedding, or anywhere else for that matter.

Another easy way to make fake vomit is to simply cook up some very thick oatmeal. Once your oatmeal is cooked and cooled, add water and mix lightly until you get a nice vomit look.

Of course you can add corn or any other extras you like.

I hope this gives you a good start on your vomiting. Try adding a few things to your vomit to make it just the perfect grossness for you.

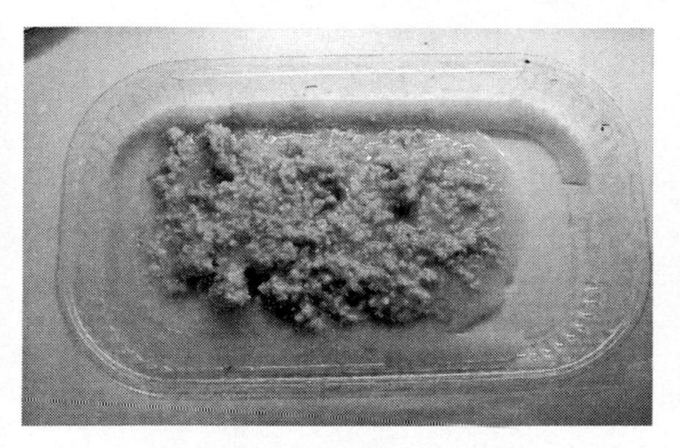

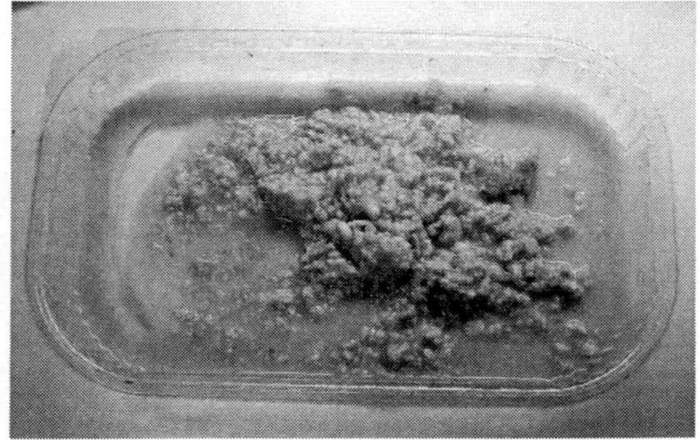

***Left:* Very thick oatmeal mixed with water makes another good vomit recipe. *Right:* Adding corn to oatmeal water vomit makes it even tastier looking.**

WORMS

Here's a helpful little tip. Fake worms, as well as assorted other bugs, can be found at your local sporting goods store. Just look in the fishing section. Some of these little critters are very real looking, and can be used to creep up a corpse or for any of hundreds of other uses.

A MASK IN THE BUSH IS WORTH TWO IN THE HAND

Many masks today come with a set of coordinated gloves to make your hands match the mask. Normally you would have to put these on an actor to

The hands are placed next to the mask to give the effect of a monster jumping out of the bush.

make an effective display. I have come up with a little trick I like to use that can make an effective display without an actor. I simply slide the mask over a wig form, and place it in a bush. The hands are then placed next to the mask to give the effect of a monster jumping out of the bush.

THE STEAMING SKULL

Here is a fun little prop I like to call the steaming skull. While the effect is somewhat dramatic, the prop could not be easier to build.

The skull in the picture below seems to be spewing smoke or steam from its mouth. How is this effect accomplished? You start by propping the skull's jaw open. This is very easy to do. Just take a small piece of stick and prop the backside of the jaw open as shown below.

The steaming skull is a fun and dramatic prop that is very easy to build.

Now, that you have propped the jaw open, you have just completed the most difficult part of the prop. Now all you need to do is place the skull with the open jaw over your secret steam generator.

In case you do not recognize the steam generator, it is an ultrasonic humidifier. These are devices that turn ordinary water into a very fine mist which can be used to add moisture to the air in a room. You can find these at most any appliance, department or drugstore for as little as $20.

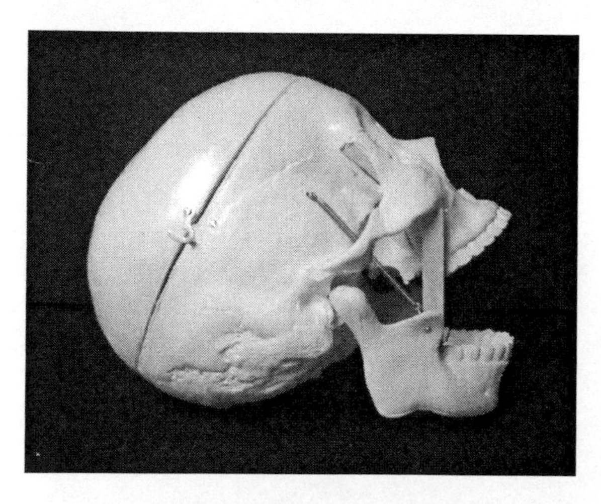

Start by propping the skull's jaw open.

Of course, having your skull sitting on the humidifier will look odd, so you will have to find a way to camouflage the humidifier so that the skull will stand out. One thing you will need to be careful about is that you will find that at times you may have a bit of water collecting around the skull and on anything near the humidifier. You will need to take care that anything you use to make this prop or use near this prop will not be damaged by water. More importantly, you must make sure that you do not have a water buildup on the floor where people may slip and injure themselves.

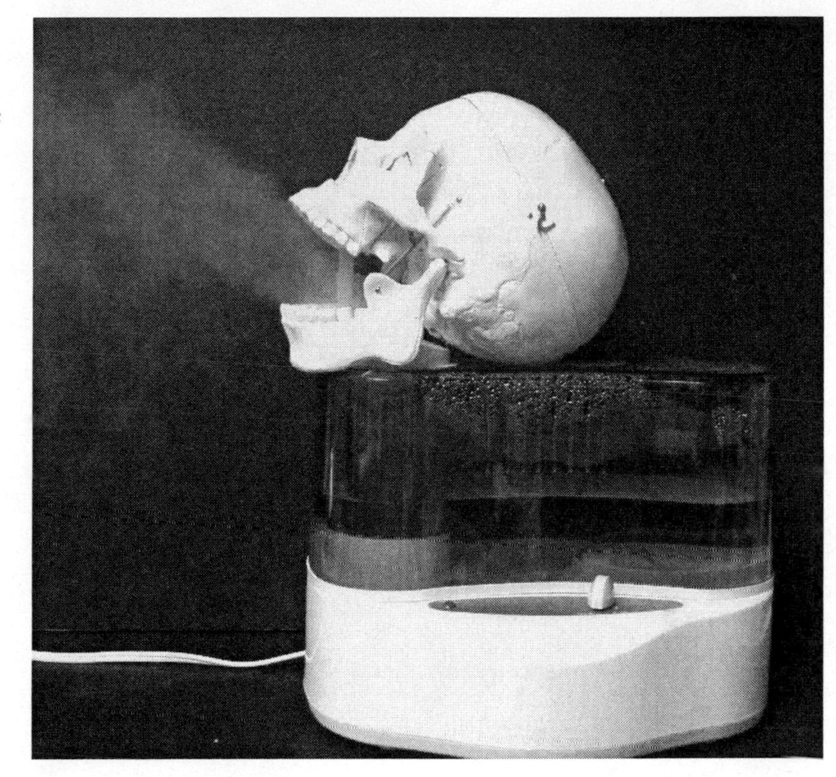

The secret behind the steaming skull.

PART III
REFERENCES

WHERE CAN I FIND...?

Throughout this book I have talked about using a number of items to build your props. Some of them have been everyday items you most likely have around the house. Others have been common, easy to find items that everyone knows where to buy. Some items are not so common, and many people would have no idea where to get them. That is where this section of the book comes in. Here I will give you a list of sources for the items that I have mentioned in this book. I have done business with most of the companies listed here, and I have been satisfied with the service that I have received. As an individual company may supply several items, rather than giving you the full contact information for the company after the item, I will simply give you the company name. The company name can then be looked up in the Suppliers section.

1" × 2"—1" × 2" boards are available at almost all lumberyards and many home centers. These pine boards are very inexpensive and are great for framing out fake walls where strength is not important.

Art Supplies—Various art supplies can be found at local art and craft stores. If you cannot find what you need locally, try Dick Blick, which offers a very large line of art products and carries many of the items I used for my props.

Artificial Flowers—Artificial flowers are available at most craft and hobby stores.

Battery Packs—Available at electronics stores and some hobby centers. Also available at Radio Shack and often from American Science and Surplus.

Black Lights—Once next to impossible to find, black lights are becoming much easier to find. Many party centers and even hardware store now carry either complete black light fixtures or black light bulbs or tubes, which can be used in fixtures you provide. If you cannot find them elsewhere they can be ordered from The Anatomical Chart Company.

Bones—Many interesting props can be assembled from assorted loose bones. If you cannot dig them up elsewhere, they can be ordered through the mail or over the Internet from The Anatomical Chart Company.

Brain-Shaped Gelatin Mold—If you cannot find a brain-shaped mold at your local party center or hobby shop, they can be ordered from The Anatomical Chart Company.

Clear Coat—There are many clear coat products available today. Among these are varnish, shellac, and polyurethane. The purpose of a clear coat is to protect the finish underneath without changing its color. Some clear coats add a shine to the finish; these are call gloss or high gloss. Other clear coats add protection without adding shine; these are called satin finish. If you are using a clear coat over a finish that is meant to be black light reactive, remember to purchase one that does not claim to be UV protective. The chemicals used to protect the finish from UV light will keep your prop from glowing under black light. Clear coats can be found in most paint, hardware and art stores.

Corn Syrup—Corn syrup can be found in the baking section of most grocery stores. It comes in both light and dark; the light is best for use in making stage blood.

Corobuff—Corobuff is sold primarily for store displays and other commercial use. It can be hard for the home haunter to find. The first time I used Corobuff, I was fortunate enough that a local party store would sell me some it had left over from a display. Recently, I was able to find flagstone Corobuff, as I used in Bucky's remodeling, available via mail order from the Fright Catalog.

Cotton Swabs—Cotton swabs can be found in most drugstore and beauty supply stores.

Crackle Paint—Crackle paint can be found in many hardware stores, home centers, craft stores and art supply stores. If you cannot find it locally, it can be ordered through the mail from Dick Blick.

Electrical Tape—Electrical tape is available at most hardware stores and electrical and electronic supply houses. If you wish to order it through the mail, Radio Shack carries a large assortment; they even have different colors.

Expanding Polyurethane Foam Sealant—Expanding polyurethane foam sealant can be found in most hardware stores and home centers. Its most common use is for insulating around doors and windows. Look for it in the door and window section of the store, or you may also find it near the insulation or in the plumbing section. It is surprising how many uses people have found for this product besides prop building.

Eyes of Terror— Eyes of Terror gum is sold in many grocery, party and Halloween stores during the Halloween season. Recently I have seen the same style gum sold under the name of Spooky Eyes.

Fabric Whitener— Fabric whitener is sold in many grocery and department stores. It can be hard to find; look for it by the laundry detergents. The brand I used was Rit.

Fake Fingernails— Fake fingernails can be found in many drug and beauty supply stores. You can usually find them near the nail polish.

Flagstone Corobuff—*see* Corobuff.

Floral Moss— Floral moss should be available where you buy your artificial flowers. Look for it at craft and hobby stores or garden centers.

Flowerpot— Flowerpots can be found at craft and hobby stores or garden centers. You should have a large selection to choose from.

Food Coloring— Food coloring is available in most grocery stores. Look in the baking section.

Gel Stain— Gel stain is available in many locations where you would buy regular wood stain. It is thicker than regular oil- or water-based stains, which makes it better for horizontal surfaces and on shiny surfaces when a dark color is required. Look for it in the stain section at many paint and hardware stores.

Gelatin Molds— Gelatin molds can be found at many party and cookware stores. If you are looking for Halloween shapes they can be harder to find. If you need a brain-, heart- or hand-shaped mold, they can be ordered from The Anatomical Chart Company.

Glow-in-the-Dark Polymer Clay— Polymer clay is available at many craft and hobby stores. Look for it near the modeling clay. If you cannot find polymer clay locally, it can be ordered through the mail from Dick Blick.

Glycerin— Glycerin can be found at many drugstores, but the bottles are usually small and high priced. I buy mine mail order, in gallon bottles, from the Chemistry Store.

Granite Paint— Granite paint is great for getting the look and texture of stone in an easy spray application. Granite paint can be found in many paint, hardware, craft and art stores. If you cannot find it locally, you can get it by mail order from Dick Blick.

Hand-Shaped Gelatin Mold—If you cannot find a hand-shaped mold at your local party center or hobby shop, they can be ordered from The Anatomical Chart Company.

Hot Melt Glue Gun—You cannot beat a hot melt glue gun for quickness and ease of use for many applications. It can be found at many hardware stores and craft stores.

LEDs—LEDs, or light emitting diodes, can be purchased from your local electronics supply house. If you do not have a local electronics supply house you can order them through the mail from Radio Shack. If you are looking to save a little money, you can also try American Science and Surplus. They often carry surplus LEDs at discount prices.

Liquid Latex—Liquid latex can be hard to find. It is carried by some art supply stores, but not many. It can be ordered through the mail from Dick Blick or less expensively from Poly Products.

Liquid Laundry Starch—Liquid laundry starch can be found in many grocery and department stores. Look for it by the laundry detergents.

Mirrored Window Film—Mirrored window film can be found in many hardware and home centers. Look for it by the window treatments (near the blinds and shades).

Moss—Moss can be found in many craft shops and garden centers. Look for it near the flowerpots.

Newspaper—Newspaper should be easy to find. Look for it at newsstands and bookstores. There are even companies that will deliver a fresh supply to your doorstep every day.

Paint Tint—Paint tint can be found at many paint and hardware stores.

Pearlizing Agent—There are probably other places which carry it, but the only place I know of to order pearlizing agent is from the Chemistry Store.

Petroleum Jelly—Petroleum jelly can be found in most drug and cosmetic stores.

Polyester Batting—Polyester batting can be found in most fabric stores. You can also often find it in other stores around Christmastime; it is used to simulate snow under a tree.

Polymer Clay— Polymer clay is available at many craft and hobby stores. Look for it near the modeling clay. If you cannot find polymer clay locally, it can be ordered through the mail from Dick Blick.

Prop Eyes— Prop eyes can be ordered through the mail from The Anatomical Chart Company.

Rubber Gloves— Rubber gloves (or latex gloves) can be found at most drugstores as well as many craft stores.

Sea Dye— Sea Dye can be found at some boating supply stores or ordered through the mail from Landfall Navigation.

Sealaver—Sealaver is the seaweed wrap used to make sushi. It can be hard to find but is carried by a few grocery stores. If you have an Oriental food market in your area, it would be a good place to look. Look for it in the seaweed section.

Silicone Adhesive—Silicone adhesive is available at most hardware stores as well as many craft stores.

Skeleton Hand— Finding a skeleton hand can take some digging. If you cannot find one elsewhere they can be ordered from The Anatomical Chart Company.

Skeletons—Can't turn up a skeleton? If you cannot find one elsewhere, they can be ordered from The Anatomical Chart Company.

Skulls— Finding a skull can be difficult. If you cannot find one elsewhere, they can be ordered from The Anatomical Chart Company.

Stain— Wood stain is available at most paint and hardware stores.

Staple Gun— Yon can buy a staple gun at most hardware stores.

Tonic Water— Tonic water can be found at most grocery and liquor stores.

Transparent Skulls—Finding a transparent skull can be difficult. If you cannot find one elsewhere, they can be ordered from The Anatomical Chart Company.

Twinkle Eyes— Twinkle Eyes can be found in many grocery and craft stores around Halloween. Look for them in the Halloween section or by the pumpkins.

Unflavored Gelatin— Unflavored gelatin can be found at many grocery stores. Try looking in the baking section.

Wire— Wire can be found at many hardware stores. For smaller gauges you may need to try an electronics store. If you need a smaller gauge wire, try Radio Shack by mail order.

Wire Wrap Tool— Wire wrap tools are available at electronic supply stores. If you need one, try Radio Shack by mail order.

SUPPLIERS

Below you will find a few companies who supply items useful to the haunta-holic.

American Science and Surplus
Address: P.O. Box 1030, Skokie, IL 60076-8030
Phone: 1-847-934-0722
Fax: 1-800-934-0722
Web site: www.sciplus.com

American Science and Surplus is a company which specializes in closeouts and parts removed from larger items. Most of their items tend to be of a scientific or mechanical nature, hence the name. In their catalog, or in one of their three retail stores, you will find a wide assortment of doodads and whatnots. Common items you will find are electric motors of various sizes, gears, LEDs, battery packs and many other items which may be of use to the haunter. Since their items are surplus and take-outs, the product line changes often, and quantities may be limited. Prices often tend to be a small fraction of the normal retail price of the items; however, all items are sold without warranty.

I have dealt personally with this company, and have been well pleased with the products and service.

The Anatomical Chart Company
Address: 16522 Hunters Green Parkway, Hagerstown, MD, 21740
Phone: 1-800-621-7500
Fax: 1-301-223-2400
E-mail: (for Halloween products) mlack@anatomical.com
Web site: www.buckysboneyard.com (click on Halloween products)

The Anatomical Chart Company started as a company selling a small line of charts for medical use, and has grown to include a full line of anatomical charts and models. Noticing that a small number of their models (skeletons and skulls) were being ordered by haunted attractions, they decided to develop a line of products aimed specifically at the haunt industry. Today, this line is a standard in the haunt industry. They have a large line of what they call fourth quality items. These are made using the same molds as the medical quality products, but may contain flaws ranging from minor to, in rare cases, major. While you take what you get as far as quality, the prices are half or often far less than half of those of the first quality. Haunters love these items, because not only are they much cheaper, but the defects actually often add to the appearance of the items when used.

The company offers a full line of skeletal items, as well as a few Halloween novelty items. Some of their most popular items include: skeletons in several sizes from a few inches to life size, skulls in several sizes and assorted loose bones sold by the pound. Wholesale prices are available to businesses, and individuals may order retail with a minimum order of $25.

I have dealt personally with this company, and have been pleased with the products and service.

The Chemistry Store

Address: 520 NE 26 Court, Pompano Beach, FL 33064
Phone: 1-800-224-1430
E-mail: sales@chemistrystore.com
Web site: www.chemistrystore.com

The Chemistry Store offers a line of soap and candle making products, as well as chemicals for home hobbyists. Many of the items offered for soap and candle making can be adapted for use in your haunt, and with a little knowledge of chemistry, you can find a number of safe uses for some of the chemicals they offer.

The Chemistry Store was my source for low-cost glycerin, as well as pearlizing agent. They carry other items that may be of use to the imaginative hauntaholic, such as Mica Tints and sulfur.

I have dealt personally with this company, and have been pleased with the products and service.

Dick Blick Art Materials

Address: P.O. Box 1297, Galesburg, IL 61402-1267
Phone: 1-800-447-8192
Fax: 1-800-621-8293
Web site: www.dickblick.com

Dick Blick is a large retailer of art supplies. They have a very large catalog (nearly five hundred pages for the one I have), and carry just about any art materials you could want. In addition, they operate over thirty retail stores in thirteen states.

Many of the products offered by Dick Blick have uses in making your own Halloween props. Many of the items I used in this book are available by mail order. Among the many items available are: crackle paint, granite paint, fluorescent paints and glow-in-the-dark polymer clay.

I have dealt personally with this company, and have been well pleased with the products and service.

First Imperial Trading Company
Address: 5901 E. Telegraph Road, Commerce, CA 90040
Phone: 1-888-277-6659
Fax: 1-323-726-0890
Web site: www.straightfromthegrave.com

The First Imperial Trading Company does business under the name of Straight from the Grave. They sell a variety of Halloween items at very low prices, as long as you are willing to order in case quantities. While some of the larger items come in a case quantity of only one, some smaller items may be packed two dozen or more to a case. If you need a dozen black light tubes, or a case of twelve quart bottles of fog juice, this just might be a company you want to check out.

Products available will change from time to time. Some of the mainstays are Styrofoam tombstones, fog machines, cheap prop weapons and cheap plastic skeletons (not very real looking).

I have dealt personally with this company, and have been pleased with the products and service.

Fright Catalog
Address: 100 Barber Avenue, Unit F, Worcester, MA 01606
Phone: 1-888-437-4448
E-mail: service@frightcatalog.com
Web site: www.frightcatalog.com

Fright Catalog carries a large assortment of Halloween related products, and is the one place I have found where flagstone Corobuff may be purchased by mail order. Those of you wishing to order flagstone Corobuff from Fright Catalog, please note that they call it graystone.

I have not yet personally dealt with this company.

Haunt Master Products
Address: 107 Mirandy Court, Bridgewater, VA 22812-9567
Phone: Cell preferred, 1-540-421-0695; Other, 1-540-828-4244
E-mail: jim@hauntmasterproducts.com
Web site: www.hauntmasterproducts.com

Owner-operator Jim Kadel started Haunt Master Products in 1997. The company specializes in electronic products for the haunt industry, sold at prices that make them affordable to the home haunter. Jim designs the products he sells himself, and besides the items in his catalog, he will also build to the customer's specifications.

The company's product line features controlled LEDs to be used as eyes in your props, as well as lighting control devices. The product line is being added to regularly, so check out the Web site for the latest items available.

I have not yet personally dealt with this company.

Landfall Navigation

Address: 151 Harvard Avenue, Stamford, CT 06902
Phone: 1-800-941-2219
E-mail: info@landfallnavigation.com
Web site: www.landfallnavigation.com

Landfall Navigation sells a line of boating, navigation and safety items, including Sea Dye Markers. The dye from Sea Dye Markers can be used to turn a very large quantity of water black light reactive. The water will glow a bright greenish-yellow when exposed to black light, great for simulating toxic waste.

I have not yet personally dealt with this company.

Midnight Syndicate

Address: 10035 Woodview Drive, Chardon, OH 44024
Web site: www.midnightsyndicate.com

Midnight Syndicate produces a line of music CDs with a horror theme. These are not sound effect CDs with screams and rattling chains. Instead, they contain classical music with a horror feel, the type of music you may find as background music in a good horror movie. The production is excellent and the music a pleasure to listen to. The music contained on these CDs is great for setting the mood outside a haunt or at a horror themed party. You can listen to samples from their CD's at their Web site.

I have dealt personally with this company, and have been pleased with the products and service.

Polyproducts

Address: P.O. Box 42, Roseville, MI 48066
Phone: 1-800-521-1005
Fax: 1-586-778-7775
Web site: www.nexusscales.com

If you were to look only at their Web site, you would think the only thing you can get from Polyproducts is scales. Give them a call, however, and you can order high-quality liquid mold latex at a great price. Due to their location in the Midwest, liquid latex ships only May through October.

I have dealt personally with this company, and have been pleased with the products and service.

Radio Shack

Address: More than 7,000 locations
Phone: 1-800-843-7422
Web site: www.radioshack.com

Radio Shack is a retailer of home electronics and electronic components. With more than 7,000 stores throughout the U.S., there is usually one near anyone who lives in the country. If you do not live near one, you can still order from their catalog, or from the Web site. I do not have space here to list all the Radio Shack locations; just check their Web site or give them a call to find the location nearest you.

Radio Shack is a great place to look if you need any electronic components in small quantities. If you need a larger quantity of any item, they will even give a discount on quantities. If you need LEDs, transformers, bulbs, sockets, wire or any components, check at Radio Shack and odds are you will find it there.

I have dealt personally with this company, and have been pleased with the products and service.

Spooky F/X

Address: California
Phone: None
Fax: none
E-mail: SpookyFX@aol.com
Web site: spookyfx.com

Spooky F/X has been haunting since 1982. The Internet-based company was founded in 1997. The company now markets exclusively through the Internet. The company was the first to bring out can air brush propellant powered products, cassette player interface, safe ultra low PSI designs, the first to offer affordable Electro-field motion detectors as well as many other design innovations. In fact, each year Spooky F/X develops dozens of product designs, and then produces at least two of these as new products. Their products are designed to be of high quality and yet affordable.

The products this company manufactures are mainly large, moving props, as you would find in a professional haunted house. If you are looking to spend only $10 or $20, look elsewhere. If you are looking for a centerpiece prop for your haunt and are willing to spend as much as a few hundred dollars, check them out. Many of the props they offer will require an air compressor to power them, so if you do not own one, you may want to take this cost into consideration before ordering.

Spooky F/X accepts orders only by e-mail or over the Internet, another way they keep costs down so that they can pass the savings on to you.

I have not yet personally dealt with this company.

APPENDIX: MERRY HALLOWEEN

One of the best times to look for bargains on Halloween prop-building materials is right after Christmas. There are usually a large variety of items available at 50% or more off the pre–Christmas price.

You might wonder how items which are meant to be pretty or cute can be changed into items to terrorize young children. Well, with a little imagination, it really is not very difficult. Throughout this book, I give you a number of examples to get you started. The rest is up to your imagination.

Items I suggest you be on the lookout for would include: light sets, bulbs, animated figures, extension cords, fake candles, cotton or polyester batting or just about anything your imagination can distort into something gruesome.

Light sets can be easily cannibalized for bulbs and sockets that can be used as skull eyes or in any

Christmas lights come in literally dozens of different sizes, shapes and colors, allowing for hundreds of Halloween uses.

The author was able to purchase all these items at an after Christmas sale for around $120. They can be used to build literally hundreds of props.

number of interesting ways. You will usually find it much cheaper to take the bulbs you need from a set of lights than to buy the replacement bulbs. The replacements tend to sell for about $0.20 each while you can find a set of 100 lights for around $4.00 or $0.04 per bulb. Besides being less expensive on a per bulb basis, buying the set gives you handy little holders for your bulbs. I show you in this book how you can remove individual lights and sockets from these sets and convert them to work off batteries. This will allow you to use your props anywhere without worrying about extension cords or the possible dangers of higher voltage AC current.

Another item of interest is the relatively new LED light sets. Instead of conventional incandescent bulbs, these sets use light emitting diodes, which use much less power. While they are somewhat more expensive than the conventional sets, they do offer a few advantages. In general LEDs will have a longer life than a regular bulb, making them ideal for applications where it would be difficult or impossible to change the light. They also generate almost no heat so they can be safely used where some other lights cannot. And since they use less power, they offer a much longer battery life when used in battery powered applications.

You can also often find extension cords in the after–Christmas sale section. While most of the props I show you how to build do not use AC power, extension cords are always useful for black lights, fog machines, etc., as well as, being handy around the house the year round. And, as long as you have to buy extension cords, you might as well buy them on sale.

The author's idea of how to decorate a tree. Yes, those are skulls on the tree.

As for fake candles, they always look good in the top of a skull and can be used to give an ancient feel to your dungeon or torture chamber. You will most often find these candles as lights with a simulated flame, which makes them look a little more realistic.

Cotton or polyester batting, which is sold to simulate the look of snow, can be used to stuff corpses or just old clothes for an easy dead body look. I recommend the polyester because it will hold up better should it get wet.

There are a great variety of animated figures sold at Christmastime. With a bit of work these can be stripped of their cute exteriors and the guts used to animate skeletons or other Halloween characters. Consider taking a Santa waving a lantern, put a hockey mask and a new set of clothes on it, then replace the lantern with a bright shiny knife (a plastic prop knife for safety). Or, put a Wolfman mask and a little extra fur on a herd of reindeer, and let the pack loose to terrorize the world. For every cute animatronic made for Christmas, you should be able to come up with several scary modifications. Just use your imagination.

Of course, Christmas is not the only holiday time when you should be looking for raw materials. Just about any holiday can provide a wealth of ideas. Turn bunny ears into horns, use Hanukkah candles in skulls; the opportunities are endless if you just look hard enough. Moreover, as can be seen in the picture on the previous page, you can always use your Halloween items year round too!

EPITAPH

I hope you have enjoyed this book and perhaps picked up a few ideas along the way. When I started writing it, I had no idea what a long, drawn-out process it would be. Now that it is complete, I feel it was well worth the effort. I hope you agree. At this time I would like to invite you to send me any comments you may have. I welcome any suggestions on how I may improve or clarify the instructions I have given. If there are things about this book you liked or did not like, please let me know. I can be reached by e-mail at: tipsfromthecrypt@ameritech.net. I plan to keep this e-mail address active for several years after this book is first published. I do not know how long copies of it may be in circulation; therefore, I cannot guarantee it will be active forever. I will try to answer each e-mail I receive. Since I have no idea what kind of response I will receive; it may take me some time to answer your e-mail.

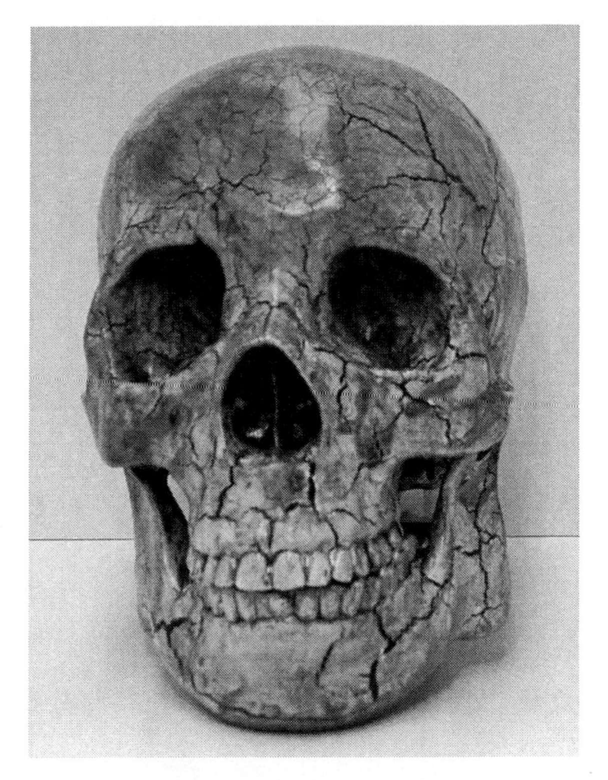

One of the many props this book shows you how to make.

INDEX